THE SACRAMENTS

Louis-Marie Chauvet

THE SACRAMENTS

*The Word of God
at the Mercy of the Body*

A PUEBLO BOOK

The Liturgical Press   Collegeville, Minnesota

A Pueblo Book published by The Liturgical Press

Design by Frank Kacmarcik, Obl.S.B.

This book was first published in French by Les Éditions de L'Atelier / Les Éditions Ouvrières, © 1997 by Les Éditions de L'Atelier, Paris.

Library of Congress Cataloging-in-Publication Data

Chauvet, Louis-Marie.
    [Sacrements. English]
    The sacraments : the Word of God at the mercy of the body /
Louis-Marie Chauvet.
        p.   cm.
    "A Pueblo book."
    Includes bibliographical references and index.
    ISBN 0-8146-6143-2 (alk. paper)
    1. Sacraments—Catholic Church.   2. Catholic Church—Doctrines.
I. Title.

BX2200.C4313   2001
234'.16—dc21   00-067164

Contents

Introduction

We are going to treat of the theology of the sacraments, which is also called "sacramental theology." Theology was defined by St. Anselm as "faith seeking understanding." This expression, which is still valid, connotes two things on which we must be in agreement from the start.

First, theology is a believer's task. Faith is not at the end but at the beginning of this task. To make an act of faith does not mean simply either to believe that God exists ("believe that" is in the domain of opinion) or to believe ideas about God, beautiful and generous as these ideas may be (to believe for example in science, the immortality of the soul, or astrology, still pertains to a purely intellectual thought process), but to believe *in*, which means to have trust in someone, to put one's faith in that person. This is never the product of a merely intellectual reasoning. Because it necessarily involves us as persons in a vital relationship with another, "to believe in" (a spouse, a friend, and so on), belongs more to the relational than to the rational order; "desire" holds a decisive place in such a relationship.

We often deem that the act of faith, although not rational, is nevertheless reasonable. But is it always so? This question is in any case unavoidable when we speak of believing in God. In the last analysis, it is this question which dominates the whole of Christian theology: Is the faith that I have received from the church, through my native milieu or from such and such a person, not rational (because the revelation of God always goes beyond reason), but reasonable?

As a consequence, here are the believers "in search of understanding" their faith. To achieve this, they construct a discourse. This discourse is based first on the Scriptures, because they are the primary place of the revelation of God, along with their authentic interpretation through the official magisterium of the church. However, at the same time, this discourse cannot be constructed without dialogue both with the theological work of the past and with modern culture and, more particularly, with the new findings of contemporary disciplines, each of which has its place in the field of knowledge (exegesis, philosophy, history, anthropology, and so on). Theology as discourse about God is therefore a critical discourse utilizing all the resources of reason. Nonetheless, these remain contained within faith.

These few remarks on the subject of theology are important. About to embark on the path of language and symbol, we do not in any way claim to explain the mystery of God's communication with humankind, a mystery operating in the sacraments. We receive this mystery from the church and we make it our own from the start. For all this, we are not reduced to the unquestioning faith that believes without understanding and even without seeking to understand. (In any case, one is allowed to ask what such a way of believing means since it evades all questions.) On the contrary, theology is one form of the courage to be: no question should be silenced with the excuse of "mystery." But as the frequent expression, "Oh, how I understand you!" shows, it is perfectly possible to understand someone without pretending to explain everything about that person in a scientific way. Likewise, one understands a poem without ever being able to fathom its whole depth through explanatory commentaries. And if one understand what love is, it is precisely inasmuch as one renounces to explain it rationally; otherwise, it would not be love anymore.

It is this sort of understanding that we have in mind here. Obviously, it requires a properly intellectual process, and a rigorous one, but above all, it is at the service of, first, living, from which it originates and to which it returns. For the question of sacraments is not simply outside ourselves: in a manner of speaking, it carries us along since we are—or wish to be again, provided a number of theoretical and practical difficulties be elucidated—their believing practitioners. It has a vital importance.

THE BASIC PASTORAL QUESTION

Among the many questions that can be raised, there is one which often seems to come to mind, even though not fully consciously. This pastoral question can be formulated by reference to the dialogue of Jesus with the Samaritan woman at Jacob's well. She wants to know whether one must continue to "worship on this mountain" (Mount Garizim, the high place of Samaritan worship) or "in Jerusalem" (the center of Jewish worship). Jesus answers, "Woman, believe me, the hour is coming when you will worship the Father neither on this mountain nor in Jerusalem. . . . God is spirit, and those who worship him must worship in spirit and truth" (John 4:20-21, 24). Of course, according to the theological vocabulary of John's Gospel, "to worship in spirit and truth" does not mean praying in a wholly interior or purely mental way, but worshiping according to the Holy Spirit that Jesus will give after his resurrection and that leads to the true knowledge of the Father. Nevertheless, even though Jesus does not specify here the concrete forms which the true worship of God must take, he is clear about the spirit in which it must be conducted.

Then why not ask: In order to worship the Father what need do we have of all these rites which unfold in a more or less obligatory fashion and make use of antiquated gestures and movements, of preprogrammed formulas, of materials imposed in the name of "tradition," without speaking of the ostentatious and solemn ceremonies with which the church surrounds them? Does not all this run counter to the spirit Jesus speaks of or at least hamper it? And thus we are led to dream of a "truer," therefore necessarily more spare religion in which contact with the pure word of God would at last be possible.

This is pure imagining! Nonetheless, the question underlying this dream expresses an intuition that deserves to be considered: that the church can never be in serene possession of its liturgical rites, that it must constantly resist the temptation to imprison itself—as well as God—within them. For these rites, which have Christian meaning only if they are filled with the word and in-dwelt by the Spirit, contest the word of God in the very moment they attest it. In this sense, the temptation to do away with them can be salutary. Probably one must have wrestled with this temptation at a given moment before being able to be reconciled with them and to live with them in a genuine Christian manner. Actually, what the present book is really about is reconciliation with the liturgical rites. Of course, first there will be criticism, but in the end, reconciliation.

THE BASIC THEOLOGICAL QUESTION

Such a reconciliation must be theologically justified. This justification, as will be seen, is fundamentally connected with the theological question which recurs throughout this whole book and which is: What do we learn about Christian faith and Christian identity from the fact that the sacraments have always been their very fabric? Let us explain. We are basing our argument on a fact: from its origins, the church has always celebrated the sacraments, in particular baptism and Eucharist; and ever since then no one becomes a Christian except by receiving these sacraments. We do not seek to justify this fact, that is to say, to explain it as necessary; the best we could do, as the medieval theologians did, would be to supply arguments that would show the "fittingness" of the sacraments within the reality of the incarnation. In other words, we do not try to answer the question *why* in relation to the sacraments because we take into account the fact that they were born with the church, that they are always-already contemporary with it and every Christian. The question we are seeking to answer is: What does it *mean* for the faith that things are so?

The answer that will be given throughout this book and that validates the reconciliation mentioned above can be formulated as follows: the fact that Christian identity cannot be separated from the sacraments (in particular those of initiation) means that faith cannot be lived in any other way, including what is most spiritual in it, than *in the mediation of the body,* the body of a society, of a desire, of a tradition, of a history, of an institution, and so on. What is most spiritual always takes place in the most corporeal.

This being the case, it is possible to perceive the concern of this (fundamental) theology of sacramentality: nothing less than a Christian reconciliation with the body (or better, as shall be made clear, with corporeity). Are not the sacraments the most powerful expression of a faith that exists only "at the mercy of the body"? As a consequence, what is at stake here is the overall way Christians understand themselves as Christians, speak of themselves as Christians, lead their lives as Christians.

Overture:
Three Theoretical Models

As we have emphasized above, theology's point of departure is the faith of the church. It is in the very nature of the church to confess that the sacraments it celebrates in faith in the name of Jesus Christ have a spiritual efficacy called "grace," a beautiful term. The most forceful expression of this grace is no doubt that extremely sparing one given us in the dialogue of eucharistic communion: to the statement, "The body of Christ," Christians answer, not with the description of their feelings or the difficulties that their intellect might struggle with, but simply with the "amen" of faith. This amen comes from the mouth and the heart, of course, but also from the whole body since it is manifested by the opening of the hands into which the pure gift of God is placed. The gratuitous communication of God with the believers, such is the salient point of the sacraments. Any weakening of this affirmation—provided it is correctly understood, as we shall see—would rob the sacraments of their essential originality.

For the time being, the question for us is not what the expression "sacramental grace" means; we shall have many opportunities in this book to closely examine it. The question centers on the various ways in which theologians of the past have attempted to elucidate the interconnection, essential in every sacrament, between the action of the living God of Jesus Christ and the human action of the church.

Among the different models of answers to this question, three are of more particular interest for us: the objectivist model proposed chiefly during the Scholastic period of the twelfth and thirteenth centuries, eminently by Thomas Aquinas (1228–1274); the opposite subjectivist model, in reaction against the foregoing, which prevailed in certain circles of the Catholic world and—for entirely different reasons—in the work of the great Protestant theologian Karl Barth (1886–1966); and the model of Vatican II, which, while following Thomas Aquinas, makes important corrections to his thought. It is precisely the dynamism of the Vatican II model that will lead us to wonder whether another model is not possible today, a symbolic model which would change the approach of the three preceding models.

OBJECTIVIST MODEL

First of all, let us underline that while the following development, based on the catechism of 1947, is on the whole in agreement with the theology of the great Scholastics of the twelfth and thirteenth centuries, it considerably hardens their thoughts. Thomas would recognize the matrix of his theology but certainly not the flexibility which, like every great thinker, he knew to inject into his discourse.

In the 1950s, the catechism taught to children defined the sacraments as "visible signs instituted by our Lord Jesus Christ to produce and increase grace in our souls." The first characteristic of a sacrament is to be a sign, "a sacred sign" or, as Augustine said, "a sign of a sacred reality," a term used later on by Thomas Aquinas. But in the catechism definition, the accent is not placed on the aspect of the utilized sign's efficient "significance": for instance, no one was shocked when, to symbolize the immersion into death with Christ through baptism (Rom 6), the celebrant poured three barely visible drops of water on the baby's forehead and, along with this vague gesture, pronounced a barely audible formula, in Latin to boot. In this catechism, the accent is placed on the production of grace; the important thing is the objective efficacy of the sign. In other words, the sacraments are regarded less as *revelatory signs* than as *operative means* of salvation.

This clearly appears in the images employed:

(a) Image of the sacrament as "instrument." This image has the disadvantage of suggesting the idea of a quasi automatic production, as long as the instrument is properly utilized by the minister. Besides, grace thus "produced" risks being seen precisely as a product, a product-which-is-an-object.

(b) Image of the sacrament as "remedy." This image carries the same connotation of automatic production as the one above because the sacrament is more or less understood as a sort of magic potion to restore spiritual health. Moreover, this image is negative: one celebrates what human beings lack as a consequence of sin, not the possibility of a different history.

(c) Image of the sacrament as "channel." One sees immediately the major limitation of this image, which evokes the narrow pipe or bottleneck through which grace would "flow." Let a priest happen by chance upon the dying victim of an accident and give this person extreme unction in extremis, and here is this person saved, or at least surer of being saved. The same thing applies to the unbaptized child in danger of death. We know well how this type of reflex has fed the fear of millions of Christians for centuries.

(d) Image of the sacrament as "germ." This biological and no longer merely instrumental image has the advantage of suggesting the dynamism of a possible development. However, it remains linked with the idea that through the sacrament, God would deposit "something" in the "soul."

It is obvious that such images favor quite questionable representations of the efficacy *ex opere operato*[1] of the sacraments and, as a corollary, of the "power" of the priest. The priest is seen primarily less as a pastor and minister of the gospel than as a sacred intermediary *(sacerdos)* in charge of building a bridge *(ponti-fex)* between God and human beings, that is to say, of opening the gates of heaven to them.

Furthermore, the whole perspective is rather individualistic: the church as a community of faith and mission is absent; when it is mentioned, it is essentially as an institution endowed by Christ with supernatural powers for the benefit of individuals. This perspective is also "interioristic": the important thing is the salvation of the "soul."

It is evident that the insistence on the objective efficacy of the sacraments is done at the expense of the concrete existential subjects, who are not taken into account. True, the catechism of that period asks that they have the "piety" and the "right intention" in order to receive the sacraments fruitfully. However, this pertains not to the "nature" or the "being" of the sacraments but only, if one can so put it, to their "well-being." In the 1947 catechism's sixteen lessons on the sacraments, the word "faith" never appears; the same is true of "church" (except once to designate it as an institution into which baptism incorporates its members). The one instance of the concrete subjects being taken into account is the condition sine qua non, that they not place any obstacle (mortal sin or canonical sanction forbidding

---

[1] The expression is difficult to translate. Let us say that it means "by the very fact that the (sacramental) act is (understood: validly or legitimately) accomplished." Employed by the Scholastics, it was officially used again by the Council of Trent in the sixteenth century. Any magic interpretation of this formula is nonsense, as we shall see. On the contrary, the expression means (1) negatively, that God's offering of the gift of grace in the sacraments is not conditioned by the subjective quality of the faith or the holiness of the minister or recipient and, therefore (2) positively, that God is sovereignly free: God's grace is absolutely gratuitous.

access to the sacraments) to the reception of grace that comes down through the sacraments.

We have said it above: the analysis that we have briefly presented here is similar to that of the great Scholastics only at the level of the overall model. They carefully strove to purify the images enumerated above through analogy. By this method they meant to show that they were not duped by the vocabulary they used. In the spiritual order of grace, all concepts and images are approximate: while the spiritual reality is partially similar to what these terms mean, it is simultaneously partially different. In other words, the sacraments function "a little like" instruments; while they contain grace, it is not like a vase containing a remedy (Thomas Aquinas enumerates eight ways in which, according to Aristotle, a thing can be said to be in a place). The way the sacraments produce grace is only a "quasi" production, irreducible to that of a machine, and it would be monstrous to say that grace is a product-which-is-an-object. Thus, for instance, Thomas Aquinas specifies that if "grace is in the sacraments . . . [it is only] according to a certain instrumental power transient and incomplete in its natural being."[2] It is easy to see the importance of the differences between the doctrine of eminent theologians (any reification of their thought can only be a misinterpretation on the reader's part) and what becomes of it in pastoral manuals of catechism and liturgy not always concerned with nuances.

Nevertheless, it is as we have said, the same overall pattern of thought which is present in both cases and can be visualized by the following diagram:

God $\xrightarrow{\hspace{1cm}}$ Sacrament $\xrightarrow{\hspace{1cm}}$ Humankind

The accent is placed on the upper arrow: God sanctifies and saves human beings through the sacraments; these are primarily *means* of salvation. In return, humans can make of their whole daily lives a "spiritual offering" (see Rom 12:1; Heb 13:15-16; 1 Pet 2:4-10) which they present to the glory of God in the sacraments; these are then *signs* of salvation, that is to say, of God's grace present in daily life.

[2] Thomas Aquinas, *Summa Theologica*, Part III, q. 62, a. 3, in *The "Summa Theologica of St. Thomas Aquinas, Part III,* literally trans. by fathers of the English Dominican Province, No. 3 (qq. 50–83) (New York: Benziger, 1914) 35.

Thomas was not ignorant of this twofold circuit. He had even sketched the place the sacraments could have in the "moral" part of his Summa, and more precisely in the framework of his analysis of the "virtue of religion." In this latter case, the sacraments, seen according to the direction of the lower arrow of the diagram, would have been considered the summit of the Christians' ethical life, the revelatory expression of their daily life inasmuch as it is lived in the theological virtues of faith and charity.[3] Unfortunately, Thomas did not develop this perspective for itself. This is regrettable because it would have helped to balance his sacramental discourse, too strongly centered on the objective efficacy of the sacraments as "source" of salvation.

SUBJECTIVIST MODEL

This second model has appeared time and again under many different forms in the course of church history (illuminism of the Gnostic kind,[4] numerous movements of renewal more or less opposed to the institution, and so on). The adjective "subjectivist" applies as well to the group-subject as to the individual-subject; besides, it is taken in a broad sense to qualify a common trait of this trend, that is, the reaction against the church as institution. This reaction can take three principal forms.

(a) The first one is extremist and would offer little interest were it not for the fact that it exists, in ways more or less diffuse, among a fair number of our contemporaries. According to this type, which we shall call A, there is disaffection toward the church: the gospel, yes; the church, no. In this case, there is a tendency to identify orthodoxy (the truth concerning the revelation of God in Jesus Christ) with orthopraxis (good conduct), to subject objective truth to the criterion of subjective sincerity, and the quality of faith to that of generosity. Because the reign of God is (indeed) wider than the institutional church

[3] The theological virtues (faith, hope, and charity) are given by God and have God's very self as their object, whereas the moral virtues have their origin and principal end in human beings.

[4] "Gnosis" or "knowledge" is characterized by a tendency to rely on direct illumination by a private revelation made to an "inspired" person and as a consequence to bypass the mediations necessary for the true knowledge of God. Obviously, this does not prevent (rather the contrary) certain Gnostic sects from developing their own institutional apparatus, rite, and "dogmatic," in general even more constraining than that of the church.

and the Spirit "blows where it chooses" (John 3:8), the criteria for belonging to the church are erased and replaced by the good will and sincerity of every person. "Everybody is beautiful, everybody has generosity in their hearts; therefore, everybody is Christian." The value of the sacraments is primarily linked with the *subjective sincerity* of every person. This type A, as can be seen, tends to completely absorb the church into the reign.

(b) Types B and C are much less radical than the preceding because they are careful to reserve a real place for the church and the sacraments. They developed recently, even though their roots—like subjectivity itself—go back to the seventeenth century and even to the Renaissance. Type B represents a rather frequent tendency in certain milieux of the post-conciliar Catholic Church: objective criteria of belonging to the church and holding to the orthodox faith are recognized and claimed, but (hence its subjectivist character) these criteria are determined on the basis of values which the group declares to be evangelical. The problem is that the determination of these values, often strongly colored by ideology, is made by the group: militant generosity, particular reading of salvation history, emphatic valorization of "research" and "freedom," tendency to reject de facto church groups differing in their sensibility and analyzing political and institutional matters in another way, suspicion of parishes too widely open to anyone, tendency to think of themselves as Christians finally becoming adults, and so on. Instead of receiving the criteria of evangelical and ecclesial life from the living tradition of the church, even if it means they should unmask its possible failings, these groups seek criteria in their own methods of analysis, which leads to ostracizing, at least in practice, the church "of diversity" and "sociological" religion. One senses several pitfalls due to this model, visible on three planes:

(1) On the ecclesiological level, the pitfall of elitism. By wanting to push, if not pressure, Christian communities and individuals into being the living sign (but according to what criteria?) of what they celebrate in the sacraments, one ends by losing sight of the *eschatological* condition of the church and Christian life as well as Jesus' word, "I have come to call not the righteous but sinners" (Matt 9:13).

(2) On the level of Christian anthropology, the pitfall of (neo-) pelagianism. Pelagianism is the heresy, vigorously opposed by Augustine in the beginning of the fifth century, which, by minimizing the role of God's grace, sees in it a mere auxiliary to the moral energies and good works of human beings. In fact, by dint of wanting "to celebrate the

lived experience" or "to celebrate Jesus Christ in the lived experience," one ends by being unable to celebrate in common except with other participants who have lived "worthily" (always according to the group's criteria). The celebration amounts to being the *reward for the right living* of the group.

(3) Finally on the pastoral level, the pitfall of rigorism. By being suspicious of the "authenticity" of the faith manifested (always according to the group's criteria) by a certain sort of behavior in human and ecclesial life, persons who ask for baptism or a wedding are requested, for example, not only to have faith (which is a legitimate request) but to have a faith *conscious of itself*. This is simply to forget that faith is never reducible to the consciousness one has of it; that faith is not only, not even first of all, a matter of intellectual analysis (even though it also demands this) but a matter of the assent of the whole person to the living God revealed in Jesus Christ, in whom one places one's entire trust, to whom one gives one's faith; and that it is possible to be deeply believing without finding "the words to say it."

Of course this model does not exist in a chemically pure state. There are many variants between groups and individuals. Nevertheless, there is also a common matrix. Logically this viewpoint leads one to see in the sacraments primarily the "celebration of the lived experience" or rather "the celebration of Jesus Christ in the lived experience." They are essentially ecclesial acts of recognition (therefore joyful and festive) *of* what God has done and acts of gratitude *for* what God has done in the believers' lives. Where the objectivist model emphasized their function as operative means, and therefore as source of salvation, this model on the contrary stresses their function as revelatory signs and therefore as summit of the salvation already given, at the risk of erasing more or less their character as instruments.

Type B can be represented by the following diagram:

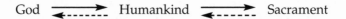

God ⇄ Humankind ⇄ Sacrament

The accent is placed on the upper arrow: God acts freely, through the Spirit of the risen One, in the lives of human beings; the sacrament is the festive expression of this action. Where the objectivist model understood the sacrament as an instrument of *production* of grace, this model understands it as an instrument of *transmission* of grace, already given by God, into daily life. As indicated by the lower arrow, this function of recognition of what God has done allows humans, in return, to regard the sacrament as an expression of gratitude *for* what God has done.

(c) Type C of this subjectivist model has an eminent representative in the person of Karl Barth. It reproduces the same scheme as the preceding one, although Barth's point of departure is opposed to that of type B. As we have seen, type B starts from below, in opposition to the classical scheme; it insists on reintroducing the existential subjects and the ecclesial communities into the sacraments. On the contrary, Barth, the faithful disciple of the Reformers, Calvin in particular, starts from above, that is to say, from the sovereign freedom of God, which nothing, and especially the church, can hinder.

Barth abhors any theology of the "and" (God's action and human action), which he interprets as a "synergistic" collusion by which the action of the church would in some way "be added" to God's; this calls into question the supreme efficacy of God's word in Jesus Christ. If the sacraments are efficacious *ex opere operato,* then, Barth fears, they negate the freedom of God who saves humans when and how God wants, independently of any ritual institution which would function as an instrument of salvation. The sacrament is therefore only "a purely human action responding to the word and action of God." The sacrament has the sole function of "recognizing," "proclaiming," "attesting," "reflecting," "following" the antecedent and gratuitous gift of justification and sanctification of humans by God. Its function of simple *response* to God does not, however, make it optional since (at least this is the case for baptism and holy communion) it is mandated by Jesus Christ; as such, it is even a "holy" action.[5]

All this has not prevented Barth from writing superbly on the liturgy. It is simply, as he himself writes concerning baptism, that he consciously took a stand, "by principle and *ab ovo,*" against "every ancient and very strong ecclesial tradition, as well as all its variants."[6] With regard to salvation, the sacrament is revelatory, but not operative: through it the Christian community manifests its recognition of the already-present gratuitous grace of God and festively expresses its gratitude toward God.

[5] Here we are referring to the very last volume of Karl Barth's *Dogmatique* (IV/4) devoted to baptism as "foundation of Christian life," pp. 133 and 165. [Karl Barth, *Church Dogmatics* (New York: Scribner, 1955–)]

[6] Ibid., pp. 106–107.

As in type B—but this time with arguments carefully developed by a theologian of great stature—the sacraments are seen primarily ? as instruments of transmission of the grace already given to the human subjects (hence its subjectivist character). Barth was so intent on respecting the gratuitousness of salvation and the free efficacy of God's word that he was led to deliberately contradict the preceding sacramental model. But the two models are less contradictory than contrary, which means, as Aristotle had pointed out, that their opposition is within a common genus, that is, on the same terrain or at the same level: "contrary propositions are within the same genus." In fact, the approach in both cases is that of the sacrament as instrument, that is, either an objective instrument of the production of grace as in the first model or an instrument of transmission of grace as in the second.

THE VATICAN II MODEL

The latest council did not formally develop a sacramental model. But while taking up the essential of the Scholastic sacramental doctrine which had been the standard at the Council of Trent, it corrected it and thus redressed its equilibrium. This redirecting process is largely dependent on what affected the theology of the church as sacrament of salvation or sacrament of the reign of God. This does not mean that we have here an eighth sacrament but the foundation on which the understanding of the seven sacraments is based. It goes without saying that the church is this fundamental sacrament only because it is totally dependent on the source-sacrament of God and the encounter of humanity with God which is Christ.

With regard to the question that occupies us here, let us keep in mind that such a sacramentality of the church means two things.

It means first that the church is not the reign itself; it is *only* its sacrament. This reminds us that the reign is larger than the church, even though the latter is its condition and its primary expression. The reign extends beyond the church in all directions, like the Spirit that "blows where it chooses" (John 3:8) and the word of God that grows slowly, but irresistibly, and works invisibly in the human dough (parables of the mustard seed and the leaven in Matt 13). Besides, it is important to underline that Vatican II is the first council which officially declared (although many theologians had said so for a long time) that "the holy Spirit offers to all the possibility of being made partners, in a way known to God, in the paschal mystery" and that those who "seek God with a sincere heart and, moved by grace, try in their actions to do his will . . . may attain eternal salvation."[7]

But on the other hand, the church *is* the sacrament of the reign. Inasmuch as it is a sacrament, it is a sign of the presence of the reign. It must show the marks of its being a sign of the reign. Among these marks, the first one is the confession of faith in Jesus as Christ on the basis of the Scriptures. Therefore, since the church is only a sacrament, one can be saved by God in Jesus Christ, the one Savior of all human beings, without being a Christian; conversely, since the church is a sacrament, one cannot be a Christian without being within the church, that is to say, without making one's own the confession of faith in Jesus Christ from which it was born. In this sense, we can substitute for the saying "Outside the church there is no salvation," the formula of Bishop R. Coffy, "Outside the church there is no recognized salvation" (that is to say, salvation confessed as such).

The sacraments, and above all, the two major sacraments, which according to tradition are baptism and Eucharist, belong to these marks of the reign which give the church its identity. Although Vatican II has adopted the traditional doctrine of the sacraments as means of salvation, it has strongly emphasized their function as signs of salvation. In connection with the Constitution on the Liturgy and the liturgical reform mandated by the Council, liturgists everywhere have sought to promote the signifying quality of the sacramental signs. To achieve this, they strove to counteract:

(1) their reification, by insisting on the self-explanatory authenticity of materials, gestures, languages, and the mode of celebration;

(2) the excessive objectivism that was prevalent, by taking into account the lived experience of human beings;

(3) a conception judged overly concerned with the point at which the sacrament is realized, by emphasizing the diffuse sacramentality of the life lived in faith: Is not the sacrament of reconciliation already begun when one takes the initiative of getting reconciled with another? Does not the effective practice of sharing with the poorest persons already possess a texture of sacramentality in relation with the Eucharist as the sacrament of sharing the body of Christ?

[7] "Pastoral Constitution on the Church in the Modern World," no. 22.5 (cf. "Dogmatic Constitution on the Church," no. 16), in Vatican Council II, *The Basic Sixteen Documents: Constitutions, Decrees, Declarations*, rev. trans. in inclusive language, ed. Austin Flannery (Northport, N.Y.: Costello, 1996) 186.

(4) an excessively individualistic mentality and a tendency to reduce the sacraments to their interior effects, by stressing their ecclesial dimension. Every sacrament is first of all a church event; it is in that capacity that it reaches individuals. The question was then posed: Is the church, the concrete local community itself, in its actions, statements, appearance the living sign of what it celebrates? When it seems to contradict in its pastoral practice what it otherwise proclaims theologically in the sacraments, it is called to conversion. If it is not a reconciling agent in the world, is it not in contradiction to the sacrament of reconciliation that it celebrates in the middle of the world and as a sign for the world? If it does not concern itself with the immigrants, does not it give a counter-testimony when it baptizes the immigrants' children and claims to welcome them into its bosom in the name of Christ?

Prior to celebrating the sacrament of the sick, must not the local community establish a true pastoral care of the sick and the handicapped? If, in its catechesis and different types of chaplaincies it does not worry enough about opening children and teenagers to faith, if it does not sufficiently apply itself to confirming their faith, is not the sacrament of confirmation a challenge to its spiritual dynamism and missionary potential? And so on. One can clearly see that the sacraments symbolically proclaim to the world what the church is; they attest it. But they contest it in the very moment they attest it.

This same insistence of the fundamentally ecclesial dimension of the sacraments also served to correct the excessive inflation of priestly "powers." "The active subject of the liturgy" is the ecclesia as such, that is to say, the concrete assembly of the baptized, as is shown by the constant "we" of the liturgical prayers.[8] Obviously, the priest has a specific function of presidency, "in the name of Christ," but this does not place him above the church; theologically, the priestly function can be rightly understood only within the church. One presides; all celebrate. In any case, the ministry of presidency exercised by the priest can in no way justify the sort of clerical omnipotence which all too often has prevailed in the church.

This sort of questioning, formulated in a jargon, often quite theologically approximate and not always innocent of a polemical intention toward the past with which one had a quarrel, was not without

---

[8] Yves Congar, "L'Ecclesia ou communauté chrétienne, sujet intégral de l'action liturgique," in *La liturgie après Vatican II*, ed. Jean Pierre Jossua and Yves Congar (Paris: Cerf, 1967) 241–282.

danger. Pushed too unilaterally, it risked ending in the deviations we have listed above when speaking of model 2. However, one cannot neglect calling attention to the considerable benefit that pastoral theory and practice has derived from it: liturgical celebrations have challenged Christian communities, often most vigorously, regarding their structures, their ways, and their very being, and they have been the source of an authentic missionary zeal. We are empowered by this dynamism even today, probably more serenely than in the 1970s. May this dynamism not fade away!

Be that as it may, the concern of the council to counterbalance the theology of sacraments as means by their role as signs is unmistakable: "The liturgy is the summit toward which the activity of the church is directed; it is also the source from which all its power flows," says the Constitution on the Liturgy (no. 10).[9] By using again the three terms of the preceding diagrams, one can visualize the sacramental theology of Vatican II in the following way:

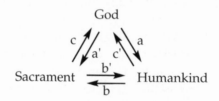

The movement of the external circuit is the newest (although, as we have seen, model 1 was not ignorant of it but hardly gave it a prominent place). It shows: (a) that God acts in people's lives in a perfectly free fashion, that God is not obliged to use the sacraments to save them, and that the reign is wider than the church; (b) that the sacraments are the summit of the life sanctified by God's grace and the revelatory expression (the sign) of this sanctification; (c) that they are acts of gratitude toward God. In this perspective, one sees what was profoundly right in versions B and C of model 2, and in particular in Barth's position, too unilateral in other aspects.

As to the internal circuit, more classical, it shows: (a') that the operating subject of the sacraments is always God (through Christ and in the Spirit); (b') that the sacraments are source or operative expression

⁹ "Constitution on the Sacred Liturgy," no. 10, in Vatican II, *Sixteen Documents*, 122.

(means or cause) of sanctification; (c') that, thus sanctified, human daily life becomes liturgy or spiritual offering to God's glory.

This diagram, being triangular and no longer linear like the preceding ones, is perfectly balanced. Must we stand here in complete satisfaction? Not necessarily, and for the reason we are going to give. Indeed, the two movements of the circuit are no doubt well put together; the two categories of sign and cause are closely interwoven, so closely that, as Thomas Aquinas had astutely pointed out, in the sacraments the sign has this altogether singular trait, to exist only by mode of causality, and that, conversely, the cause has this altogether singular trait, to produce its effect only by mode of sign. To use a comparison, we are presented with two mechanical parts perfectly tooled and combined. Yes, but sign and cause are two concepts differing in nature and in level. The two parts are not made of the same material; they are heterogenous. This observation may appear abstract. In fact it is heavy with consequences from the viewpoint of contemporary culture.

It is not the business of a council to take sides on such problems reflecting different schools of thought. This ecclesial task is that of theologians, if it is true that their function is to translate the church's faith into terms understandable to the culture of the time. Now, it appears that by way of language and symbolism it is possible to go forward theologically in this domain, that is to say, to present a general sacramental theory whose two most important parts are made of the same alloy and therefore are homogenous. That this is possible does not mean that we are more perspicacious or more intelligent than the theologians of past generations. It is due simply to the fact that we are situated in another cultural age and that we possess instruments of investigation not available in the past. We are not better than our ancestors; we are different. To each culture its theological discourse. Shall we try?

Structure: The Symbolic Order

The Sacraments: One Element of Christian Existence

For every single person, the body is the place in which the most internal and most external meet or the external place in which the internal finds its structure. Such a structure is "symbolic" (with a meaning we shall explain). It is an "order," that is to say, according to the definition in the *Petit Robert*, "an intelligible relation between a plurality of terms."[1] The *symbolic order* precisely designates this meaningful organization of the many elements that compose a properly human existence. It precedes every single person since it is within it that one becomes a "subject" (or a "person").[2] This is what we shall establish in the first chapter; in the second, we shall draw the proper consequences concerning the Christian subject; and we shall discuss the relation of these elements in the third.

---

[1] Paul Robert, *Le Petit Robert: Dictionnaire alphabétique et Analogique de la langue française*. ed. Alain Rey et al. (Paris: Société du Nouveau Littré, 1976).

[2] The two terms "subject" and "person" are practically equivalent. However, "person" has a moral connotation which the more neutral term "subject" does not have. For this reason, we shall more often use the latter, which is adequate to define the human being from the anthropological viewpoint.

Chapter 1

The Human Subject in Language and Culture

From the anthropological viewpoint, therefore independently of faith, the sacraments are expressions in word and rite proper to the particular religious group that Christians are. Inasmuch as they are expressions, they belong to what is called language: first verbal language, of course, but also the language (or quasi language) of gestures, postures, movements, which are all forms of body language.

Now, what is language? This is a vast and complex question. For our present purpose, we want to retain at least this: language is not an "instrument" but a "mediation." The least one can say is that this statement is far from self-evident. It is so far from being self-evident that such an *instrumentalist scheme*[3] corresponds not only to the common sense representation of language but also to the whole of philosophical tradition which, underneath its many variants, has prevailed in the West at large. This metaphysical scheme has come to us from the ancient Greeks, beginning with Plato. Let us explain this scheme before attempting to show its more or less hidden presuppositions.

LANGUAGE AS INSTRUMENT

One can visualize the instrumentalist representation of language by the following diagram:

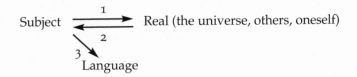

---

[3] The term "scheme" is borrowed from the great philosophical tradition. It is close to the usual term "schema." But while the latter designates a mental codification of experience as such, the former refers, beneath thought and intentions, to a sort of constitutive structure of human beings. Kant speaks of "a priori schemes."

Arrow 1 in this diagram means that the subject is in an immediate relation to reality; arrow 2 means that reality enters the subject's mind in a natural way and as a perfect replica under the form of a mental image, representation, or concept; arrow 3 means that as a consequence, the subject can communicate to others (or to herself or himself as to another) what she or he has perceived of reality. We said it above: such a representation of things seems so natural that common sense has quasi spontaneously adopted it and the philosophical tradition dominant in the West has largely depended upon it.

It is important to understand clearly that in this diagram language is treated as an instrument since the human subject (or the person) is posited (at least logically) before it. Of course, some people will be quick and forceful in pointing out that language is a very particular instrument, if only because it is the most precious and most malleable of all since it is used for communication. Even so, people continue to hold on to an instrumental approach in which one presupposes an ideal subject who would stand outside language, therefore outside mediation, that is to say finally, outside body and outside history. The human being would be some kind of lame angel.

What hides behind this approach? It is probably the *immediacy* which we assume characterizes the relation of the subject with reality. It is granted that the frailty of human beings is such that this relation is always somehow blurred by errors of perception, of transmission, of reception. But it is surmised that, thanks to the progress which each one can make and the amelioration of procedures, these errors are corrigible, at least partially, in this world. Ideally in any case, there should not be any errors. This ideal corresponds to the self-understanding of human beings. In this perspective, they realize themselves the better as they succeed in surmounting mediations as so many obstacles to their truth and self-realization. Finally, what seems to be hidden here is human beings' desire, largely unbeknownst to themselves, that reality be transparent and they be fully present to themselves by evading the contingency of the sensible, bodily, social, historical mediations.

With regard to language, it is remarkable that the metaphysical tradition has unrelentingly tried to minimize its mediational value by favoring the speaking voice. Indeed, verbal signifiers, that is, the sounds produced by the voice, vanish as soon as they are uttered. The result is that very rapidly one forgets that they too are concrete mediations made of sensible matter organized by culture, and one perceives only what is nearest to self and has an immediate proximity to the soul and the ideal nature of meaning.[4] Another theory is to see in language, as Augustine, then Thomas Aquinas[5] did, a consequence of original sin, which presupposes that human beings had been created without language. Besides, for Augustine, "language is assumed to be necessary neither for framing one's thoughts nor for identifying one's desires. Prior to and independently of all ability to talk, one is supposed to be already aware of one's mental states and acts."[6] In this perspective is not the ideal to recover the original condition of human beings, who were enlightened by the "interior word" of God?

As we have already suggested, this devaluation of language as primary mediation betrays the devaluation of all mediations. Among these devaluations one can list giving preference to the intelligible over the sensible, to "what is not transient" over history, to right reason over desire, and finally to the soul over the body. In the last analysis, everything which is in process of development, of "becoming," is suspect; what is permanent, stable, eternal is preferred. Is not the true "philo-sopher," "friend of wisdom," according to the statement which Plato attributes to Socrates, the person who chooses a life "in which there is neither joy nor pain, but thoughtful thinking as pure as possible"?[7] In other words, human beings are realized only inasmuch as they subject what is "in process of becoming" to what is "essence," what is "desire" to what is "thought," what is "body" to what is "soul"—which is ultimately accomplished by death when the body is literally "put down" to the benefit of the immortal soul.

Of course, this devaluation is relative: in view of what their condition is in this world, human beings must "live with" language, body, what is of the sensible order, history, desire. They are even capable of doing great things, provided they have the benefit of education and self-discipline. It nevertheless remains that these mediations are

[4] See Jacques Derrida, *De la grammatologie* (Paris: Minuit, 1967) 21–31; [*Of Grammatology,* trans. Gayatri Chakravorty Spivak (Baltimore: Johns Hopkins, 1976) 6–26].

[5] Thomas Aquinas, *Summa Theologica,* pt. 1, q. 94, a. 1.

[6] Fergus Kerr, *Theology after Wittgenstein* (New York: Blackwell, 1986) 41. Here the author comments on Augustine's celebrated passage regarding the acquisition of language by the young child, in *Confessions* 1.8.43.

[7] Plato, *Philebus* 55a, in *The Tragedy and Comedy of Life: Plato's Philebus,* trans. and comment. Seth Bernadete (Chicago: University of Chicago Press, 1993) 67.

obstacles to their self-realization and to the possession of truth. Even Christianity, in spite of a more positive view of matter because it is created by God and of the bodily condition of human beings because it has been assumed by the Word of God itself in Jesus, has never fully cast away this suspicion of the sensible. Christianity has indeed recognized in the sensible matter of the sacraments of faith mediations of communication between God and humankind, but this is primarily because the sacraments are seen as "remedies" according to the Scholastics' classical and most often used expression, remedies adapted by God to the human condition in order to heal it.

The instrumentalist scheme of language is laden with consequences. It walks hand in hand with the most characteristic dualisms which we have inherited from the dominant metaphysical tradition: visible/invisible; body/soul; internal/external; in-process-of-becoming/essence. This scheme is controlled by the desire to seize the "thing" in an *immediate* way, to be fully present to oneself, to be totally transparent to others. Thus, Fergus Kerr, commenting on the philosopher Ludwig Wittgenstein, writes, "Our dependence for our status as rational agents upon the materiality of signs, once overlooked, soon tends to be played down and even denied. Thus the metaphysical paradigm [model] of the self is generated. (The metaphysical tradition might even be defined as the age-long refusal to acknowledge the bodiliness of meaning and mind.)"[8]

Therefore, what unconsciously dominates the conception of language as instrument is the presupposition that sensible mediations are obstacles to the truth. It is this very presupposition that has been questioned through the epistemological revolution led by the contemporary sciences and philosophy of language. What if, instead of being obstacles to truth, sensible mediations of language, body, history, desire were the very milieu within which human beings attain their truth and thus correspond to the Truth which calls them?

LANGUAGE AS MEDIATION

An eminent contemporary linguist, Emile Benveniste, writes this:

"The comparison of language with an instrument must fill us with distrust, like every simplistic notion about language. To speak of instrument is to oppose humankind and nature. The hoe, the arrow,

[8] Kerr, *Theology after Wittgenstein*, 136.

the wheel are not in nature. They are fabricated objects. We are always inclined to naively imagine that at the beginning, a complete human being would discover another human being similar to herself or himself and equally complete, and that little by little, a language would develop between them. This is pure fiction. We never see human beings separate from language and we never see them inventing it. We never encounter human beings reduced to themselves and contriving to conceive the existence of other human beings. What we find in the world are speaking human beings speaking to other human beings, and *language teaches us the very definition of human being.*"[9]

The import of these words is clear: language is contemporary with human beings—with humanity which begins with it, and with every single individual. To treat language as an instrument is to suppose, as we have seen, that the subject could, at least logically, preexist it. While human beings existed before inventing instruments such as the hoe or the arrow, they did not exist before language (and consequently culture).[10] There exists only speaking subjects, and speaking to another speaking subject (even if this other speaking subject is anthropomorphized nature). One can be a human being without knowing tools such as a pencil or a table; one cannot be a human being without language. In order to be able to "invent" language, one must think of it; but in order to be able to think of it, one must already be in language. It is therefore true that "language teaches us the very definition of human being" and that, as Benveniste adds, "it is in and by language that human beings are constituted as subjects."

Consequently, with respect to language, the notion of instrument will be replaced by that of mediation, that is to say, the *milieu* in which the subject becomes subject. This milieu is to be regarded as a sort of womb. This term has the advantage of bringing us back to the fetal condition; from the time of pregnancy, the child is enclosed in a maternal womb which is not only biological but already cultural since

---

[9] Emile Benveniste, *Problèmes de linguistique générale*, vol. 1 (Paris: Gallimard, 1966) 259; [*Problems in General Linguistics*, trans. Mary Elizabeth Meek, Miami Linguistics Series 8 (Coral Gables, Fla.: Miami, 1971)]. Emphasis is ours.

[10] "Culture" is understood here, as in the whole of this book, not as the culture of learned people "who are cultivated," but in its fundamental meaning: every human group, every society, and within it every human subject, has a "culture," in the full sense of the term. "Culture" and "language" go hand in hand.

the mother (modern psychology insists on this point) already speaks to her baby, shares with it, consciously and especially unconsciously, her emotions and feelings, and begins, most often without realizing it, to transmit to it the cultural heritage of the group, the mother tongue to begin with. In summary, the fact that speaking begins in the mother's womb must be considered a necessary condition of any humanization. Not a sufficient condition to be sure: when he was discovered, the wolf-child, who had received from his parents the complete chromosomal equipment necessary for walking and talking like other humans, walked on all fours and could not speak. The "education" after birth, through which the system of values formed by the culture is inculcated in the child, is obviously capital in this affair. Such an inculcation is programmed by the group; but this is only the tip of the iceberg: the invisible part, that dictated primarily by the parents' unconscious and ready to penetrate the child's psychic makeup, notably under the form of superego, is much more important. It is perhaps no exaggeration to say that the cultural air that children receive through every pore of their skin is in some way as decisive for enabling them to live as subjects as the physical air which fills their lungs for enabling them to live at all.

To understand language as mediation is to assent to the following diagram:

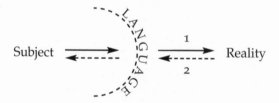

In this diagram arrow 1 indicates that the relation of the subject to reality, therefore any properly human or signifying relation, is mediated, consequently *constructed*, by language and, in a more general sense, culture; arrow 2, that it is precisely *by* constructing reality as "world" that the subject constructs *itself* as subject. Language is thus a construction game in a twofold sense: objective, of construction of reality as world and, subjective, of construction of the subject—a little like the Legos with which children learn how to build, at their whim, all sorts of machines with pulleys or all sorts of castles and thus how to build themselves.

This diagram intends to call attention to two principal points. On the one hand, in relation to the subject, language is no longer regarded as an instrument but as a womb: the subject arises and is maintained within it. However, there is no question of substituting the precedence of language for the precedence of the subject, as shown in the previous diagram, since here subject and language (culture) are contemporaneous. On the other hand, the diagram indicates that every properly human relation to reality is culturally constructed. A bit of explanation is in order here.

In the film *The Gods Must Be Crazy* we see a tribesman of the Kalahari, hardly out of the Stone Age, discovering by chance a bottle of Coca-Cola thrown out of an airplane a while before. For him and for us this bottle has everything necessary to be a bottle: if it had fallen on his head, he would have felt, like us, a keen *sensation* of pain. But the *perception* he has of the bottle is such that for him, as for the people in his tribe, this object is not a bottle. Indeed, not only do they have no word for bottle in their language; they are equally ignorant of the existence of glass, of which it is made, and have no word for it. Furthermore, none of the tribe knows what this strange thing is for: one of them moves it, like a mirror, toward the sun to create pretty reflections; another blows into the neck of the bottle to create musical sounds; a third uses it as a sort of rolling pin, and so on. Then it happens that, coveted by all for its many possibilities and at the same time feared as a foreign (therefore dangerous) object, the doodad (Is not this the word that fits the situation?) sows discord in the village and a man must go and throw it into the abyss, at the end of the world—which cannot be very far. And obviously, here begins the adventure of our man.

This example suitably illustrates our topic. In the tribe's language and culture there is no such thing as a bottle. This does not exist for them; what exists is a thing, at once captivating and dangerous, which they try to fit into the meaningful mapping of the world which their language, their culture, their social organization provide. Not only do they lack the idea of a bottle (which would at least postulate that they have the word), but they do not even have the perception of it. Similarly, even though every forest in the world is a fairly vast surface occupied by trees and thickets, the aboriginal people whose home is the rain forests of equatorial Africa do not perceive a forest in the same way as the Chicagoan who goes to the woods for a weekend of fresh air. Or to use another simile, even though the physical composition of snow is the same everywhere, it is not perceived in the same way by us Westerners and the Inuit who possess a score of words in their language to describe snow. For us, it goes without saying that work and play are separate, if not antagonistic, activities, but the same is not true of the Australian Aborigines, who have one word for both.

Clearly, the ordering of the world varies according to languages and cultures. And this is true of realities that appear most evident to us. Thus, the notion of person in traditional Balinese society has little in common with ours (on the contrary, it has all the traits of what we would call depersonalization).[11] Among the ancient Greeks the notion of god designated a function, even "a plurality of functions,"[12] rather than the personal transcendent being that it means for us.

These few examples are sufficient to facilitate the understanding of what we mean by mediation of language and culture. It can be compared to a filter, or better to a lens which forms on the human eye in the womb. Such a lens is invisible; furthermore, used by everyone since the first instants of life, it attracts so little notice that it is constantly forgotten and causes everyone to qualify as "the most natural thing in the world" what is in fact a wholly cultural one. For everything is filtered through it, and it is precisely this filtering that makes raw reality into a world.

What does language do? In his famous lecture on the "stage of the mirror," Jacques Lacan has shown that between the age of six and eighteen months, the human child does not spontaneously identify the image it sees in the mirror as a self-image. At first, the baby sees a body (and at the very beginning only the unrelated parts of a body). In order to be able to identify itself, that is to say, to recognize that it is a "symbolic" whole of another order than the image in the mirror, the baby must hear itself *named* by someone, someone using its first name and subsequently a personal pronoun. It is this *distancing*, this break of immediacy that opens the child to symbolic recognition. After the first name, the personal pronoun has this quite singular characteristic: it includes the subject (here, the child) by representing it and at the same time it excludes the child by only representing it. The subject is born

[11] Clifford Geertz, *Bali: interprétation d'une culture* (Paris: Gallimard, 1983) 109–164.

[12] Jean Pierre Vernant, *Mythe et société en Grèce ancienne* (Maspéro, 1974) 103–120; [*Myth and Society in Ancient Greece*, trans. James Lloyd, European Philosophy and the Human Sciences 5 (Atlantic Highlands, N.J.: Humanities, 1980)].

precisely in this inner split effected by language, or in Lacan's jargon, "It is by its partition that the subject proceeds to its parturition."[13]

The equally well-known analysis of Claude Lévi-Strauss on the origin of the prohibition of incest reveals this same distancing effected by language. This taboo has two specific characteristics: first, it is "the only rule among all the rules that has a universal character";[14] second, it is less one rule among others than the *"fact* of the rule" itself. In other words, the law of separation between the immediate satisfaction of sexual desire, the law which is at work in the prohibition of incest, that is, the law of difference, or better, of deferral (what causes the desire for immediate gratification to be deferred), is THE law. The emergence of humanity from animality is linked to this law of the renunciation of immediate gratification, which is the law that creates the space, the emptiness within which all other laws will find their place. One could discern the same fundamental conviction either in Freud's famous Oedipus complex or more recently in R. Girard's "mimesis."

Like humanity in general, every single individual accedes to the status of subject thanks to this law of separation between desire and immediate satisfaction, separation effected by language. For such is really the primordial function of language: it places reality at a distance by representing it in sounds and chains of coded sounds and thus makes it signifying. It commits "the murder of the thing" (Lacan), inasmuch as it is a raw thing, in order to make of it a "speaking" thing. From this moment, everything speaks, not only in the intransitive sense when nature speaks to us, but also in the transitive sense when we are spoken by it. When I speak, it is always in some way according to my culture and my desire. Thus, "what the perception brings is not the tree before me

---

[13] Jacques Lacan, *Écrits* (Paris: Seuil, 1966) 843. [*Ecrits: A Selection*, trans. Alan Sheridan (New York: Norton, 1977)].

[14] Claude Lévi-Strauss, *Les structures élémentaires de la parenté* (Presses Universitaires de France, 1949) 10; [*The Elementary Structures of Kinship*, trans. James Harle Bell, John Richard von Sturmer, and Rodney Needham, editor (Boston: Beacon Press, 1969)]. Let us specify that whereas the rule itself is universal, the concrete prescriptions vary. Thus, among the 250 societies studied by George Peter Murdock, *Social Structure*, 8th ed. (New York: Macmillan, 1963), none tolerates sexual relations between persons at the first degree of kinship (for instance between a man and his mother, his daughter, or his sister), and all of them extend the prohibition of incest beyond this first degree. However, it is on this last point that there are important differences between cultures.

but a certain vision which the tree provokes in me and which is my response to the call of the tree."[15] In the same way, the water which I observe is never a purely "natural" thing but is necessarily grasped by my understanding as "signifying" to some degree, therefore bearer of my own culture and desire: "The water which I look at, drink, in which I bathe, is always deep, clear, pure, fresh. . . . Its reality is to be immediately a metaphor of my existence."[16] From the landscape which I observe, I retain only some features reflecting the cultural system which has been inculcated in me since my earliest days and which I have interiorized to such an extent that these features appear to me the most natural in the world; they also reflect the various forms of the singular history of my desire. As François Flahault writes:

"Linguistic activity is never confronted (except in physical sciences, and even there, it is not evident) with a physical universe that would be heterogeneous to it, but rather with a world always already filled with signification, always already ordered, always already socially organized. Certainly, material reality has an existence independent of the awareness that human subjects have of it; but precisely, it is not with this universe that infants are initially confronted; it is in a world *inhabited* by other humans that they must make their way. . . . The same thing is true for adults: the acts of getting dressed, eating, residing, moving, working, suffering, finding pleasure—all these continually plunge us into a world filled with symbolic reference points. . . . *Although it is the physical reality which affects the senses, it is the thick semiological layer it is covered with which is perceived.*"[17]

From a directly philosophical viewpoint, Martin Heidegger says nothing different on the first page of *On the Way to Language:*

"According to an ancient understanding, we ourselves are, after all, those beings who have the ability to speak and therefore already possess language. Nor is the ability to speak just one among man's many talents, of the same order as the others. The ability to speak is what

[15] Brice Parain, *Recherches sur la nature et la fonction du langage* (Paris: Gallimard, 1942) 61.

[16] Antoine Vergote, *Interprétation du langage religieux* (Paris: Seuil, 1974) 64.

[17] François Flahault, *La parole intermédiaire* (Paris: Seuil, 1978) 84–85. Emphasis, the author's.

marks man as man. This mark contains the design of his being. Man would not be man if it were denied him to speak unceasingly, from everywhere and every which way, in many variations, and to speak in terms of 'it is' that often remains unspoken. Language, in granting all this to man, is the foundation of the human being."[18]

To say that "there is speaking" constantly in human beings is to say that every perception of reality is mediated by their culture and the history of their desire. In the absence of these, this reality would be left to its raw factualness and would be only a chaos or a meaningless jumble. In order for the subject to reach and retain its status of subject, it must build reality into a "world," that is to say, a signifying whole in which every element, whether material (tree, wind, house) or social (relatives, clothing, cooking, work, leisure) is integrated into a system of *knowledge* (of the world and of society), *gratitude* (code of good manners, mythical and ritual code ruling relationships with deities and ancestors), and *ethical behavior* (values serving as norms of conduct). The infant as well as the adult have to deal with this world, *always-already* constructed, and not with things in their crude physical state. By these means, the universe and events form a coherent whole which is called "the symbolic order." Subjects can orient themselves by it because each thing can find in it its own signifying place.

The implications of this approach are weighty. The sensible, cultural, institutional mediations are no longer obstacles which ideally should be surmounted in order for subjects to walk toward truth. On the contrary, they are, even in their very ambiguity (for they are necessarily ambiguous), the milieu within which human beings learn, at their expense, to accede to their own truth and, by the same token, accept to hear the call of truth, which is greater than themselves. At this point, one can glimpse the possibilities open to Christians with regard to their living relationship with God through the sacraments, these sensible and institutional mediations which are so ambiguous.

THE SYMBOLIC ORDER

We mentioned symbolic order above. We must be more precise about what we mean by this locution. First of all, one can ask why not

---

[18] Martin Heidegger, *On the Way to Language*, trans. Peter D. Hertz (New York: Harper and Row, 1971) 111–112. The text of the lecture "Die Sprache" (Speech) goes back to 1950.

simply speak of cultural order. The two expressions are practically equivalent, as readers will have understood. However, the term "symbolic order" has a threefold advantage.

(a) "Symbol" comes from the Greek *sym-ballein* which means "to put together," to place side by side the elements of a whole, somewhat like the different pieces of a puzzle. But in contrast to the term puzzle, the term symbol connotes the idea of contract, of pact or covenant. In antiquity, when two or three persons (or groups legitimately represented by these persons) made a contract, they were given the pieces of an object shared among them. At any time, even after decades, these persons or their descendants could exhibit their piece of the object, join it to the other pieces, and thus prove themselves to be partners in the contract. For the time being, let us leave aside this power of identification inherent in the symbol. What interests us here is the idea of *placing side by side*.

This idea can be transposed to the level of a social group. For a human society to exist, it is necessary that the subjects which compose it agree, which presupposes a common code of values, norms, roles, functions, and, above all, a common language. This code itself is the object of a convention. This convention is most singular since, at least with regard to language, it does not exist because someone some day would have decreed it. Language, together with the most important social functions, is part of a heritage existing from time immemorial. This convention creates the *social pact* enabling people to live together and in agreement. This convention constitutes the symbolic order, that is to say, the coherent ensemble of social, cognitive, ethical, aesthetic, philosophical, political values as well as rules concerning dress and cooking. All these are inculcated from earliest infancy and are so deeply embedded in everyone that they bespeak the symbolic order most openly and are so taken for granted that they cannot be put into question. That this ensemble forms a coherent world means that every element of universe, society, individual life has meaning only by finding its place, its right place, in it. It is also possible to speak of "structure," this term having the advantage of immediately stressing that the meaning of each element rests on its relation with all the other elements which compose the structure. In a structure, everything holds together! By altering the traditional way of working, as is happening for instance to African societies subjected to the pressure of Western technology, one also undermines the traditional stability of the village, therefore social and familial relationships, therefore the myths that are their foundation, therefore the whole religious system, therefore the most vital symbolic expressions of the culture, without even mentioning the villagers' eating habits, their traditional dwellings, their mode of dress, or the economic and political problems that arise at the same time, and so on.[19]

(b) To speak of "symbolic order" is precisely to indicate that all the elements of the cultural puzzle are joined to one another and that each element acquires it significance only by being put back into this conventional ensemble as diversified as human societies are. By the same token, it is to distinguish the symbolic from the "imaginary." This last term comes to us from Lacan's psychoanalytic theory. It designates this psychic agency (in the same way as Freud speaks of the "agency of the superego") which, in distinction to the real and the symbolic, is characterized "by the prevalence of the relation to the image of what is the same."[20] This means that whereas the symbolic places the real at a distance by representing it and thus enabling it to be integrated into a culturally significant and coherent whole, the imaginary tends to erase this distance in order to regain the immediate contact with things. As a consequence, things are only the mirror into which the subject projects itself and where it attempts to find (of course unconsciously) its own "image," only embellished. This is an erasing of the difference or otherness in order to find again the "image of what is the same." Everything always returns to the "same," that is, to the subject itself, unavoidably idealized.

This agency of the imaginary, inherent in every person's psychological makeup, does have positive aspects. Among other advantages, it functions as a goad impelling the subject to progress toward this ideal ego whose image the subject bears within itself. But left to itself, the imaginary is deadly, as the story of Narcissus shows: wishing to join the beautiful image of himself he saw in the water of the fountain, he leaned forward so far that he drowned. Instead of being reinserted into the fabric of cultural and social rules where they find their signifying place, the elements are isolated and by the same token desymbolized:

[19] One can see that the serious problems which the Third World knows today are cultural problems, the technological and economic ones being only the most obvious expression.

[20] Jean Laplanche and J. B. Pontails, *Vocabulaire de la psychanalyse*, 6th ed. (Presses Universitaires de France, 1978) 195; [*The Language of Psycho-Analysis*, trans. Donald Nicholson-Smith (New York: Norton, 1974)].

"One cannot isolate a symbol without destroying it and causing it to slip into the ineffable imaginary."[21]

Such an isolation occurs on several levels. It can be in its relation to the overall culture, in which case, one ends in madness. It can be in its relation to a lesser ensemble of this culture: for instance, for someone to make the sign of the cross in isolation from Christianity, in which it finds its meaning, is to treat it imaginarily and give it just about any meaning at all according to the imagination of the moment (gesture to brush off a fly, tic, warning given to someone, and so on). It can be in its relation to the sequence of signifiers within which the element has its own meaning: for instance, a neurotic subject retains from a whole discourse only the word or expression which feeds its obsession; instead of replacing this signifier within the whole of the sentence or speech which gives it the meaning recognized by other people, the subject isolates it and uses it in an imaginary fashion. All this clearly proves that it is possible to hear someone's words correctly but only in the measure in which one "comprehends" the world of the speaker. This point is especially important in the religious and, even more, the ritual domain.

(c) The third element of the symbolic is its reference to the "other." This other is neutral: it designates the agency under which or in the name of which the subjects agree with one another. Thus, to come back to the example cited above, a contract can be made only when two (or any number of) partners act under the agency of the other represented here by the law. It is by means of this reference to the law (at least implicit) that the contract can be recognized as valid and legitimate by the partners and that they can feel obligated to the duties and entitled to the rights specified in the contract. Besides, this law can take quite diverse forms, depending on the societies and the times. It can be, as in our society, the law written in due form, or else the nation; it can be the "tradition" from time immemorial or the "ancestors"; it can be the founder of the society or religious group, whether mythical or historical (Moses, Jesus); it can be God; it can be the society as such. For example, the simple fact of speaking English between us requires that we act under the agency of this other which is the English-speaking linguistic community (past and present).

[21] Edmond Ortigues, *Le discours et le symbole* (Paris: Aubier-Montaigne, 1962) 221.

There is no symbol, and beforehand, no symbolic order without this "subjection" of partners to the other.

Most often, such a subjection (which is the condition of freedom) is not conscious. But in a certain number of cases it must be made explicit. This is particularly evident in the most strongly ritualized official documents, such as the signing of a contract, the appointment of someone to a position, the execution of a decision taken by the legitimate authority. "In virtue of the power vested in me by the people," the President will say; a justice of the peace will declare X and Y united in marriage "according to the law of the state of Z"; the minister will baptize "in the name of the Father, and of the Son, and of the Holy Spirit." But let us repeat, the process underlying the whole of the cultural and social order is present even when not made explicit as in these examples.

* * *

What is valid for human subjects in general is of course valid for Christian subjects. To attain their identity as Christians, they must be part of the symbolic order proper to the church. This symbolic womb, within which each person is born as Christian through initiation, is unique. Of course this symbolic order is rooted in the general culture, but it reconfigures it, that is to say, it brings to the culture new directions, so new that Christians understand the meaning of their own lives differently from atheists or Muslims. One becomes a Christian only by adopting the "mother tongue" of the church. Sacraments are an important element of this tongue. However, they are only one element among others. This is what we shall develop in the following chapter.

Chapter 2

The Christian Subject
in the Language and Culture of the Church

To acquire Christian identity one must assent to faith in Jesus as "Christ," "Lord," "Son of God." This means that one must assent to the confession of faith from which the church was born. From the first, two points must be made clear: one concerning the notion of identity; the other concerning the relationship of the individual Christian to the church.

First, when we speak of *identity,* as will happen often in what follows, we are not placing ourselves on a merely juridical or administrative level. Of course, there is no identity without an institutional process requiring at the minimum, as in traditional societies, the conferring of a name recognized by all, and in our societies a name duly recorded at the Office of Vital Statistics.[1] Such a process is much deeper than the mere application of an official stamp on a membership card of a political party or a club. It touches the very possibility of existing as a subject because a person without an identity, and especially without a name, can only be excluded from society and cannot live as a subject. For instance, a stranger without any identification and struck with amnesia cannot exist as a subject unless other people, being unable to ascertain the stranger's own name, give her or him a name. Clearly, to speak of identity as subject is to touch the most sensitive point of what makes a human being a person.

The more so when it comes to Christian identity. "The more so" because what is at stake here is the recognition of the Christian not only as a human subject but as a believing subject. Christian identity is linked to the confession of faith Christians make their own and as a consequence to the meaning which, on this basis, they give to their lives. Christian identity entails a personal commitment. However, this

[1] See ch. 6, n. 1, on p. 117.

identity does not bypass the church as institution. Christian identity is not self-administered; to obtain it, one must receive baptism, and one does not baptize oneself; one is baptized by another person acting as the minister of the church in the name of Christ.

In the second place, although this identity has an undeniable personal dimension, it is bestowed only *within an ecclesial pattern* common to all Christians. It is this "pattern" which we are going to analyze now. Another specification is in order. A seamstress cutting a dress makes it from a common pattern in which at least a neckline and armholes are provided; but from there on, she can cut the dress from a solid or flowery material, make it more or less long, decorate it with frills and flounces or laces, and so on. Similarly, there is a general pattern of Christian identity: it is impossible to call oneself a Christian if one does not adopt as one's own the few marks characteristic of a Christian, just as it would be impossible to put on the dress we were speaking of without passing the neck and arms through the openings prepared for them. This pattern is not for a ready-made garment that would fit everyone. One person came to faith through the reading of the gospel, another at a eucharistic celebration which she or he attended by chance; one person is moved by the social commitment of Christians, another by the mystical dimension of faith; one person intends to work in catechesis, another wants to act in service to the neediest. There might be one common pattern, but anyone can still "dress Christian" in an individual way.

This common pattern is the symbolic order proper to the church, that is, as we have seen, a structure. Let us look into what this structure of Christian identity is all about.

THE STRUCTURE OF CHRISTIAN IDENTITY

This structure is given to us especially in St. Luke's two works, the Third Gospel and the Acts of the Apostles.

Three Key Texts

Some of Luke's texts concerning the way one comes to faith seem built on the same model. In particular, there is a parallelism between the story of the disciples of Emmaus (Luke 24:13-35) (A), that of the Ethiopian's baptism (Acts 8:26-40) (B), and the first account of Saul's conversion (Acts 9:1-20) (C). They show us a common mold.

(a) In the three cases Luke places us in the *time of the church* according to his theology in which, after Jesus' resurrection, everything starts from Jerusalem in order to go to "all Judea and Samaria, and to the ends of the earth" (Acts 1:8). This is indicated by the movement in A from Jerusalem to Emmaus (even though, in this early phase, which is that of the first recognition of the risen One, there is a return to Jerusalem), in B from Jerusalem to Gaza, and in C from Jerusalem to Damascus.

(b) In the three cases we deal with an *initiative on God's part:* in A, through the risen Christ when the two disciples' eyes are shut; in B, through God's Spirit when the Ethiopian's mind is not open; in C, again through the risen Christ when Saul's eyes are going to be closed.

(c) Most importantly, in the three cases this divine initiative, which alone allows the witnesses to accede to faith, happens through the *mediation of the church.* This mediation of the church is attested at three levels:

(1) First, in A, it is that of the kerygma of the church announcing that Jesus' death and resurrection are the key to "all the scriptures" (Luke 24:27); in B, the major passage of the Suffering Servant in Isaiah 53 which the Ethiopian reads without understanding since he cannot comprehend its meaning without a "guide" (the guide for reading that precisely the church supplies); as for C, it implies this same announcement of the crucified Jesus' resurrection, since the voice from heaven shows that he is alive in his church ("I am Jesus whom you are persecuting").

One can note that in each case this initiative of God sets in motion a journey toward faith, which prompts the witnesses to request something: in A, "Stay with us"; in B, "What is to prevent me from being baptized?"; in C, "What am I to do, Lord?" (Acts 22:9).

(2) However, this faith remains incomplete as long as it is not "informed" by a "sacramental" gesture: that of the breaking of the bread in A; of baptism in B; of the laying on of hands and baptism by Ananias in C. Only then, in A and C, are the "eyes opened," is the "sight restored."

(3) The eyes open but on an absence: in A, the risen One disappears as soon as he is recognized; likewise in B, Jesus' witness, Philip, is "snatched away" by "the Spirit." This absence knows itself to be henceforth in-dwelt by a presence. It is precisely the fact that this presence has become invisible that urges the witnesses to proclaim by their missionary commitment: the two disciples in A, just as Saul in C, are from now on heralds and witnesses, while the Ethiopian in B "went on his way rejoicing," with this joy so frequently mentioned by

Luke and which in his theological code designates "the joy of the messianic times, the joy of salvation in faith"[2]

Chapter 24 of the Gospel of Luke

The key to understanding how one comes to faith, which is given to us in the three preceding texts, can be studied in a deeper way in the first one. However, it is not useless to situate the story of Emmaus within the whole of chapter 24 where it finds its place.

Here again, we must record parallelisms between the three principal pericopes of this chapter: (A) the announcement of the resurrection to the women who came to the tomb (vv. 1-12); (B) the story of Emmaus (vv. 13-35); (C) the appearance to the disciples (vv. 36-49). In the three cases, the protagonists begin with a desire to "find," "to see," "to touch": in (A), the women "did not find the body," whereas Peter "saw" the linen cloths; in (B), the women "did not find his body," whereas the disciples who went to verify their testimony "did not see him"; in (C), beset by confusion and doubt, the eleven are urged by the risen One to "see" and "touch." For the time being let us observe that all these verbs occupy a common terrain, that they are at the same level, or that they have a common trait: they all refer to the *corpse* of Jesus (what did they expect to "find" or to "see" if not his dead body?) or the marks of his death ("to see" the linen cloths, "to touch" his wounds).

Next, it is remarkable that the freeing of the witnesses from their quandary is effected in each case by a recourse to the Scriptures: (A) "Remember . . . that the Son of Man must"; (B) "slow of heart to believe . . . was it not necessary?"; (C) "everything . . . must be fulfilled . . . thus it is written." All these "necessaries" are evidently to be understood from the viewpoint of God's revelation and God's "plan" of salvation in the Scriptures ("Moses and all the prophets" in B; "the law of Moses, the prophets, and the psalms" in C). The Christian rereading of the whole of the Scriptures as announcing the death and resurrection of the Messiah of God or, in the reverse direction, the rereading of this death-resurrection as "in accordance with the Scriptures" (see v. 44) is the key of interpretation, the hermeneutics (see v. 27), the opening of the minds (see v. 45) from which the church was born.

---

[2] Note of the *Traduction œcuménique de la Bible,* 2 vols. (Paris: Cerf, 1975–1976), on Acts 1:8.

If therefore, as is the case at Emmaus, the sacramental gesture of the "breaking of the bread" or, as in the two preceding texts, that of baptism plays an important role in access to faith, it is always on the basis of this new interpretation of the word of God in the Scriptures and of the faith in that word.

The Story of the Disciples of Emmaus

In the background of this account there is a question, a question which was that of the two disciples of Emmaus, one of them named Cleopas. But a question which is that of any disciple of Jesus, today as yesterday: "If it is true that Jesus arose and that he is alive, how is it that we do not see him, that we cannot see/touch/find him?" (see above for the status of these verbs in the whole of chapter 24). Luke responds to this question, which is the central question of faith, with a catechesis in the form of a story, a story that has an exemplary value for every believer.

The round trip Jerusalem-Emmaus-Jerusalem, which is the framework of this account, can be read on three levels: first, geographical; then, theological—Luke concentrates all the appearances of Jesus in Jerusalem, the one focus toward which his whole Gospel converges and from which everything departs "to the ends of the earth" after the resurrection and Pentecost; finally, symbolic—it is the inner reversal happening to the two disciples, their conversion, which is symbolized by this geographical round trip.

Such a conversion is a *performance*, that of the passage from non-faith to faith, from closed eyes to open eyes, from lack of comprehension to recognition. Such a performance is exactly what every human being must realize in order to become a disciple of Jesus, the Christ. The only thing is that in order to succeed in such a performance Cleopas and his companion must obtain the necessary *competence*.

The story describes how this competence is obtained. Three indicators having to do with time mark it: a first stop on the road: "They stood still, looking sad" (v. 17); the rest at Emmaus: "So he went in to stay with them" (v. 29); the return to Jerusalem: "That same hour they got up and returned to Jerusalem" (v. 33).

(a) The first temporal indicator corresponds to the beginning of the dialogue between the two disciples and the person who has just joined them. They know everything about "Jesus of Nazareth" (v. 19) and especially about his dramatic last moments. They know everything about him, but they have understood nothing of him. They regard him as a "prophet" but only as a prophet. True, they had been close to considering him the Messiah, "the one to redeem Israel"; but this political interpretation of Jesus' messianism had misled them. True again, "angels" have declared to some women that he is alive; but neither they nor the other disciples after them "saw" him. Everything is at a standstill in their minds: they have allowed themselves to be shut up in the tomb of death with Jesus, and their difficulties are as heavy as the stone that closed that tomb.

The unblocking of this impasse begins at the moment they let the stranger take the initiative and speak, an initiative characterized by the appeal to the *Scriptures*. In fact, it is a completely new hermeneutics (*diērmēneusen*, "he interpreted") of all the Scriptures that he proposes to them. It is summed up by Luke in one sentence: "Was it not necessary that the Messiah should suffer these things and then enter into his glory?" Luke tells us that the key to understanding God's whole plan according to the Scriptures is the death and resurrection of the Messiah.

Through these words of Jesus, condensed to the maximum by Luke, it is all-important to glimpse as if through alabaster the discourse of the *church*. For what does the church do? (Let us remember that at the time of the final redaction of our Third Gospel, about 80–85, the term "church" designated the local assembly of the Christians in any given city.) Every "first day of the week" (the Jewish term for Sunday) it reads, as was the custom in the Jewish synagogue, two scriptural texts: one from Moses, that is, the Torah (the Law, corresponding to our Pentateuch) and one from the Prophets, texts which were then explained in the homily. By bringing the two texts together and linking them to another passage from Scripture, a psalm verse for instance, which the homilist used as an opening, the homily aimed at showing the always timely meaning of the word of God. It is this same rabbinical technique of reading and homily that the early Christian communities quite naturally adopted in their meetings.[3] However, if the technique is the same, the interpretation is new: "Moses and the prophets" (plus "the psalms" in verse 44) are from now on interpreted in relation to the death and resurrection of Jesus, as verses 25-27 of our text show in exemplary fashion.

[3] On this point, see Pierre Grelot and Marcel Dumais, *Homélies sur l'Écriture à l'époque apostolique*, in *Introduction à la Bible: le Nouveau Testament*, vol. 8 (Paris: Desclée, 1989).

If it is indeed the foundational discourse of the church (its kerygma) we perceive here behind the discourse of the risen Jesus on the Scriptures, the issue which dominates the whole of our story becomes clear: you cannot arrive at the recognition of the risen Jesus unless you renounce seeing/touching/finding him by undeniable proofs. Faith begins precisely with such a *renunciation of the immediacy* of the see/know and with the assent to the mediation of the church. For it is he, the Lord, who speaks through the church each time it reads and interprets the Scriptures as referring to him or, conversely, each time it rereads Jesus' destiny of death and resurrection as "in accordance with the Scriptures." In other words, each time the assembly in church proclaims and hears the Scriptures as being his very word ("He is present in his word since it is himself who speaks when the holy scriptures are read in church," Vatican II will declare, as the apostolic tradition had said),[4] it is his spokesperson, his representative, therefore his sacrament.

(b) But we have not yet found the definitive issue. For it is only around the table, therefore at rest, that their eyes are opened. Then "he took bread, blessed and broke it, and gave it to them." It is not at random that these four verbs follow one another; they are the four technical verbs which we find in our accounts of the Last Supper.[5] The addressees of Luke's Gospel could not hesitate: when hearing this passage, they could not help but think of the story of the Last Supper, which they knew by heart since this story, as transmitted in the New Testament (and as early as the sixth decade, according to 1 Corinthians 11 where Paul carefully applies himself to "[handing] on" what he had "received" from the tradition going back to the Lord), was read every Sunday. In the same way they had previously recognized their own practice of reading and interpreting the Scriptures in church in the

---

[4] "Constitution on the Sacred Liturgy," no. 7, in Vatican Council II, *The Basic Sixteen Documents: Constitutions, Decrees, Declarations*, rev. trans. in inclusive language, ed. Austin Flannery (Northport, N.Y.: Costello, 1996) 121.

[5] However with a variant: the use of the verb "to bless" (translated by "to pronounce the blessing") is typically Semitic and corresponds to the blessing that the head of the household or of the group addressed to God over the bread at the beginning of meals; this expression is impossible in Greek. This is why Paul (1 Cor 11:24) and Luke (22:19), who address communities of Greek culture, used the verb "to give thanks" *(eucharistein)* where Mark (14:22) and Matthew (26:26) have kept the Semitism "to bless" *(eulogein)*.

"was it not necessary?" of Jesus, they more clearly recognize here, if that is possible, their own practice of celebrating the *Eucharist* in memory of him. The lesson is similar to the preceding one about the Scriptures. Here again, we must see the church as if through alabaster behind Jesus. What Luke tells us is that each time the church takes the bread, pronounces the blessing, breaks it, and gives it in memory of the Lord Jesus, it is he who does it through the church. The gestures the church makes, the words it pronounces are his gestures and his words. In the fullest sense of the word it is the "sacrament."

So, the "performance" of the passage from no-faith to faith requires the same separation from the desire for immediate proof as previously and the same assent to the mediation of the church: it is in the church celebrating the Eucharist as his prayer and his action, as it is in the church welcoming the Scriptures as his word, that it is possible to recognize that Christ is alive.

(c) The two disciples' eyes opened but on emptiness because, as soon as he was recognized, "he vanished from their sight" (v. 31). However, this emptiness is now for them full of a presence which they are going to announce "that same hour." It is impossible to recognize the risen Jesus without oneself being impelled to "rise" in newness of life, therefore without being entrusted with announcing it.[6] In any case, the classical pattern of the stories of Christ's manifestation in the New Testament attests to this: after stressing the initiative of the risen One, who "shows himself," and the recognition by the witnesses of his being "the same" as the crucified Jesus but in another form, it always ends on a command to go on a mission: "Go and tell." Having returned to Jerusalem where they begin by receiving the same testimony from the eleven, based on that of Simon (v. 34), [we surmise] the two disciples will leave the city very rapidly.

This missionary witness has in Luke, especially in Acts, an important ethical dimension. In the short depictions (rather idealized) that Acts gives us of the activities and behavior of the first Christian community of Jerusalem, the "communion" between sisters and brothers occupies a large place: half of Acts 2:42-47, three fourths of Acts 4:32-35. This

---

[6] The expression in v. 33 "that same hour they got up" (*anastantes autē tē hōra*) in which the verb *anistēmi*, which means "to get up" and is one of the two principal verbs used when speaking of Jesus' resurrection in the New Testament (he "got up" from the dead), suggests this "rising" of the disciples.

communion *(koinōnia)*, based on faith in Jesus, was first of all that of hearts "united" (see 2:44), "unanimous" (see 2:46). But—Luke emphasizes—it concretely translated into attitudes and gestures of sharing: they showed that they had "one heart and soul" by having "everything they owned . . . held in common" (4:32). It is important to understand that for Luke this ethics of sharing between sisters and brothers, with preference for the neediest, did not have just a moral value but a theological one: "the fact of not having destitute persons among them had the value of a sign: Moses' promise has been accomplished in their behalf, for they are the messianic community become present."[7] In other words, in Luke's theological code this ethical sharing has the value of a missionary testimony rendered to Jesus' resurrection.

In John's theology, this theological dimension of the ethics of service to others is even more accented. The Fourth Gospel intentionally substitutes the washing of the feet for the institution of the Eucharist; it replaces the command concerning the ritual memorial of the Lord Jesus ("do this in memory of me") with a command concerning this memory translated into acts: "I have set you an example, that you also should do as *[kathōs]* I have done to you" (John 13:15). In virtue of the very strong sense which John habitually gives to *kathōs*, Xavier Léon-Dufour writes, "It is as if Jesus were saying, 'By acting this way, I give you the power to act in the same way.'" It is not a question of simply imitating Jesus in an external way: it is he who gives his disciples the power to act as he acts; it is he "who performs in his disciples the service that is their distinguishing mark."[8] There is something sacramental about their ethics of service inasmuch as it carries the gift that Jesus made of himself.

Whatever this rapid detour through John's Gospel teaches us, Luke's exemplary lesson is clear: you cannot, he says to his addressees (and therefore to today's believers), realize the performance of the passage from non-faith to faith, that is, this opening of the eyes which enables you to recognize Jesus as risen and always living, unless you obtain from him the "competence" to accomplish it. For it is

[7] Jacques Dupont, *Études sur les Actes des Apôtres* (Paris: Cerf, 1967) 510. The author explains that holding possessions in common probably did not mean that they were the object of a legal transfer but that they were to be used by all according to need.

[8] Xavier Léon-Dufour, *Sharing the Eucharistic Bread: The Witness of the New Testament,* trans. Matthew J. O'Connell (New York: Paulist, 1986) 250 and 380.

he who explains the meaning of the Scriptures; it is he who presides at the breaking of the bread; it is he who continues his service to humans through that of his disciples. To obtain all this, you must *disenthrall* yourselves from your (quite natural) desire for immediate proofs of him. Failing this, you can only reduce him to your own ideology and your own preconceptions: he no longer is for you the living One (see Luke 24:5); by submitting him to your desire and your previous convictions, you manipulate him and thus make him a corpse again, as is indicated by the three closely related verbs "to see," "to find," "to touch" in chapter 24. In order to accede to faith, the two disciples of Emmaus have had to overturn their own Jewish convictions and accept something monstrous for any good Jew, a Messiah who would have to go through death. You too must convert your desire for immediacy and *assent to the mediation of the church.*

Living in God, the Lord Jesus has left his place on earth, as the story of the ascension shows (Acts 1:6-11). From now on, this place is occupied by the church. Of course, the church occupies this place symbolically, that is, by maintaining the radical difference, for the church is not Christ, but his symbolic witness, which means that its original and constant raison d'être is to direct everything back to him. It is in the church that faith finds its structure because the church is in charge of keeping alive, in the midst of the world and for its good, the memory of what he lived for and why God raised him from the dead: memory through the *Scriptures,* read and interpreted as speaking about him or being his own living word; memory through the *sacraments,* (here the breaking of the bread) recognized as being his own salvific gestures; memory through the *ethical* testimony of mutual sharing, lived as an expression of his own service to humankind.

We can visualize this structure of Christian identity in the following diagram:

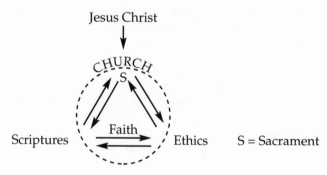

Christian identity, not the salvation of human beings, is the object of the above diagram. It does not say, "Outside the church circle there is no salvation," but "Outside the church circle there is no recognized salvation," therefore no Christian. One can be saved without being a Christian, that is, without belonging to the visible church (See Vatican II quoted in the opening section of this book, pp. xxi–xxii); but one cannot be a Christian without belonging to the church because Christian identity begins with the confession of Jesus as Christ, confession which from the origins has constituted the church. In this sense, there are no "anonymous Christians."

Moreover, the circle is not closed; it is made up of dotted lines. This signifies that the church is not a ghetto, but that it has existence and meaning only because of its relationship to the *reign,* which in the world is wider than it, as we have seen in the section opening this book. It is not the reign; it is only its sacrament. But the fact of being its sacrament, as we said in the same place, demands that it be the sign of the reign, and therefore that it show the marks of the reign. These *marks* are many but can be reduced to the three we have named.

Scriptures/Sacraments/Ethics

(a) The first one is the particular way of reading the *Scriptures* portrayed in the New Testament, which itself is only the unfolding of the apostolic church's confession of faith. Under the paradigm "Scriptures" we can classify everything that pertains to the *knowledge* of God's mystery revealed in Jesus Christ: the Bible in the first place of course since it contains all the foundational texts of the church's faith; but also all the theological discourse of yesterday and today, because theology is at bottom nothing else than the orderly and critically organized elucidation of the difficulties present in our foundational texts. Catechesis belongs also, at least in large part, to this pole of Christian identity which immediately depends on biblical revelation.

(b) The second is the *sacraments,* and in a wider sense the various forms of celebration which the church performs in memory of Jesus' death and resurrection. Among these forms there are first the "two major sacraments" or "two principal sacraments," according to Scholastic terminology, that is, baptism and Eucharist (this is an important observation from the ecumenical viewpoint, notably with regard to Protestants who recognize these two sacraments). They are "major" simply because they are the "sacraments of Christian initiation" (confirmation was added to these two and can only be understood as the completion of baptism, from which in any case it was not separate in antiquity, either in its celebration or in its theological understanding). It is through these two sacraments that every person is initiated into the mystery of Christ, that is, becomes a member of his living "body." Eucharist is the summit of the initiation because it is through participation in Christ's eucharistic body that one is fully integrated into the ecclesial body.

The strict notion of sacrament is analogical, which means that it is not verified in the same way or to the same degree in all cases (what the Council of Trent meant to say when officially reminding Christians that sacraments are not all "on an equal footing"). This led to placing on a lower degree the other five ecclesial rites which the theology of the twelfth century recognized as "sacraments properly so-called": for instance, confirmation is understood as the development of baptism, and penance as a return to baptism.

But we can classify under the rubric "sacrament" all the church's forms of celebration: the Christian funeral, which is not a sacrament because sacraments are for living beings only, is replete with sacramentality (is it not, according to the very rite of the church, the fulfillment for everyone of her or his "passover" with Christ, inaugurated at baptism?). Monastic or religious profession, not recognized as a sacrament because it does not produce super-Christians endowed with a super-baptism, is nonetheless full of sacramentality since it is also in its own way a renewal of baptism, and this time undertaken with the energetic resolution of an adult. The same is true of a penitential celebration conducted in church without a priest, therefore not sacramental, and of a celebration of the word in a large or small group, and so on. Under the paradigm "sacrament," we classify everything that pertains to the thankfulness which the church expresses to God.

Prayer could be placed here. For, on the one hand, the model, and even the source, of every really Christian prayer is the liturgical prayer of the church addressed to the Father through the Son in the Spirit and expressed in the form of thanksgiving and petition. The Eucharistic Prayer is exemplary in this regard. On the other hand, free as its form may be, every Christian prayer formula, even the most spontaneous, as well as every posture or gesture are in large part (even though people are not conscious of it) the effect of ritual behaviors learned in the liturgy and interiorized for a long time and thus little by little "incorporated" by everyone. If prayer does not appear as such in our diagram, it is not because it does not belong with the characters that identify believers but because, if it is genuinely Christian, it is inspired by the model which the church gives in its liturgy and participates in it.

(c) The third mark is the *ethical* conduct by which Christians testify to the gospel by their actions. Let us specify that this ethics does not extend just to interpersonal relationships but also to collective problems which, although in the last analysis formulated by private persons, are the result of forces other than the united forces of individuals and require solutions of another order than those which work for individuals or small groups. Under the paradigm "ethics," we place all that pertains to *action* in the name of the gospel (therefore also, and even primarily, in the name of humanity).

(d) If we widen the perspective, we see that the relation between Scriptures, Sacrament, and Ethics is superposed on a probably fundamental anthropological structure which we have named "knowledge," "gratitude," and "action." For the human subject cannot live as subject without at once thinking the world (the logic of theoretical reason at work especially in philosophy and science), singing the world (the aesthetic value of poetry, music and the feast, whether religious or not), and acting in the world (ethics, not technique—as indispensable as this may be in other respects—constituting the essential human mode of action). It goes without saying that this anthropological structure is reconfigured, and so "converted," when it is taken up by Christian faith.

The Priority of the Ecclesial "We"

The diagram (p. 28) shows that the church precedes the individual. "Here we run up against this same fundamental truth, namely it is not a question of Christians uniting to form the church, but of the church forming Christians"[9] In other words, it is not that women and men, in some way attached directly to Jesus Christ, would be Christians separately and by banding together would form the church. In order to be Christian, one must belong to the church. The church is primary. The gospel is communitarian by its very nature. To believe in

---

[9] Yves de Montcheuil, *Aspects of the Church,* trans. Albert J. La Mothe (Chicago: Fides, 1955) 50.

Christ is to be immediately gathered together by him who is confessed as "our" common Lord.

Baptism, which is precisely the sacrament of entrance into the church, shows this in an eminent way: Paul underscores at least three times that the barriers which, according to the ordinary concepts of the time, separated the two parts of humankind (Jew and Greek), the two social statuses (slave and free), and the two sexes (women were subject to men, this subjection being religiously made visible by the inferior place granted them both in the Jerusalem Temple and in the synagogues) are abolished (Gal 3:26-28; cf. Col 3:10-11 and 1 Cor 12:13). Did not Christ die, says the letter to the Ephesians, to tear down the "dividing wall" and to "create in himself one new human- ity in place of the two" and "reconcile both groups to God in one body" (Eph 2:14-16)? Thus, as Col 3:9-10 shows, is baptism anything else than this gesture of faith by which each one "strip[s] off the old self" and puts on "the new self," this new self which designates not only the person of Christ but also this collective "body of Christ" (in the same way the "Adam" of Genesis 2 designated the generic "human being," the "old self" in Col 3:9) in which "there is no longer Greek and Jew, circumcised and uncircumcised, barbarian, Scythian, slave and free; but Christ is all and in all" (3:11)? Differences are no longer partitions; on the contrary, they offer to the "body of Christ" this rich diversity of members and functions which any body needs. The other is no longer to be considered a rival or a potential enemy, especially on the religious plane; the other must be welcomed as a brother or a sister.

The creation of this new "we" by baptism is expressed particularly in the Eucharist (but this applies also to the whole of the Christian liturgy) in which every prayer is said in the first person plural: "we pray to you," "we give thanks to you," "we implore you," "we offer you," and so on.[10] Linguists tell us that the pronoun "we" does not designate the sum of the "I" and "you" but is "a complex person" from the start. Therefore, if, in the wake of Vatican II, liturgists rightly insist that the agent of the celebration is the church as church understood in the pri-

---

[10] Two exceptions confirm the rule: the "I confess to Almighty God," be- cause it comes from a personal apology by the priest in the Middle Ages; and the Apostles' Creed, because it comes from a baptismal liturgy in which each one was obliged to personally profess his or her faith.

mary meaning of assembly,[11] it is not (or it is not first of all) due to a democratic ideology but to a properly theological reason. The priest who presides (for if all celebrate, one presides) manifests "sacramentally" or "ministerially" that it is Christ himself who presides and exercises his unique priesthood in the midst of the assembly and on its behalf; it is precisely *because* it is Christ who presides that all the members of his body act together with him, on the basis of faith and baptism.

In this strictly theological perspective, not only is it erroneous to say that "such and such a priest celebrates" (what the priest does is preside "in the name of Christ"), but it is insufficient to think that the community celebrates only by uniting itself to what the priest does. In fact, this community acts; it acts *as a body,* as a constituted body, as body of Christ, even though the roles and functions, the priest's in the first place, are distributed within it in different ways. Consequently, the more one stresses that the liturgical action is that of Christ himself risen through the Spirit—what is attested by the presence of an ordained minister—the more one is led to emphasize that the assembly, which is his present body of humanity, is the active sacramental mediation of his action, in particular of his praise to the Father and his supplication for his sisters and brothers. Nothing is more traditional, although this view has been generally forgotten since the Middle Ages. Paul himself attests to this: in 1 Cor 11:17-34, it is always to the common "you" that he speaks of the "Lord's Supper." And in chapter 10 of the same letter, the subject who blesses the cup and breaks the bread is the "we" of the assembly (which in no way prevents that there be a "minister" presiding over the assembly):

"The cup of blessing that we bless, is it not a sharing in the blood of Christ? The bread that we break, is it not a sharing in the body of Christ? Because there is one bread, we who are many are one body, for we all partake of the one bread" (1 Cor 10:16-17).

Lex orandi, lex credendi ("the rule of ['liturgical' is understood] prayer is the rule of faith") is a well-known saying. *The church believes as it celebrates.* The liturgy is therefore a theological locus of first importance. It shows us, not by mode of reasoning but by mode of

---

[11] Yves Congar, "L'Ecclesia ou communauté chrétienne, sujet intégral de l'action liturgique," in *La liturgie après Vatican II,* ed. Jean Pierre Jossua and Yves Congar (Paris: Cerf, 1967) 241–282.

symbolic action,[12] that no one becomes a Christian except by being taken into the common "womb" of the church. Therefore, it is with good reason that one can and must say, according to the already quoted formula, "It is not a question of Christians uniting to form the church, but of the church forming Christians."

The Celebrating Assembly

As we have suggested, the primary locus of the church is the celebrating assembly. This of course does not mean that Christians belong less to the church when they are scattered during the week but that the "one, holy, catholic, and apostolic" church manifests its identity best as a concrete liturgical assembly. This observation is in agreement with the New Testament, where the word "church" is used to designate first of all the local assembly of Christians. This usage has two precedents: first, the Jewish assembly in the desert (*qᵉhal*, translated in the Septuagint by *ekklēsia*); second, the use of this term in ordinary Greek to designate the citizens' assembly which was in charge of deliberating on the measures to be taken for the good government of the city. Hence the frequency of the plural "churches" in the New Testament. This allows us to emphasize three important theological points:

(a) First, a church without an *assembly* would be a contradiction in terms. To designate the Christian phenomenon in the process of birth, Christians did not find anything better than applying to it the word "assembly" or "church." This is to say that the gathering—with the understanding that this gathering is called or convoked by God or Christ, as indicated by the etymology of the word *ek-klēsia* from the verb *kaleō* ("to call")—is the major characteristic of Christians. From this point of view, Christians are people who join their sisters and brothers in an assembly in the name and memory of Jesus. Such an assembly is the Christians' *primary mark* or, in the language we used previously, the "fundamental sacrament" of the risen Christ. This reinforces what we have said above on the ecclesial "we."

(b) Second, if there are necessarily different forms of church assembly, the most typical is the *diversified Sunday assembly*. Again, these two features do not mean that outside of this type of assembly, one is less a Christian but that here, too, it is this type of assembly which is "sacramentally" exemplary of the nature of the church.

---

[12] This point will be developed in the chapter on rituality.

(1) First, *Sunday* assembly. The Christian Sunday, the day on which the memorial of Jesus as risen Lord is celebrated, is quasi contemporaneous with the beginning of the church. The unanimous mention of the resurrection of Jesus "on the first day of the week" (the Jewish name for Sunday) does not aim at chronological accuracy but has a theological and, more exactly, liturgical value: this mention makes manifest the foundation of the habit taken by the first Christian communities as early as the sixth decade[13] to gather on that day in memory of Jesus' resurrection.[14] What motivated this choice is perfectly obvious: not the rest of God on the seventh day of creation, as for the Jewish Sabbath (the Christian Sunday became a day of rest only in Constantine's time at the beginning of the fourth century), but the resurrection of the crucified Jesus. The Christian Sunday is the memorial-day of the paschal event. Therefore, one can speak of the "sacramentality" of this memorial-day. For in the same way baptism and Eucharist are the memorial of the resurrection through the sacramental medium of the bread and the wine, Sunday is the memorial of the resurrection through the sacramental medium of time (the day that Sunday is) and more exactly of the assembly that characterizes that day.

Of course, the Eucharist was bound to occupy the center place. Many testimonies from the Fathers of the church attest that the celebration of the Eucharist took place on Sunday in all the churches. However, progressively and at different periods depending on the churches, it was celebrated on Wednesday and Friday, then also on Saturday, then on every day of the week.[15] But although the Eucharist

---

[13] See for instance 1 Cor 16:1-2, where Paul's text shows that this custom already exists in Corinth as well as in Galatia (and one can surmise in the other churches which Paul founded); Acts 20:7, on the breaking of the bread in Troas *"on the first day of the week."*

[14] Nevertheless, it is likely that this custom took root some time later in the Judeo-Christian communities because of their attachment to the Sabbath.

[15] There is a clear attestation to this difference—regarded as normal—for instance, in Augustine's *Letter* 54.2 (ca. 400), "In some places no day is omitted in the offering of the [eucharistic sacrifice], in others it is offered only on Saturday and Sunday, or even only on Sunday." (Augustine, *Letters*, vol. 1, trans. Sister Wilfrid Parsons, S.N.D., Fathers of the Church (Fathers of the Church, 1951) 253. Similarly, Basil's *Letter* 93 (ca. 372). Daily Eucharist seems to be attested by Cyprian in Carthage in the middle of the third century. But the extension of this practice to all churches is clearly discernible only from the end of the fourth century.

as such is at the heart of the Sunday assembly, although it is not secondary, it takes the second place because it is subordinated to the gathering itself held in memory of Jesus risen from the dead. Such a gathering has a theological value in itself. As we have said, it is the "primary sacrament" of the risen One. As a consequence, where in the absence of a priest the local community cannot celebrate the Eucharist, it is nevertheless "convoked" by its Lord to "make church" in his memory. This is the major theological foundation of the "Sunday assemblies without a priest."[16]

It is significant that during the first centuries, bishops did not ask their faithful to "go to Mass" on Sunday (this will change in the high Middle Ages), but to "go to church," an expression that designates the assembly and not, at least before 350, the building.[17] To be a Christian is to belong to the church, and to belong to the church is to take part in the Sunday assembly. Here we have proof that the Fathers of the first four or five centuries saw spontaneously the "identity between participation in the ecclesia-assembly and belonging to the church."[18] In this perspective, one understands the argument of the bishop in the *Didascalia Apostolorum* (Syriac version of the 3rd century):

"Since now you are the members of Christ, do not scatter yourselves from the church by not assembling. Because you have Christ for your head, as He counselled and promised—that you are partakers 'with me'—do not neglect yourselves, and deprive our Savior of His members, and do not tear and scatter His body. But on the Lord's day leave everything and run eagerly to your church for she is your glory."[19]

---

[16] "Sunday assembly in the absence of a priest." On this phenomenon, which has been particularly important in France for some twenty years and is of increasing importance in other Western countries, and on the opportunities it offers, but also the risks it incurs, see Monique Brulin, "Assemblées dominicales en l'absence de prêtre.—Situation en France et enjeux pastoraux," *Maison-Dieu* 175 (1988) 111–167.

[17] Christine Mohrmann, *Études sur le latin des chrétiens*, 4 vols., Storiae e letterature 65, 87, 103, 143 (Rome: Edizioni di storia e letterature, 1958–1965).

[18] Pierre-Marie Gy, "'Eucharistie' et 'Ecclesia' dans le premier vocabulaire de la liturgie chrétienne," *Maison-Dieu* 130 (1977) 19–34.

[19] Vööbus, Arthur, ed. and trans, *The Didascalia Apostolorum in Syriac*, Corpus Scriptorum Christianorum Orientalium 408 (Louvain: CorpusSCO, 1979) 135.

(2) Because Sunday is the memorial-day of the passover of the Lord Jesus, the assembly held on that day has a significance that is sacramentally particular. But this is fully unfolded only in *diversified* assemblies, that is, those made up of persons of all ages and social conditions. Indeed, in such assemblies the "new humanity" inaugurated by Christ and conferred on all at their entrance into the church through baptism—"there is no longer Jew or Greek . . ."—is symbolically presented to be seen and lived by. What has just been said does not devaluate more homogeneous assemblies of young people or of persons of the same socio-cultural milieu. Here as before, we are speaking on the plane of the identity of the church and its sacramental manifestations. We are simply declaring that it is in this type of assembly that the church shows most clearly what it is in the midst of the world. The pastoral consequence is that Christian identity could avoid being obscured in Christians who take part in the Eucharist only "when it pleases" them, on any evening of the week, and/or only when the assembly shares the same cultural values or the same musical sensibility, even the same type of political analysis as themselves.

(c) Finally, our third theological observation concerning the term "church" is as follows: if from the sociological viewpoint the local church is really a part of the universal church, from the theological viewpoint it is the concrete *integral* realization of this same church of Christ, one and universal, in the particularity of a given place or time. Vatican II, insisting on this doctrine of the New Testament and the Fathers, neglected in the Middle Ages and erased in the modern period, said of the local church (in this case the diocese) that it is "the principal manifestation of the church" and that "it is in and from these (the local churches) that the one and unique catholic church exists." The council also applies this notion of local church to eucharistic assemblies (thus Constitution on the Church, no. 26), showing as a consequence that *every eucharistic assembly truly realizes the church of God*, with the condition, as the same text says, that it be "lawful," that is in particular, that an ordained minister in communion with the bishop and therefore in communion with the other church communities preside.[20] This means that the church of Jesus Christ is not to be sought at

---

[20] "Constitution on the Sacred Liturgy," no. 41, in Vatican II, *Sixteen Documents,* 133; "Dogmatic Constitution on the Church," no. 23, in ibid., 31–33; "Dogmatic Constitution on the Church," no. 26, in ibid., 37. On the "Copernican revolution"

the ends of the world but in the concrete community in which Christians live.

Pastoral Consequences

Finally, the liturgical assembly, inasmuch as it is church, is for everyone the chief *concrete mediation* of her or his relationship with the living God revealed in Jesus. The temptation to succumb to the desire for an immediate relation with Christ or a direct illumination from the Holy Spirit is strong. The Christian faith tells us, on the basis of the incarnation of God in Jesus, that the encounter with God goes through the encounter with others. The church, and first as a local assembly, is the concrete expression of this principle. True, to attend Mass on television is a good thing when one cannot do otherwise. However, even if "it's so much better on TV than at the parish" (no noisy children, no neighbors singing out of tune, no incompetent organist, no homily that seems vacuous or poorly prepared, and so on), the church asks Christians to go to the assembly. For Mass is not meant to favor an intimate relation to God—in that case it might be better to follow Mass on television. It is a church action. It is lived as a church, a church made up of men, women, and children who are sinners but who dare to acknowledge themselves as the "holy church" of God; a church made up of different members, often divided among themselves but, however, given to the world as "body of Christ"; a church made up of persons reluctant to commit themselves to conversion or mission but which dares to recognize itself in faith as the "temple of the Holy Spirit," the Spirit that renews all things. "It is great, the mystery of faith!" Before it applies to the Eucharist, this expression applies to the concrete assembly as church. Here there is both mystery and scandal. This is what is not self-explanatory, and for the believing intelligence the scandal of the presence of Christ in the Eucharist risks serving as a mock scandal (that is, merely intellectual) if one ignores this primary scandal, an existential one: the encounter of the living Christ which is possible only through the mediation of a church, indeed holy but composed of sinners, indeed body of Christ but made up of divided members, indeed temple of the Holy Spirit but so parsimoniously missionary. The con-

---

effected by the Council, see H. M. Legrand, "L'Église se réalise dans un lieu," in *Initiation à la Pratique de la Théologie,* ed. Vernard Lauret and François Refoulé, vol. 3: *Dogmatique* 2 (Paris: Cerf, 1983) 145–180.

crete assembly of every single Sunday confronts Christians with the
harsh reality of this mediation that everyone seeks to forget.

FAITH OR THE ASSENT TO A LOSS

The stumbling block that the church is, and we are speaking of the
actual church, indicates clearly where the difficulty of faith lies. For to
accept the mediation of the church is to renounce direct contact with
Christ. To return to Luke's language, it is to renounce the immediacy
of the see/find/touch.

The Temptation of Immediacy

Of course we know well—our own experience, added to that of two
thousand years of church, convinced us long ago—that we cannot directly reach the body of the Lord Jesus. Yes, "I know . . . but still. . . ."
Everyone knows that she or he is not the most beautiful, the most intelligent, the strongest. Long ago life inflicted this truth on everyone;
it has become a conviction. "But still. . . ." This restriction comes
from the deepest level of everyone's unconscious desire. It is formulated only on rare occasions when "it escapes me," when "I can't
help." Psychoanalysts would tell us that precisely these involuntary
utterances—which we cannot stop and which we sometimes regret
the same instant, placing our hand before our mouth in order to show
that we really did not think, that we have made a blunder, that we
should not have said this, but that we could not help—are the manifestations of the unconscious "desire." These outbursts occur when
attention is relaxed, that is, when "censure" is no longer operative.
They are the more significant as they come from the unconscious and
are not fully intentional. Most of the time the "but still" is not expressed; nevertheless, it is present in the ellipses, the blanks in our
speech, the corrections, the slips of the tongue, the tone of voice, and
so on. One may be convinced of not being the strongest; but whence
is it that one never ceases to be jealous of a given person who seems
to have a right to more consideration than oneself on the part of one's
colleagues? Between knowledge and desire there is often an abyss.

The same holds true with regard to the relationship with God. Certainly Christians know that they do not have a direct line to Christ.
But still . . . they are no less possessed by the same fundamental desire for immediacy than the addressees of Luke's Gospel. This desire
can take a multitude of forms. It is possible to link its *three principal
forms* to the three poles of our structure of Christian identity.

(a) The overvaluation of the *Scriptures* can entail such a veneration of the letter of the Bible that one falls prey to fundamentalism. "You are asking questions on the meaning of your life or you are uncertain about a decision you must take. Open your Bible and God will surely give you the answer." Some groups do not hesitate to follow this path. In a more subtle way, it is the overvaluation of the same category (that of knowledge, as we have said) that leads some Christians to classify others according to their theological knowledge or their ability to express their relationship to God in a critical manner. In this perspective, the model Christian would be the "critical" Christian.

(b) Whereas the above temptation flourished more in the Protestant churches, the second, which is the overvaluation of the category *sacrament*, is more characteristic of the Catholic world. Because the sacraments are seen as "means of salvation" and because they act *"ex opere operato,"* one has such a trust in them that they tend to occupy the whole sphere of Christian life. In this perspective, which verges on magic, the model Christian is the "practicing" Christian.

(c) The tendency to overvaluate the category *ethics* is transconfessional. It can take two principal forms: a political one in which the model Christian is the "activist" who, by means of her or his commitment to justice, advances the reign of God on earth, and in which orthodoxy is measured by orthopraxis. The other form is more emotional; there the model Christian is the "charismatic" whose personal testimony, strengthened by that of the group, proves in a convincing manner the presence of Christ and the action of the Spirit.

It goes without saying that these are theoretical types. Concretely, all nuances exist. What we simply want to show by these theoretical types linked to Scripture, sacraments, and ethics is that any overemphasis on one is at the expense of the others. Focused on this imaginary "point of fixation," Christians manipulate God, Christ, or the gospel, assign to it its fixed place, reduce it to their own ideologies, codes of analysis, and convictions. Christians make of the gospel the mirror of their own desires (especially "spiritual" ones). They convert the gospel instead of allowing it to convert them. Thus God becomes an "idol"; thus they change Christ back into a corpse instead of letting him be "the living." These are as many ways of getting a hold on Christ.

Maintaining a Distance

Faith lives only from the *space* between the three poles. It is precisely this space which *concretely mediates the distance between God and us,* our respect for God's difference. This space is uncomfortable because it constantly maintains an emptiness. But this emptiness, which the imaginary unceasingly strives to fill, is what lets Jesus truly be the living One and respects his lordship. It is also what gives Christians room for "play" by allowing individuals to breathe freely within the faith of the church, instead of submitting them to the uniform mold of one ideology. To be healthy, faith requires that Christians find their own balance on this "tripod." Not that they should sit on it once for all: in a domain which must remain in motion like faith or life, the right balance is, as in walking or bicycling, always unstable. From this point of view, it is normal that at times everyone relies more on one of the three poles. At least, the image of the tripod is a help to understanding that if the whole weight of Christian identity rests on only one pole, the center of gravity is displaced and a fall is unavoidable.

How could the reading of the Scriptures still be genuinely Christian if it were not connected both to the liturgy where the act of proclamation in the church assembly attests preeminently that these Scriptures are the word of God for today and to the ethical life in which they demand to be embodied?

How could participation in the sacraments still be genuinely Christian if it were not connected both to Scripture—which founds liturgy not merely as the celebration of God but also as the celebration of the God revealed in the life, death, and resurrection of Jesus—and to the ethical life—by which Christians are called to "veri-fy," that is, "make true" what they have celebrated and received in the sacraments?

How could ethical practice still be genuinely Christian if it was not confronted by the Scriptures, its source, and at the same time rooted in the liturgical celebration? Let us develop this last point further. What makes ethical life a Christian reality is neither its scope (it is the same for every human being) nor its degree of refinement (Kant's maxim, "Do not do to others what you would not want others to do to you," was known to Gentiles and Jews in the time of Jesus) nor its level of generosity: this generosity can go as far as giving away all one's possessions or handing over one's body for a noble cause, without its being Christian (1 Cor 13:3). What makes it Christian is not its "matter" but the "form" which is given it by love understood as a response to God's love, which came first (1 Cor 13). The liturgy is the place where this priority of the love of God freely bestowed is attested (see the gesture of eucharistic communion). In the measure in which the ethical life of service to others is lived as a response to this primary gift, and therefore takes its source in the sacraments, in that same measure it finds its Christian identity.

Our diagram of Christian identity is a *structure*. Now a structure is a whole of which each component is an integral part and in which each component finds its value only by reference to the others. This is what we have just demonstrated. This is why it would be absurd to think or say that one could be a Christian without any ethical concern for others; it would be equally absurd to think or say that one can be a Catholic "without going to Mass." Certainly only love matters, which, as Paul says, "is the fulfilling of the law" (Rom 13:10) and on which we shall be judged in the evening of our life (John of the Cross) according to the symbolic picture of Matthew 25. But how could this love for others be lived as love for God if it were not rooted in the word and the Eucharist? To declare bluntly that what is important "is not the Mass, it's others," is to exhibit a singular incomprehension of the Christian mystery.

Each of the three poles has its own place and role. Biblical and theological knowledge does not do away with either the Eucharist or the practice of love for others. Attendance at Sunday Mass is in danger of becoming merely a pious exercise if it is not sustained by a minimum of biblical culture and theological reflection and is reduced to a sort of parenthesis "for God" at the end of the week. As for ethics, whether militant or centered on sisters and brothers, it dispenses Christians neither from the theological elucidation without which it risks getting bogged down in mere ideology or feeling nor from its revitalization in the liturgical reception of God's gift.

Chapter 3

Relations between the Elements of the Structure

In a structure, as we have seen, each element has relevance only inasmuch as it is in relation with the other elements. We must now analyze more closely the relations between the Scriptures and sacrament and between sacrament and ethics.

RELATIONS BETWEEN THE SCRIPTURES AND SACRAMENT
We would like to demonstrate that there is something sacramental about the Scriptures, in the sense that they are the sacrament of the word of God, and that, conversely, the sacraments of faith exist only as the crystallization of this word.

The Scriptures, Sacrament of God's Word
It is absolutely traditional to affirm that the Scriptures are sacramental. First of all, let us remember that Eastern Christians still use the word "mysteries" when speaking of the sacraments, our word "sacrament" coming from the Latin translation of the Greek *mystērion*. Besides, the Latinized form, *mysterium,* of the Greek word was employed as often as *sacramentum* by the Latin Fathers. In the first two centuries, these terms, the Greek and the two Latin ones, were applied first of all to the Scriptures. Their extension to the church's rites began only in the third century before becoming a current usage in the fourth. But even in this case, and this is true until the twelfth century, the primary reference of the word "sacramentum" or "mysterium" to the Scriptures is not forgotten. All Fathers, whether Greek or Latin, whether Antiochenes or Alexandrians, could have endorsed Augustine's formula, "'Sacramentum,' that is to say, every word of holy Scripture," or Jerome's, also about the Bible, "every word contains a sacrament; there are as many mysteries as there are words."[1]

---

[1] Augustine, *Letter* 55: "sacramentum, aut aliquis sermo de sacris litteris"; see *Letters*, vol. 1, trans. Sister Wilfrid Parsons, S.N.D., Fathers of the Church

The Bible is replete with mysteries or sacraments in conformity with the use of "mystery" in the Jewish writings of the apocalyptic current, replete with revelatory signs of God's secret design for the world. The Bible is therefore the first sacrament of the word of God (Christ being the source-sacrament: Does not Paul speak of the "mystery of Christ" in Col 4:3 and Eph 3:4?). All this suggests three theological reflections.

(a) The first concerns the veneration traditionally shown the book containing God's word, almost on a par with the Eucharist. In this regard this excerpt from a homily of Origen in the third century is significant.

"You who are accustomed to take part in divine mysteries know, when you receive the body of the Lord, how you protect it with all caution and veneration lest any small part fall from it, lest anything of the consecrated gift be lost. For you believe, and correctly, that you are answerable if anything falls from there by neglect. But if you are so careful to preserve his body, and rightly so, how do you think that there is less guilt to have neglected God's word than to have neglected his body?"[2]

Likewise, he does not hesitate to compare the homily to the multiplication of the loaves: "Consider . . . now how we break a few loaves: we take up a few words from the divine Scriptures and . . . many thousand men are filled. But unless the loaves have been broken, unless they have been crumbled into pieces by the disciples, that is, unless the letter has been discussed and broken in little pieces, its meaning cannot reach everyone."[3]

Therefore, there is nothing surprising about the marks of veneration of which the "tabernacle" of the word is the object: the rich deco-

---

(Fathers of the Church, 1951). Jerome, *Commentarioli in Psalmos* (Little commentary on the Psalms), in *Opera exegetica,* ed. Germanus Morin, vol. 1: *Hebraicai quaestiones in libro Geneseos; Liber interpretationis Hebraicorum nominum; Commentarioli in Psalmos; Commentarius in Ecclesiasten* Corpus Christianorum, Series Latina 72 (Turnholt: Brépols, 1959): "singula nomina habent singula sacramenta; quot enim verba, tot mysteria." Here one notices the equivalence, equally frequent in Augustine, between "sacrament" and "mystery."

[2] Origen, *Homily on Exodus 13:3,* in *Homilies on Genesis and Exodus,* trans. Ronald D. Heine (Washington, D.C.: Catholic University, 1982) 380–381.

[3] *Homily on Genesis 12:5,* in ibid., 182–183.

ration of the evangelaries; processions with lights, incense, and song; acclamations addressed to the "word of God." Vatican II's Constitution on Divine Revelation is significant in this regard:

"The church has always venerated the divine scriptures as it has venerated the Body of the Lord, in that it never ceases, above all in the sacred liturgy, to partake of the bread of life and to offer it to the faithful from the one table of the word of God and the Body of Christ."[4]

It is therefore in the word and the Eucharist that the "bread of life" is offered. To communicate in the Eucharist without having previously ruminated on the word appears nonsensical.

(b) The second reflection aims at attracting attention to the interval that exists between the Scriptures and the word. Of course, the Scriptures are truly the sacrament of the word, but precisely, they are *only* its sacrament. There is no pure and simple identity between the two. This is why for Christians the word of God is not immediately the Book (Christianity is not a religion of the Book), but someone, the One who "fulfills" the Book, Jesus, the Christ. The consequence of this is that there is no "sacred language" in the strict sense of the term. Paul's "neither Greek nor Jew" can perfectly apply here: the letter can be Hebrew, but also Greek, Latin, English, Chinese, whatever. On this point, there is a great difference between Christianity on the one hand and Judaism and Islam on the other. In the same way Jesus' "being the Christ" cannot be understood without going through his "being a particular Jew" but extends beyond this by being universal, the revelation of God, historically made through Hebrew and Greek—which remain the tongues of our foundational Scriptures—extends beyond these two languages, as the story of Pentecost shows so well. The fact that in 1546 the Council of Trent officially recognized the Greek version of the Bible, called the Septuagint (a version much more commonly used in the New Testament than its Hebrew source), along with its Latin translation, called the Vulgate, as "authentic" Bible, is significant in this regard.

The Christian interpretation (the hermeneutics) of the Scriptures as fulfilled in Jesus Christ presupposes that, in the wake of Judaism, the reader sees the letter of the Scriptures as a sacrament only inasmuch as it

[4] Dogmatic Constitution on Divine Revelation, no. 21, in Vatican Council II, *The Basic Sixteen Documents: Constitutions, Decrees, Declarations*, rev. trans. in inclusive language, ed. Austin Flannery (Northport, N.Y.: Costello, 1996) 111–112.

announces something other than itself. Or to use Paul Beauchamp's words, the reader sees the letter of the Scriptures as splitting, dividing itself in two so that it forms a "figure," the first creation, the first exodus, the first covenant, the first manna, and so on, announcing a renewed creation, a new exodus, a covenant "new and eternal," a "true manna," and so on.[5] Therefore, this hermeneutics is constitutive of the Scriptures as word of God in their letter itself. To which one must add that in any case the Bible remains a dead letter as long as it is not shown to be relevant to the readers' present frame of mind and concerns.

As can be seen, the sacramentality of the Scriptures prohibits any fundamentalist reading. Indeed the letter is here, absolutely impossible to bypass since it is, irreplaceably, the original source. This letter must be respected in its historical and cultural otherness: it is through it, through the historical evolution to which it attests (as indicated notably by the concept of "figure" mentioned above) that God revealed divine self to humankind to the point of becoming visible ("Philip . . . whoever has seen me has seen the Father") through the singular Jewish identity of Jesus-the-man. The Spirit is not found in spite of the letter but through it. However, through the letter it is the Spirit that we must find. The condition under which we find it is that we accept that the letter does not deliver the word of God to us in an immediate way. And this constantly requires the interpretation, the hermeneutics we have been speaking of.

(c) This interpretation needs a guide.[6] This guide is the church. This is what happens for the New Testament, which is nothing else than a rereading, as a church (that is, as the assembly), of Moses and the Prophets in the light of the death and resurrection of Jesus. This means that the Bible is in the liturgical assembly as a fish in water. By its very constitution it is made to be proclaimed in the assembly, not to be read in a book open flat on the desk in one's office and in an individual manner (whatever the legitimacy and fruitfulness of this practice may be in other respects). The biblical revelation of God reaches us *always-already* within the ecclesial matrix. This is why Stanislas Breton could write, "The church is the impossibility of the *scriptura sola*

---

[5] Paul Beauchamp, *Le récit, la lettre et le corps, essai biblique*, Cogitatio fidei 114 (Paris: Cerf, 1982) ch. 2.

[6] See the story of the Ethiopian's baptism in Acts 8, analyzed in the preceding chapter (pp. 20–22), and in particular the dialogue between Philip and him: "Do you understand what you are reading? . . . How can I unless someone guides me?"

[scripture alone]." That the Scriptures as word of God are sacramental by their essence means that the place that is home for them is the church assembly. What we call the Liturgy of the Word is not merely a festive excrescence of our Scriptures as word of God but really the sacramental manifestation of the essence of the biblical text. In other words, the Bible never reaches its truth as word of God as fully as in the liturgical act of its proclamation where the ancient text is, as it were, raised from its death by the living voice of the reader, then by that of the homilist who unfolds its timeliness.

The Sacrament, "Precipitate" of the Scriptures

The word of God does not reach us except through the sacramental mediation of the Scriptures read in church; conversely, the sacraments are like the precipitate (in the chemical sense) of the Scriptures as word. Of course, sacraments are rites, and we cannot understand them theologically without most carefully taking into account their ritual modality. However, although every sacrament is a rite, the rite becomes a sacrament only if it is converted by the word and the Spirit.

WORD AND SACRAMENT

That every sacrament is a sacrament of the word, is attested by the *lex orandi* ("the rule of prayer") of the church. The story of Emmaus already reflects a practice where the "breaking of the bread" followed the readings of Moses and the Prophets interpreted in the homily. The sequence Liturgy of the Word/Liturgy of the Sacrament, which is observed not only at Mass but also in every sacramental celebration, is not arbitrary. Is the sacrament anything else, according to Augustine's formula, than a *visibile verbum*, a "visible word," or rather the very word made visible? "In the name of the Father, and of the Son, and of the Holy Spirit," which is the sacramental word of baptism and reconciliation, is a synthesis of the Christian rereading of all the Scriptures, to such a point that these words are precisely those which accompany the sign of the cross, the Christian symbol par excellence, and condense in themselves the whole of Christian identity.

"The word comes over the element and becomes sacrament."[7] This formula, which was current in all the textbooks of the Middle Ages, has

---

[7] "Accedit verbum ad elementum et fit sacramentum." The "word" is the grammatical subject of the two verbs in the sentence, rather than the subject of only the first one, according to the rather frequent translation, "The word

become a true adage. It must be understood on three levels: (a) first, the Christological level since the Word, which through the Spirit comes over the element of bread or water, is Christ himself, the Word of God; (b) then, the liturgical level since this risen Christ who is always the same, comes "in-formed" by the liturgy or the color of the day, color that differs depending on the time one is in, Lent, Eastertide, Ordinary Sundays; (c) last, the properly sacramental level where the sacramental word, because pronounced in faith by the priest in the capacity of minister, that is, pronounced "in the name of Christ,"[8] is recognized as the word of Christ himself. Indeed, as Augustine had underscored against the Donatists, who held that the reality of the sacrament depended on the personal dignity of the minister who confers it, it is always Christ who baptizes, even through an unworthy minister.

There is no direct passage from the first to the third level: this is what we want to stress against the too frequent temptation to erase the second. The liturgical action has a twofold importance as a principle: on the one hand, it is the concrete mediation in which the always-same Christ reaches the assembly—without this, one could go directly to the "consecration"—at the same time, the liturgical action also constitutes sacramental theology—without the former the latter would drift into abstraction.

Sacramental theology is the theory of a practice. Its object is the church's celebration itself. It has nothing relevant to say that does not stem from the way the church confers the sacraments. If one had always obeyed this golden rule many deviations would have been avoided. One example of these deviations pertains to the eucharistic presence of the Lord, which has been understood in isolation independently of its purpose as nourishment for its partakers, demonstrated by the gestures, the words, and even the material elements used in the narrative of the institution. Another example of these deviations pertains to the signification of the ordained ministries disconnected from their relationship to a church community.

Despite this remark, it is clear theologically that every sacrament is a sacrament of the word, or to say it differently, *the word itself mediated under the ritual mode, different from the mode of Scripture.* Although the

---

comes to the element and here is [or 'and thus is made'] the sacrament." The whole tenor of Augustine's sacramental theology favors our translation.

[8] This is the translation of the formula "in persona Christi."

distinction between word and sacrament is a legitimate one, their dichotomy has had disastrous results. Initiated by the Reformers of the sixteenth century in the context of excessive sacramentalism, against which a reaction in favor of returning to the word is easily understandable, this reaction, recently reconfigured by the ideological opposition between "faith" and "religion," ended by establishing a true competition between the two.[9] The word, source of the "true" faith, would be endowed with all virtues of "authenticity," "responsibility," "commitment," Christian "adulthood" or "maturity" finally reached, whereas sacraments would be suspected of bordering on magic, of fostering the most dubious anthropological and social archaisms, of encouraging dependency among believers, and so on. Such reasoning shows forgetfulness of two things: first, that the word also reaches us only through the mediation of a body of writings which is as liable to manipulation as anything else and which is subject to highly ritualized uses even in the most spare liturgies; second, that the sacraments, obviously exposed to pitfalls because of their ritual character (we shall come back to this), are nothing but a particular modality of the word.

THE DISCOURSE ON THE BREAD OF LIFE

In this connection, let us dwell on the discourse on the bread of life in John 6. It is a homily built on scriptural texts according to rabbinical technique; here "He gave them bread from heaven to eat" (v. 31) is a concatenation of Ps 78:24 and Exod 16:15. It answers two major questions: Who is Jesus? And what does it mean to have faith in him? The question of Jesus' identity is marked by a twofold scandal. First, he claims to be "the living bread that came down from heaven"; we hear in the background of this expression, the manna of Exodus, which itself is the figure of the word of God that feeds the human heart and faith, according to Deut 8:3, a text quoted by Jesus in response to the first temptation in Matthew 4:4. But how can he have such a pretense: "Is not this Jesus . . . whose father and mother we know?" (John 6:42)? This first scandal is compounded by a second one when Jesus declares, "And the bread that I shall give is my flesh ['delivered' understood] for the life of the world" (v. 51, JB). For even supposing that he is really sent by God, that he "came down from

[9] The distinction between "faith" and "religion" is precious when it is used to stress the originality of the act of faith. But it is tendentious, even untenable, when it is applied to categories of persons, as sometimes happened in the 70s.

heaven," which is already difficult to accept, how could God let him go through death? Would not God send twelve legions of angels to save him? If it should be so, one thing is sure, our God would no longer be "God," God would no longer be our God, the God of our ancestors, Abraham, Isaac, and Jacob. What God is he talking about? It is simply intolerable to hear: "Who can accept [this]?" is the question coming not only from "the Jews" (the usual opponents of Jesus in John), but this time, from "many of his disciples" (v. 60). For the stumbling block is not due to concern about the presence of Christ in the Eucharist, a question which will be disputed in the church only from the ninth century on; in any case, except in verses 51-58 (to "eat the flesh . . . drink [the] blood"), the discourse is not directly about the Eucharist. The scandal, much more radical than this latter one, is about Jesus' identity and mission—which implicates God's very identity. In fact, this is what is in question: the announcement of a God who loves humanity to the point of losing life and dying like a nobody is simply a revolution for the Jewish mentality.

Therefore, what we have is a discourse whose *object* is not the Eucharist as such but the identity of Jesus and faith in him. It remains that if the object is not eucharistic, the *language* is, permeated through and through by the symbolism of the act of eating. This recalls the eating of the manna which is, from the viewpoint of the Bible itself, as we have said, the figure of the word which God gives to God's people so that by ruminating it, they may nourish their faith. But this recalls also, set against this manna background, the experience of the eucharistic communion in the Johannine communities. We are told that faith is nothing else than the daily realization of what is lived in the symbolic experience of the eucharistic meal: we must eat, masticate to the point of accepting, in heart and body, the bitter scandal of a God crucified for the life of the world. For John, the eucharistic act of eating is the great symbolic experience in which we are given, to feel and live, this scandal of the faith until it enters into our bodies, that is to say, into our life.

It is always *as word* that Christ gives himself to be eaten in the Eucharist. It is impossible to receive communion fruitfully without having "eaten the book" (see Ezek 2–3; Rev 10:9-10), ruminated the word in the Spirit. Here again, nothing is more traditional. Thus Ambrose in the fourth century, speaking of the Scriptures: "Eat this food first, in order to be able to come afterward to the food of the body of Christ"; or Augustine: "Sisters and brothers, see that you eat the heavenly bread in a spiritual sense. . . . so that all this may help us, beloved, not to eat the flesh and blood of Christ merely in the sacrament, as many of the wicked do, but to eat and drink in order to participate in the Spirit."[10]

What we just said is important. Important of course with regard to the nature of the sacraments: they have no more magical efficacy than the word of God transmitted through the mediation of the Scriptures, since they too are sacraments of this same word. Important also with regard to the understanding of their mode of efficacy: it is the path of the efficacy of the word, in human communication, and not the path of the efficacy of the "instrument" as in classical theology (see Overture, pp. 14–17), that we shall use in our attempt to approach the mystery of God's gratuitous communication through them. Although theoretical, this debate is, as will be seen, full of practical consequences.

Evangelization and Sacraments

Among the pastoral implications of the above reflections, we find in the first place the malaise constantly expressed by those in charge, whether clerics or laypersons, when faced with the request for sacraments (especially baptism for little children or marriage) by persons whose beliefs are far distant from the faith of the church, if not even opposed to it. We shall deal with this problem, too grave to be ignored, in the last part of this book. However, the approach just developed leads us to underscore two points right now.

ANY SACRAMENTALIZATION DEMANDS A PREPARATORY EVANGELIZATION

The story of Emmaus attests to this: the recognition of the risen Jesus in the Eucharist was made possible only because it followed the evangelization that occurred on the road. Today as yesterday the celebration of the sacraments must be preceded by a minimum of catechetical reflection and (re-) evangelization. The pastoral efforts, which have been made at the urging of the latest council, to insure an honest preparation for baptism or marriage are a proof of this theological demand, even though these efforts may appear insufficient or unsatisfactory.

---

[10] Ambrose, *Expositio in Psalmum 118*, in Migne, Jacques-Paul, ed., *Patrologiae cursus completus: Series Latina*, 221 vols. (Paris: Migne, 1844–1891) 15:1197–1526; Augustine, *Homilies on the Gospel of John* 26.11; 27.11, in Philip Schaff, ed., *A Select Library of the Nicene and Post-Nicene Fathers*, 14 vols. (1886–1890; reprint, Grand Rapids, Mich.: Eerdmans, 1980–1983) 7:171; 7:178 [adapted by the editor].

However, although it is clear that the greater part of evangelization must be done during the time preceding the celebration of the sacraments, one must not forget that every liturgical act also has a dimension of evangelization. Paul uses the same verb, "to proclaim," "to announce" *(kataggelō),* for the Eucharist where "you proclaim the Lord's death until he comes" (1 Cor 11:26) as well as for the missionary preaching of the gospel (1 Cor 9:14). The very manner of celebration is influenced when this dimension of evangelization is taken into account. Against an excessively hieratic practice of the liturgy, it fosters this minimum of imagination and apostolic boldness which mission requires.

It remains, let us repeat it, that the liturgy cannot and must not carry the whole burden of evangelization. On the one hand, the form that evangelization may take in the liturgy, a form necessarily ritualized, cannot be the same as in encounters designed for that purpose; it must even be different, at least to avoid having what is ritual by nature drift toward explanatory catechesis or didactic discourse. Moreover, if to be alive the liturgy must rest on a good "technical" implementation, it must also, and even primarily, rest on a community itself alive and missionary all week long.

Let us add that to evangelize during the liturgy, or even to evangelize the liturgy, is not to dilute the "new wine" of the gospel (cf. John 2:1-11; Mark 2:22) with so much water, under the excuse of "adapting" the liturgy to the level of the participants, that it becomes a tasteless beverage. No! Such an adaptation, necessary in certain cases, must never result in a watering down of the gospel, and at the same time the liturgy. It is the heady wine of the gospel that the participants must be given to taste. How can they set out on their journey in Jesus' footsteps if they have not known the joy caused by the shock of the good news? Still, one must measure what they can bear, lest they feel the euphoric effects of a quasi mystical drunkenness or the dysphoric effects of disgust.

EVERY EVANGELIZATION MUST BE STRUCTURED BY THE SACRAMENTS

If the breaking of the bread at Emmaus is, as it were, the keystone of the story, it is only because it is supported by the thrust of the vault, in this case the previous evangelization. Conversely, without the counter-thrust of the keystone, the vault would collapse. It is the sacramental structuration of the evangelization itself which is this counter-thrust.

This does not mean that one must hurry and propose celebrations at any moment: respect for the travelling pace of individuals or groups requires more circumspection. The sacramental structuration of evangelization (like catechesis which is one of its major forms) essentially means two things:

(a) With regard to *form:* that it be based not only on the Bible and on the lived experience of the participants, but also on the liturgical experience of the church. And, whereas the first two poles (Scripture and ethics) are generally well honored, the third one is easily forgotten. The result of this is that the original role of the sacraments in the building up of faith can hardly be perceived because they are reduced to a sort of afterthought since it seems that all the essential has been said without any need to have recourse to them. The balance of our diagram of Christian identity (p. 28) is no longer respected. And yet, how can one speak of conversion without mentioning baptism? of sharing, without making reference to the Eucharist? of forgiveness, without adverting to baptism and reconciliation? of mission, without bringing in baptism or the celebration of confirmation recently held or about to take place in the community? of the sick, the infirm, the lonely, without recalling the celebration, either recent or future, of the anointing of the sick in the parish? of covenant, without citing marriage and the Eucharist? of death, without speaking of the Christian funeral? The question is not to give a lecture each time on the appropriate sacrament but to point out the connection with it. And this begins with the catechesis of grammar school students: while it is not fitting to give a lesson on confirmation to children in lower grades since they will receive this sacrament only several years later, it is fitting to speak of this sacrament with them by bringing up the latest celebration or inviting them to attend the next one. It is thus that one honors the sacramental pole of Christian identity and the sacraments rightly appear as constitutive elements of faith on a par with other elements.

(b) with regard to *substance,* a sacramentally structured evangelization or catechesis presents a Jesus Christ who is not simply an "example" but the genuine "sacrament" of God.[11] To present a Christ who would be first of all an example to imitate is to veer toward the path of moralism, a discouraging, even a fraudulent path since the

[11] René Marle, "Une démarche structurée sacramentellement," *Catéchèse* 87 (1982) 11–27.

example to imitate is inimitable. Christ must be announced primarily as the sacrament of God (and as a consequence he is to be "imitated" in a way completely different from that promoted above). As a sacrament, that is to say, as the gratuitous gift of God and, more precisely, as Savior. He is our ferryman to God's shore. We do not have to desperately run after him to join him: he himself comes toward us, as at Emmaus, and takes us in his boat to carry us to the other shore. It is, before all else, this truth that the sacraments are witnessing to us: a pure gift from God deposited in our hands (The body of Christ—Amen).

RELATIONS BETWEEN SACRAMENTS AND ETHICS

The clarification of the relation between sacrament and ethics is also important, especially because the devaluation of the liturgy in the wake of the revolution of the 1960s was equalled only by the overvaluation of ethics, particularly in its militant version. More than thirty years later, the upheaval has markedly abated. Nevertheless, the fact that the balance between sacrament and ethics remains in an uncomfortable tension—which is constitutive of the gospel itself—always presents the danger of a tilt toward ethics which, as is seen nowadays, can take many other forms than a certain militancy. In the pages that follow, we shall attempt to show the tension which characterizes the relation between the liturgy and life in the Christian economy.

Jewish Worship

This tension has its sources in Judaism. Compared with the pagan peoples who surrounded it in the time of the Old Testament, Jewish faith has this particular trait, that it has for its object a God who intervenes *in history*. At the same time, history is the prime place for the revelation of God; and the worship, which is a memorial of this God intervening in history, especially at the time of the exodus from Egypt, commits Israel to taking charge of history in an ethical manner. Let us develop this point.

MEMORIAL

First, Israel's cult can be characterized as a memorial, the very model of which is Passover. On the seventh and last day of this feast, the day when the Passover lamb was immolated and eaten in memory of the coming out of Egypt, one obeyed the command given by God to the people through Moses (as Jews still do in the course of the

Passover meal): "You shall tell[12] your child on that day, 'it is because of what the LORD did for me when I came out of Egypt'" (Exod 13:8). The Mishna comments on this text as follows:

"In every generation a person is duty-bound to regard himself as if he personally has gone forth from Egypt, since it is said, *And you shall tell your son in that day saying, It is because of that which the Lord did for me when I came forth out of Egypt* (Ex. 13:8). Therefore we are duty-bound to thank, praise, glorify, honor, exalt, extol, and bless him who did for our forefathers and for us all these miracles. He brought us forth from slavery to freedom, anguish to joy, mourning to festival, darkness to great light, subjugation to redemption, so we should say before him, Hallelujah."[13]

Whereas the coming out of Egypt happened centuries ago ("the LORD *did,*" past tense), everyone deems that it still concerns her or him in the present ("for me when I came out of Egypt.")

Such is therefore the nature of the memorial: it involves the participants in the event which the feast commemorates. It is a "commemoration," that is, a common memory, the memory of a people. At the same time, this memory cannot be reduced to a mere subjective state of mind where images from the past arise at random in the mind, somewhat like photographs yellowed by time retrieved from the bottom of a drawer. By reducing the past to the anecdotal level, such memories in no way take account of the present state of affairs in view of a better future; such memories are apt to submerge the person in the lethargy of "the good old days," a sheer dream. As Johannes Baptist Metz writes, "People have been robbed of their future."[14] On the contrary, the memorial is an act of collective memory which causes the present to budge and open onto the future. The memory of the suffering endured, the oppression undergone, and the struggle undertaken

---

[12] Literally "you will *haggadah*"; it is the well-known Passover "haggadah" in which the father of the family, answering the ritual questions asked by the youngest participant, narrates God's marvelous deeds performed for God's people at the time of the Exodus.

[13] Mishnah Pesaḥim 10.5, in *The Mishnah: A New Translation,* trans. Jacob Neusner (New Haven: Yale, 1988) 250.

[14] Johannes Baptist Metz, *Faith in History and Society: Toward a Practical Fundamental Theology,* trans. David Smith (New York: Seabury, 1980) ch. 6.

to bring about liberation initiates movement: tomorrow will be better than yesterday, if not for us at least for our children or grandchildren. In the meantime, such a state of mind mobilizes energies in view of this future. Thus, in the memorial the past is received as present (and even as a present). The trial of the Exodus, ritually relived every year by every generation, is bearer of the promise of a new exodus—which Christians will see realized eschatologically in Christ's passover:[15] the memorial of his own victorious suffering is for them the gage of a personal and collective future which will be not only "otherwise" in this world (which it also is, against the Christian temptation of flight from the world—see in particular the Old Testament background without which the death and resurrection of Jesus are incomprehensible) but also entirely "other" in the joy of contemplating God.

In its liturgical memorial, Israel receives its foundational past as *present,* and this gift guarantees a promise for the *future.* The theme of "today" in Deuteronomy finds its source here, as attested, for example, by the "fiction" of Moses speaking in the present tense in Deut 5:2-3 of the past covenant on Mount Horeb: "The LORD our God made a covenant with us at Horeb. Not with our ancestors did the LORD make this covenant, but with us, who are all of us alive today."

THE RITE OF THE OFFERING OF FIRSTFRUITS

Even though the word is not used, the rite of offering the firstfruits of the earth in Deut 26:1-11 is a genuine memorial. It is a discourse directed by Moses to the whole people, assembled as one person for this liturgical feast and addressed as one person. There are five sections in this discourse:

A (vv. 1-2): Ritual prescriptions using the collective "you" and the future tense. The people must take some of the fruits of the harvest and carry them to the place chosen by God "as a dwelling for his name," that is, the Temple of Jerusalem.

B (vv. 3-4): Word and ritual gesture using "I" and the present tense. "Today I declare to the LORD your God that I have come into the land that the LORD swore to our ancestors to give us."

---

[15] "Eschatology": this term, frequent in theological writings, means that since the paschal victory of Christ, we are "in the last times" (Greek *eschaton*) (Heb 1:1). But although this victory is already definitively gained, it is not yet definitively accomplished. It is this distance between this *already* and this *not yet* which the adverb "eschatologically" designates here and very often elsewhere.

C (vv. 5-9): Confession of faith using "we" and the past tense (that is, memorial) telling of the settling of the Hebrews in Egypt, their becoming slaves, their crying to God, who took them out of Egypt "and gave us this land."

B' (vv. 10-11): Word and ritual gesture using "I." "So now I bring the first of the fruit of the ground that you, O LORD, have given me."

A' (v. 11): Ethical prescriptions concerning the sharing with those who do not possess anything. "Then you, together with the Levites and the aliens who reside among you, shall celebrate."

As this presentation shows, section C, at the heart of the account, is framed by two ritual sections, themselves inserted between two passages of ritual and ethical prescriptions. Section C, whose subject is the collective "we" of Israel in the past, is a typical *memorial* in the form of a confession of faith. That this past is foundational for Israel's identity, that consequently it is valid for the today of every generation in the "com-memoration" which the people make of it, is demonstrated by its position between two *ritual* words using "I" and the present tense. Long ago the people "have come into the land" (v. 3) which God has "given" them (v. 10); and yet, through the memorial and rite that surrounds it, every generation continues to arrive "today" into this land and to receive it "now" as a gift from God. In other words, the rite symbolically realizes year in year out the "performance" of the entrance of the people into the land of Canaan and their settling there. It expresses by gestures and words in the present tense what the memorial narrates in the past tense. Israel is not the owner of its land. True, it inhabits it and grows all manner of crops in it. But Israel is only the steward of the land. It is God who "causes" the fruit "to grow" (as God has "caused" Israel "to come" from Egypt) and it is God who today as yesterday gives it to the people. Therefore, the land is not raw material: it is a *gift*. This is why Israel can live in it as Israel only by constantly *receiving* it as a gift, therefore by constantly remembering. This is symbolically expressed by the ritual gesture of dispossession: through some fruit from their harvest, which symbolically represents the whole of their land and their labor,[16] they *return* to God this land which belongs to God and was gratuitously given to them; they return God's grace, they render thanks.

---

[16] One cannot not mention here the offering of the gifts at Mass, "this bread . . . which earth has given and human hands have made."

But the whole of the text is constructed in view of the final verse (A'). This verse enjoins on the people an ethics of sharing with those who have no possessions and/or no land. These are, by vocation and at the very heart of Israel, "the Levites" and, by necessity and outside Israel, "the aliens." This means that making a ritual offering to God is not sufficient in itself; Israel does not acquit itself by dint of ritual sacrifices, as the prophets have repeated often enough. The *ritual* dispossession in honor of God is meaningful only if it is "veri-fied" (made genuine) in an *existential* dispossession in favor of those in need. In other words, Israel must behave ethically toward those who possess nothing, in the same way God did toward it when it possessed nothing. The rite is the *symbolic expression* of an ethical duty. Grace is always given as a task to be performed. For Israel, ritual liturgy has no meaning unless it is fulfilled as a "liturgy of the neighbor" (Emmanuel Levinas).

Our text shows clearly the tension that exists between liturgy and ethics within the Jewish religious logic itself. Such a tension produces a *ritual crisis* because unlike pagan peoples Israel cannot live in quiet possession of its worship. The call to ethical responsibility creates a rift between pagans and Jews, a rift having immense consequences, cultural as well as religious, which our Western countries have inherited. This ritual crisis has been fostered particularly by the prophets.[17] All of them, castigating the cultic formalism which honors God with the lips only, demand that the heart and actions be in harmony with what worship symbolizes: the circumcision of the flesh? yes, but in view of the circumcision of the heart; the offerings to the Temple? yes, but in view of sharing with the Levite and the alien or with the widow and the orphan; the sacrifices? yes, but in view of the "sacrifice of the lips" to God and the sacrifice of justice and mercy to others. The way was open to the pure and simple substitution of human good deeds for sacrifices:

"The one who keeps the law makes many offerings;
    one who heeds the commandments makes an offering of well-being.
The one who returns a kindness offers choice flour,
    and one who gives alms sacrifices a thank offering." (Sir 35:1-4)

---

[17] For instance, Amos 5:21-27; Hos 6:6 (see Matt 9:13 and 12:7); Isa 1:10-20; Jer 7:1-28; Mic 6:6-8; Ps 50:12-15; Ps 51:18-19, and so on.

Because of its faith in a God who reveals the divine self first of all through history (primarily that of the Exodus), Israel can live its worship only by engaging in "works" urged by faith in response to the preceding commitment of God to Israel. To be "pleasing to God," worship must be, as it were, in a constant state of crisis. This is what Jesus will show forcefully.

Jesus and Jewish Worship

"I desire mercy, not sacrifice"; "This people honors me with their lips, / but their hearts are far from me"; the Temple must be "a house of prayer" and not "a den of robbers." It is perfectly clear that by repeating these formulas from the prophets, Jesus was endorsing their criticisms of cultic formalism.[18] Probably in a lesser degree he was also part of a wider cultural current prevalent in the Mediterranean basin: the Greek philosophers had for a long time and in different degrees denounced sacrifices, seen as a sort of haggling unworthy of both humans and gods. At the time of Jesus, the Stoic teachings were particularly severe on this point.[19]

It is precisely the confluence of these two currents, the prophetic and the Hellenistic, which we encounter in a writer contemporary with Jesus, Philo of Alexandria.[20] This Jew, devoted to the Law of Moses but strongly influenced by Greek culture, holds the sacrifices of the Temple of Jerusalem in high esteem. However, he repeatedly reminds his readers that although God prescribed these sacrifices, it is not because God needs them (*Special Laws*, 1.293) but because God wants to increase our piety toward God (*Who Is the Heir of Divine Things*, 123). In this perspective, it is the sacrifice "of thanksgiving" which has the first place among all other forms of sacrifice. But its ritual performance in the Temple has value in God's eyes only if it expresses, in thanksgiving, the offering of the good disposition of the heart, which surpasses all sacrifices (*Special Laws*, 1.271-272). For the apex of the sacrifices is the spiritual offering of the soul united with God (*On Exodus* 2.71-72). Philo goes very far in that direction,

[18] Hos 6:6, quoted in Matt 9:13 and 12:7; Isa 29:13, quoted in Mark 7:6-7 and Matt 15:8-9; Isa 56:7 and Jer 7:11, quoted in Matt 21:13 and parallels.

[19] Royden Keith Yerkes, *Sacrifice in Greek and Roman Religions and Early Judaism* (New York: Scribner's, 1952).

[20] J. Laporte, *La doctrine eucharistique de Philon d' Alexandrie*, Théologie historique 16 (Paris: Beauchesne, 1972).

"Let [those who are about to offer a sacrifice] investigate the reasons they are going to offer the sacrifice; for it must be an expression of thankfulness for kindnesses which God has shown to them" (*Special Laws*, 1.283).[21]

We understand why Jesus, who on the Sabbath regularly took part in the synagogue worship with his Jewish compatriots (Luke 4), was not backward on the subject of criticism of the Temple sacrifices. However, *"it is difficult to ascertain"* his exact attitude on this point, in the opinion of Charles Perrot: in Mark 11:16, he seems to "stop the march of the sacrificial worship"[22] but he also respects the law on the clean and unclean when he sends the leper he just cured to show himself to the priest and tells him to offer the prescribed sacrifice (Mark 1:44; see Matt 8:4; Luke 5:14). And elsewhere, he does not abolish the offering at the altar even though he demands a previous reconciliation with one's sisters and brothers (Matt 5:23-24). It is perhaps because his attitude shows "a certain compromise"[23] that among the Christians of Jewish origin there will be acute tensions between the "conservatives" and the much more open "Hellenists" (see Acts 15).

However, we have his well-known words against the Temple. These words seem to have embarrassed the first Christian communities so sorely that they transmitted to us different versions of them, a radical one coming from the Hellenists who announce its pure and simple destruction, according to Acts 6:14; another, much more moderate, emanating from the communities which, like Matthew's, lived in Jewish circles (in Matt 26:61 mention is made of the eschatological reconstruction of this same Temple) and that, on the other hand, all of these versions (except John 2) place it in the mouths of false witnesses. Be that as it may, we probably shall never know exactly the words Jesus historically pronounced on this subject. But they can have come only from him since, negatively (criterion of difference), they cannot have originated either in Jewish milieux or in Christian communities which they embarrassed and since, positively (criterion of coherence), they are in agreement with the general tenor of his positions and with the

[21] In *The Works of Philo, Complete and Unabridged,* trans. Charles D. Yonge (1854–1855; reprint, Peabody, Mass: Hendrickson, 1993) [adapted by the editor].

[22] Charles Perrot, *Jésus et l'histoire,* Jésus et Jésus-Christ 11 (Paris: Desclée, 1979) 146–147.

[23] Ibid., 145.

newness of his message. One thing is certain: the fact that these words played a decisive role in the outcome of his trial (and that of Stephen in Acts 7, which Luke composed in parallel to Jesus' trial and death) proves their importance. These words go farther than the prophets' reproaches and herald a new status of worship. But this newness could be manifested only after Easter.

The Status of Christian Worship

THE VOCABULARY OF WORSHIP

After Easter, the newness of worship appears chiefly in the vocabulary. What is happening is a true rerouting of language. True, the most common cultic terms of the Old Testament are used in the New, but they never designate either Christian liturgical activity or the ministers who preside over it. Then to what do these terms, "sacrifice," "sacrificer" (that is, priest, meaning the one who is charged with "making the sacred" and more particularly the "sacrifice" as the Latin *sacer-dos* and the Greek *hiereus* indicate), "offering," "altar," "worship," "liturgy," and so on, apply? They are used in two ways: first, when speaking of *Christ*, to underscore that he brought the Temple worship (especially the sacrifices and the priesthood) to its fulfillment and that, having fulfilled it, he abolished it; second, when speaking of the *daily life* of Christians, provided it is united to Christ by faith and love, to characterize it as becoming through him a "spiritual sacrifice," that is, in the Spirit, "pleasing to God."

Thus, Paul writes to the Romans, "I appeal to you . . . to present your bodies as a living sacrifice, holy and acceptable to God, which is your spiritual worship" (Rom 12:1). Or else, according to the letter to the Hebrews, the "sacrifice of praise" consists in offering "through him," Christ the one priest, the confession of faith ("the fruit of lips [cf. Hos 14:3] that confess his name") as well as the duty "to do good and to share what you have" (Heb 13:15-16). In the one instance Paul perceives something "sacral" or "sacerdotal" in his apostolic mission and regards himself as the "minister *[leitourgos]* of Christ Jesus," he explains that it is not because he presides at the Lord's Supper in the communities where he finds himself but because he is engaged "in the priestly service of the gospel of God, so that the offering of the Gentiles may be acceptable, sanctified by the Holy Spirit" (Rom 15:16). This is a typical rerouting of the usual Jewish vocabulary; it presents the missionary as the sacrificer, the word of God is in some way the knife, and the addressees are the sacrifice! We could multiply similar quotations from the New Testament.[24]

THE FOUNDATION OF THE NEWNESS: EASTER AND PENTECOST

It would be a grave mistake to interpret this spiritualization of the vocabulary merely on the *moral* level. Christians are not distinguished from Jews because they would or should exhibit a more elevated or more refined moral sense. When he asked that worship be in harmony with the heart and actions, Jesus was not innovating; neither was he innovating when he taught that reconciliation between sisters and brothers has priority over ritual offering or when he made the twofold commandment of love the key to understanding the Law. Many rabbis in his time taught all this. Even if Jesus was more forceful when he spoke of these things, a difference of degree is insufficient to establish a difference of identity. The latter difference is such that it is impossible to pour the new wine of the gospel into old skins of the Law and to mend its old cloak with a piece of unshrunk cloth: "a worse tear [would be] made" (Mark 2:21-22).

The key to the Christian difference is not found in the moral order but in the *theological*. This means that it concerns not human generosity but God's generosity. This is precisely what Paul emphasized in his letters to the Romans and the Galatians: the justification through which the reconciliation of God with humanity takes place has as a principle not the good works that humans accomplish but God's gratuitous work in Jesus Christ. For such is the good news which Paul announces in his missionary discourse in Antioch of Pisidia: "What God promised to our ancestors he has fulfilled for us, their children, by raising Jesus"; "By this Jesus everyone who believes is set free from all those sins from which you could not be freed by the law of Moses" (Acts 13:32-33, 39).

Here we meet again the promise of a new covenant announced by Jeremiah and Ezekiel: since Israel is constantly unfaithful to the covenant, God will write the divine law on the people's hearts (Jer 31:31-34); God will give the Spirit in order to change their hearts of stone into hearts of flesh (Ezek 36:24-28). The missionary discourses of Peter and Paul in Acts announce this inscription of God's law or God's word in the human heart through the Spirit poured out by the risen Christ

---

[24] See in particular Rom 1:9; 1 Cor 3:16; 2 Cor 6:16; 9:12; Phil 2:17; 4:18; Eph 2:22; 5:2; 1 Pet 2:4-5.

(Acts 2:33). The Christian newness is not to be sought anywhere else than in this new reading of the Scriptures; they are "fulfilled" in the resurrection of Jesus and the gift of the Spirit. Its foundation is not moral but theological (more precisely eschatological): it is *the event of Easter and Pentecost.*

It is no longer a question of "climbing" toward God by the strength of one's wrists, that is, by fulfilling the works of the Law; it is a question of welcoming by faith God who has "come down" by the Spirit of the risen One to dwell in the hearts, that is, the life, of human beings. Consequently, it is this *dailiness* of life, when lived in faith and love, which through the Spirit becomes the primary place of the "liturgy" or the "spiritual sacrifice" to the glory of God (see the use of the cultic vocabulary in the New Testament, on preceding page). The consequences are immeasurable:

(a) The sanctification of the "profane" has been substituted for the Jewish category of "sacralization" which is separation from the "profane." Daily life is left in its condition of being "profane," but when in-dwelt by the Spirit of the risen One, it can become in its entirety a "spiritual worship." Strictly speaking, one should omit the quotation marks when referring to the liturgy of dailiness, and reserve the quotation marks for the "ritual liturgy": this is the festive expression allowing believers to symbolically see and ethically practice mutual love (with its components: justice, liberation, mercy, forgiveness) as a liturgy offered to God. It is thus the whole of life that is called to become a "feast."

(b) If the primary locus of Christian worship is the ethics of dailiness, sanctified by theological faith and charity, the new "priesthood" in charge of offering it as a "spiritual worship" is the whole people of God, as Peter's first letter states: through faith and baptism, Christians are "built into a spiritual house, to be a holy priesthood" (1 Pet 2:5). God is not restricted to residing in the Jerusalem Temple made of material stones; God is present in the spiritual temple formed by Christians, "living stones" built upon the foundation of the "living stone" which is Christ (1 Pet 2:4). For as Paul writes, "We are the temple of the living God" (2 Cor 6:16); and "Do you not know that you are God's temple and that God's Spirit dwells in you?" (1 Cor 3:16). In the same way the category of "sacralization" has been replaced by that of "sanctification," the category of "intermediary" between God and humanity, which the Jewish priesthood was, has been replaced by that of *mediation*, that is, of a milieu in which communication between God and humanity takes place from now on. This milieu is daily life, historical existence, "corporeity."

(c) Of course, the function of minister is not abolished in Christianity, any more than liturgical worship, because ministers do have their place in the church structure. But this function is of an entirely different order than that of the Jewish priests since "there is . . . one mediator between God and humankind, Christ Jesus, himself human" (1 Tim 2:5), whose priesthood is "exclusive" or "permanently" held (Heb 7:24). The priests of the church are not "intermediaries"; they sacramentally manifest, in virtue of the sacrament of holy orders which they have received, the unique mediation of Christ in whose name they preside, this unique mediation which causes the whole body of the baptized to be "priestly."

(d) We do not end by "desacralizing" Christianity. "Sacred" expressions, especially in liturgical worship, do have their place. Simply, in the same way a mathematical operator is not on a par with the numbers it multiplies or divides but indicates the type of relation established between them, faith is the "operator" which indicates the conversion (one is tempted to say "the subversion") to which the "sacred" is subjected in the Christian regime. Faith modifies the sacred by a critical exponent.

In pagan religions, the manifestation is effected primarily through the cosmos, that is, in a *seeing* mode; in the Jewish religion, the revelation of God is effected through history, that is, in a *hearing* mode: God has no face (see the prohibition of the first commandment: "You shall not make for yourself an idol" [Exod 20:4] and the penalty of death for seeing God except from the back [Exod 33:18-23]). God is first and foremost revealed as word which must be listened to. Christianity adopts the two modes, especially that of hearing, but this is in order to accede to the mode of *living*, already abundantly proclaimed by the prophets. Once again, the reason for this is not to be sought in any sort of moral superiority but in the action of God in Jesus and particularly in the gift of the Spirit. Indeed, it is due to the indwelling of the Spirit of the risen Christ that daily life is called to become a living parable of God, as Paul writes:

"You yourselves are our letter, written on our hearts, to be known and read by all; and you show that you are a letter of Christ, prepared by us, written not with ink but with the Spirit of the living God, not on tablets of stone but on tablets of human hearts" (2 Cor 3:2-3).

64

The very existence of Christians, being the place where the book of the Spirit is written, thus becomes a living word revealing Christ. The place of the theological is the anthropological. The most spiritual is given in the most bodily. Is not this what is attested in particular by the sacraments?

A VITAL TENSION

The tension between liturgy and ethics which we have noted in Judaism is, as it were, doubled in Christianity. It is tempting to assuage the discomfort by either absorbing the liturgy in ethics ("What does Mass matter? The important thing is charity") or ethics in the liturgy ("I'm square with God: I go to Mass every Sunday and go to confession regularly.") In both cases, one becomes a "dualist" Christian who separates the sacraments from the lived experience. However, the good health of faith depends precisely on this discomfort. This is to say that the tension is not to be abolished but managed. Its proper management requires, as we have seen, a twofold rereading: a liturgical rereading of ethics, which shows that the life of faith and love is a "spiritual offering," and an ethical rereading of the liturgy, because the grace received in the sacraments is given as a task to accomplish, as one prayer after communion expresses: "Make us become what we have celebrated and received." Without the liturgy, ethics can be most generous but is in danger of losing its Christian identity of response to the prior commitment to God. Without ethics, sacramental practice is bound to become ossified and to verge on magic. It is the sacrament that gives ethics the power to become a "spiritual sacrifice"; it is ethics that gives the sacrament the means of "veri-fying" its fruitfulness.

Conclusion

It is written in the biblical *letter* itself that the word wants to inhabit through the Spirit the very *body* of the people of God (Jer 31 and Ezek 36 above). This body plays its role in a ritual, therefore symbolic, manner in the sacraments: (1) every individual body, through voice, gestures, postures, motions; (2) but also the social body of the church—that of yesterday, constantly remembered through words and gestures received from tradition, and that of today as well, which is the active subject of the celebration, as the collective "we" unceasingly proves; (3) finally, the cosmic body, represented by a little water, bread and wine, oil, light or ashes, and received as God's "creation."

In view of this role of the "body" thus understood, are the sacraments anything else than the symbolic expression of the passage (the "pass-over") constantly to be made from the letter to the body, that is to say, from the Scriptures to ethics?

One Element of the Structure: The Sacraments as Ritual Symbols

The sacraments, as we have emphasized in the first part, are not the whole of ecclesial life; they are one element of it, one which acquires its properly Christian sense only by its relation with both the Scriptures and ethical life.

However, in the structure of Christian identity, they exercise an *original* function. This is what we shall now try to make clear. To achieve this we must begin with their practice itself, that is to say, their celebration. And this celebration is a language having a twofold character: it is fundamentally both symbolic and ritual. Hence the two following chapters, one on symbol and one on rite.

Chapter 4

Symbol

The sacraments are expressions by means of language. But their language is of a peculiar type since it is primarily symbolic. This chapter is devoted to the notion of symbol. First, we shall study this notion. Second, we shall show what is at work in the act of symbolization, and third, we shall dwell on the question, capital for sacramental theology, of symbolic efficacy.

WHAT IS MEANT BY SYMBOL

Some Examples

Walls, there are walls all over: houses have walls, buildings have walls, works of fortification have walls. And yet, there was THE wall, the one which everyone knew, the one which the media spoke of so often in the period of the Cold War. This wall was an eminent symbol. Everyone understood it: this wall *was* Berlin, it *was* the Cold War, it *was* the communist regime of the Eastern European countries. This wall, although now no more, is still heavy with a collective memory made of sufferings and hopes, a little like that other one, the Wailing Wall, in Jerusalem. How many persons throughout the world have wanted to get a stone from the Berlin Wall, even at a very high price, and jealously keep it as a relic? On a fortunately less dramatic plane, the real Empire State Building, but also the least miniature of it glimpsed in the house of an Amazonian Bororo, is New York in the same way the flag, whether solemnly hoisted or discovered by chance, dirty and torn, in the Sahara sands where you would have lost your way, *is* the United States; or in the same way a crucifix, large or small, beautiful or ugly, *is* Christianity.

Now, let us no longer imagine objects but words. If we hear by chance someone in the street say "Kyrie eleison" or exclaim "Attention!" the world of the Catholic liturgy or of the military is instantly brought to mind without our thinking explicitly of them. Any term or expression characteristic of a political party, of the youth culture, of a sports club can likewise function as a symbol. It can also be quite simply an accent, an intonation, or else, on another plane, a manner of walking in the street or behaving in a group that links you with your home state or the middle class or an exclusive group of Ivy League intellectuals. And we could go on with odors ("Catholicism is a fragrance of incense," said Julian Green), music (organ or rock), colors (red, blue, and so on). Therefore, any element, verbal, visual, olfactory, tactile, and so on, can, depending on circumstances, function as a symbol.

It is easy to see that daily life constantly plunges us into a world of symbolic markers which enable us to situate ourselves as subjects within a culturally organized, socially organized world, that is to say, a world in which we can find our bearings. These symbols function the better the less we explicitly think of them. They are less objects of speech than *space* within which speech takes its meaning. It is thanks to a thousand symbolic "details," from the style of the furniture and the rest of the interior decoration of the parlor where you set foot to the accent and manner of your interlocutors, their clothes, whether "cool" or conservative, and so on—all these things which stand in the order of symbol because they situate you as a "subject," with your cultural "world," in relation with other "subjects," with their own "worlds"—that you are able to genuinely communicate, or on the contrary, feeling ill at ease, that you confine yourself to polite banalities. *Symbols "speak" to us before we even begin to talk.* What do novelists do but give voice to these many unperceived symbols which "make" our daily life?

Analysis

On the basis of the few examples given above, we can already characterize symbol by at least four traits which we shall call (1) fitting together, (2) crystallization, (3) recognition (or identification), and (4) submission to the communal Other. As a preliminary, let us recall what the symbol was in antiquity: a piece of an object given to contracting parties in order to allow them or their descendants to recognize themselves as parties in this contract. Such a recognition (3) was effected by "putting together" *(sym-ballein),* that is, by fitting the different fragments together (1), which were regarded as carriers of the contract itself (2), the whole process being under the authority of the written or oral law guaranteeing the legitimacy of the operation (4).

(a) If someone shows me a stone from the Berlin Wall, I symbolize by mentally *fitting* it into or joining it with the whole Wall in which it belonged. Without this joining, the stone can suggest whatever comes to my imagination: a stone that hit me in the head one day, the grey color of the sky on a rainy day, the rock seen during a hike in the mountains, or the cement of our cities, the hardness of a stony heart, and so on. As long as the element remains isolated, that is, not fitted together with the whole to which it belongs, it does not function symbolically but *imaginarily*. As Edmond Ortigues writes, "One cannot isolate the symbol without destroying it, without causing it to swerve into inexpressible imaginary."[1] The same is true of the sign of the cross made by someone in the street or the "Attention!" heard by chance: if they are not fitted together, the first with the Christian world, the second with the military world, they can suggest practically anything. The "Attention!" for instance will make me believe that I am threatened by danger or that the person who said it is crazy.

What characterizes the symbol is not its material value in quantity or quality but its *relation* with the whole to which it belongs. As soon as the stone is set in relation to the Wall, that stone functions as a symbol as well, whether it is small or large, shapeless or round or square, nondescript or pleasant to look at. Therefore, since the performance of a symbol is linked not to the value of its "content" as such but to its relation, one understands that it is impossible to transpose a symbolic element from one cultural or religious system into another or from one context (liturgical for example) into another without causing it to produce effects completely different from those it had in its original system or its initial context. A gesture perfectly effective as a symbol in an African liturgy cannot, without dysfunction, be used in a Western liturgy; a posture, very meaningful in a celebration for young people, may appear inappropriate in an adult group; a sort of language or movement, well adapted to a Mass celebrated during a weekend in the woods, is apt to create a vague malaise, even with the same group of persons, if it is transported to the parish church on the next Sunday. A purely "natural" symbol does not exist.

(b) If the fitting together we just spoke of is possible and happens spontaneously, it is because the symbolic element *crystallizes* in itself

---

[1] Edmond Ortigues, *Le discours et le symbole* (Paris: Aubier-Montaigne, 1962) 221.

the whole of the world to which it belongs. In the stone from the Berlin Wall, in the miniature Empire State Building, in the sign of the cross, in the "Attention!" we have as it were "the precipitates" of, respectively, the whole of the totalitarianism of the communist regimes, of the New York ethos, of the whole of Christianity, of the whole of the military. The symbolic element represents the whole of the world to which it belongs; better, it carries it in itself. This is why it *is* what it represents. Obviously, it is not "really" but "symbolically" what it represents, precisely because the function of the symbol is to *represent* the real, therefore to place it at a distance in order to present it, to make it present under a new mode.

This *symbolic mode of being* is of an entirely different order than comparison. The reign of God is "like" a net which contains all manner of fish. What we have here is a simple image, whereas the Berlin Wall "is" symbolically Communist dictatorship. It is so to such a point that its demolition hastened the events in the Eastern countries and became a historical date for the whole of humankind. It is imperative to observe this trait of the symbol: it works with efficacy in the real world. Imperative because in our Western languages, the word "symbol" has come to designate what is unimportant (for instance, the payment of the symbolic dollar for damages) or what is "unreal," what does not "really" exist (such and such a locution in the New Testament is "symbolic"). The liturgy has paid a heavy price for such a semantic *drift:* what does it matter if the submersion into death with Christ in baptism is celebrated with three drops of water, if no one or nearly no one receives communion at the eucharistic "meal," if the "pleasant odor" of the gospel is represented by a vague trace of ill-smelling oil after baptism, and so on, since—as everybody knows— "all this is symbolic." In the end, one is left with liturgies literally "in-significant" in which everything or nearly everything is "fake": fake candles, fake bread, fake garments, fake deacons and sub-deacons, fake catafalques, fake offices (with the possibility of anticipating vespers in the morning), and so on. As we know, Vatican II has firmly reacted; we shall come back to this point.

Such a semantic drift of the symbol is easy to understand: as we have seen, the performance of the symbol is not connected with its material "value." There is no more need of a vast pool where one can move with ease to symbolize the submersion into death with Christ in baptism than there is need of a large stone from the Berlin Wall to symbolize Communist dictatorship. A little water, a small stone are sufficient. But this "little" in the context of the Christian liturgy and contemporary history is heavy with essential human and spiritual realities. Similarly heavy with human realities are the few dollars I give to the Girl Scouts for their cookies or to the Boy Scouts for their popcorn. This is a symbolic gesture in the twofold meaning of the term: it is very little, "nothing at all" compared to the needs of their organizations; but at the same time, it is one of the most efficient ways at my disposal to establish a supporting connection with them—I place myself on their side, I compromise myself with them, I implicate myself by "recognizing" them. From this point of view the symbol is no longer in the field of the unreal; on the contrary, it is in the field of the most significant and the *most real*. Only, the real we are speaking of here is not that of raw material; it is the real humanly (symbolically) constructed into a "world," of which we have spoken previously.

It is so true that the symbol speaks to the most real that it gives rise to another deviation, a psychological one this time, no longer a semantic one, and opposite to it. This deviation, which could be called "romantic," consists in limiting the symbol to the "touching": the cherry tree bough in bloom with immaculate Mount Fuji in the background, the loaf of bread and the carafe of wine, the old chapel on a slope above a verdant alpine valley, and so on. No doubt, there is symbol in all this, but the scope of the symbol is much vaster than these romantic images.

(c) In the symbol, as used in antiquity, the joining of the elements causes the *recognition* or the *identification* of the persons as partners in the same contract. In the same way, the mental linkage of the stone with the Berlin Wall, of the "Attention!" with the military, and of the sign of the cross with Christianity allows me to recognize myself or to identify myself as a subject: in this case, as a subject sharing the values of democracy, as a subject belonging to the English-speaking community and holding such and such a position with regard to the military, as a subject sharing or not sharing the Christian faith, and so on.

Such is without a doubt one of the major functions of the symbol: it allows all persons to *situate themselves as subjects* in their relation with other subjects or with the worlds of these other subjects (with the meaning we have previously given to the term world) or with their own worlds. An instance of this would be the evocation of one's childhood world: a certain object, a certain melody, a certain expression, a certain odor or color can bring back one or several parts of one's early years. Whereas the sign, as we shall see, belongs to the order of knowledge, therefore the order of the relation between subject and object, the symbol belongs to the order of recognition, therefore to the order of the relation between subjects as such. The sign designates significations; the symbol assigns a place to the subject.

(d) Lastly, this symbolic identification is possible only inasmuch as the subjects are under the agency of the *Other*—this Other, which we have previously designated as what binds subjects among themselves, what subjects them to a common "symbolic order" and allows them to form a *community:* language, tradition, ancestors, law, God (for the believers), Jesus or Muhammad (for Christians and Muslims), ideology (Marxist for instance), and so on. In the symbol as used in antiquity, it is the law, accepted by all the partners; without it, the contract made by them would be impossible. In the case of the Berlin Wall, it is sharing in the same democratic ideal. If the historical event of its destruction has such a symbolic effect (and efficacy!), it is because it has bonded together all the "democrats" of the world. To use completely different examples, a certain odor of cleanliness and the light squeaking of shoes on the waxed floor identifies (or identified) a certain type of religious or monastic community; the hoisted flag accompanied by the blowing of taps causes the patriotic string to resonate (or not to resonate: the functioning of the symbol is not linked with the emotions it arouses but with what it identifies, in this case the homeland), and so on. The symbol is a mediator of identity only by being a *creator of community,* thus, besides the preceding examples, rap or rollerblades which connote youth, the design of furniture which connotes "modern" (see advertisements replete with symbols), the crucifix on the wall which connotes "Catholic" or the cassock which connotes "old-fashioned priest" or, better still, the rightly named "symbol of the faith" which is the Christian creed.

Sign and Symbol

TWO PRINCIPLES OF HUMAN COMMUNICATION

It can be sensed that symbol is not the same as sign. Let us enumerate some of their principal differences. The sign, Ortigues writes, "leads to something other than itself" because it implies "a difference between two orders of relations: the sensible signifying relations and the intelligible signified relations." On the contrary, the symbol "does not lead to something of another order than itself, as does the sign, but it has the function of introducing us into an order of which itself is a part."[2]

Let us give a few examples. The word "flower," like any word in the language, can function either as a sign or a symbol. I can enter a conversation about "flower(s)" because, having heard the signifier/flower/(sound perceived by the ear), I have been led back to the signified "flower" (the concept) and because, interested as I am in botany and horticulture, I find pleasure in sharing with others my knowledge of the subject. Here the word has functioned as a sign. If, on the contrary, lost, alone in the Amazonian forest after a plane crash from which, by some miracle, I have walked away unharmed, I hear in the distance the word "flower," my reaction is not to say to myself, "Well! someone is speaking about horticulture; I'll join the conversation," but "Thank God! Another human being! I'm saved!" The word as a symbol has enabled me to identify an English-speaking person because I have spontaneously connected the word I heard to the English language to which it belongs.

It goes without saying that any word or even syllable of any language, such as "bo," would have functioned in the same way under one condition: that it could be recognized as the expression of a human language, allowing me to immediately discern that it is a cultural delimitation along a scale of sounds, delimitation which differentiates it from animal cries. The signifier "bo" would not have any signification for me if I did not know the language; but it would introduce me into the human sphere to which it belongs because it is an element of a human language. From this point of view, a mere phoneme (/b/, /k/, and so on) acts as a symbol and is the zero degree of the symbol: it has no meaning; nevertheless, it takes me into the world of meaning, the world of humanity.

The same analysis applies to the other examples, linguistic or nonlinguistic, which we have supplied above. The "Attention!" heard by chance in the street is not perceived as a "sign" warning me of danger, but as a symbol which on the spot brings to mind the military world. The sign of the cross made by a person in the subway does not evoke for me the signified (Jesus' cross as expression of God's saving love) which Christians recognize when they pray; it connects me spontaneously with Christianity to which it belongs (and of which it is

---

[2] Ibid., 43.

precisely one of the major symbols). The miniature of the Empire State Building found in the hut of a Amazonian Bororo does not make me think of what is signified (the architect who conceived the building, the reasons why he did so, the weight of its structure, and so on); for me it represents New York, what makes New York New York, even what makes the United States the United States. A signpost reading "one way" is a sign when it tells me not to drive down the street the wrong way, but it is a symbol when it brings to mind the regulations governing automobile traffic, without which it would be impossible to circulate, and the law in general, without which it would be impossible to live together. The commentary accompanying a slide of this signpost can be based on either: if it is taken as a sign, it may remind someone of a little inconvenience due to the long detour during vacation; if it is a taken as a symbol, it may inspire someone to deliver a lecture on the theme of the law as a structural element of both personality and any sort of social life.

The sign belongs to the order of knowledge or information or else value, whereas the symbol belongs to the order of recognition or communication between subjects as subjects and is outside the order of value ("flower" as symbol has no value of information; the word simply indicates the presence of someone speaking English. To express oneself by words or gestures is always to signify something about something to someone (even is this someone is oneself when one speaks to oneself as to another person). The sign is situated on the side of "saying something about something," that is, on the side of the transmission of information or knowledge; the symbol is situated on the side of "saying to someone," that is, on the side of communication with a subject recognized as a subject and situated in its place as a subject.

Clearly, sign and symbol are not on the same level. They are ruled by *two different principles*. This means that symbol (and in the literary order, metaphor) must not be understood in relation with sign as if it were a more complex, more ornate, more aesthetic expression of it. It is fitting to insist on this point because the scientific and technological world in which we live is dominated by the idea that every language should be the univocal language of science.[3] No doubt the latter,

---

[3] "Univocal," that is, having one meaning only, in opposition to "equivocal" (or else "polysemous"), subject to two or more interpretations. The language of literature, and particularly poetry, is eminently polysemous.

linked with critical reason, remains indispensable. It would be most detrimental to disparage it in reaction against a narrow rationalism and against the anguish caused by some of the consequences of scientific discoveries; one could then fall into, as happens in the present, the quicksand of the most unsubstantial "symbolism" and into the most dangerous esoteric-mystical discourses. However, this univocal scientific language is unable to do justice to the whole human reality, despite the claims of scientism.

For it is true that the human being is a being-who-has-a-language, but the *primary* function of language is not to designate things in a univocal way, to label them. This, language does also and necessarily; in this regard, it comes under instrumentality. But its primary function lies elsewhere, in its unique capacity to place things at a distance by naming them, and thus representing them, thereby giving them speech. The result, as we have insistently said, is that the raw elements of the universe become a world of meaning in which human beings can dwell as subjects. *In language, it is the symbolic function which has priority:* it makes possible this communication without which the subject could neither arise nor perdure as subject. Every language is "poetic" in essence, in the etymological meaning of the Greek verb *poiein* which means "to make," "to act": it is language that "makes" the universe into a world. Heidegger wrote that the most banal everyday language "is a poem escaped . . . a poem exhausted by use."[4] For his part, Paul Ricœur thinks that in language there is a "fundamental metaphoric function" linked to the essence of "being," and notably to the fact that in any statement, constantly present at least implicitly, the copula is "the most intimate and ultimate locus" of the metaphor.[5] Consequently, even though it is always connected with the sign (understood in the sense explained above), the symbol (or in a discourse, the metaphor)[6] is in some way the *original language* of human beings.

[4] Martin Heidegger, *Acheminement vers la parole* (Paris: Gallimard, 1976) 35; [*On the Way to Language,* trans. Peter D. Hertz (New York: Harper & Row, 1971)].

[5] Paul Ricœur, *La métaphore vive* (Paris: Seuil, 1975) 11; [*The Rule of Metaphor: Multi-disciplinary Studies of the Creation of Meaning in Language,* trans. Robert Czerny, University of Toronto Romance Series 37 (Toronto: University of Toronto, 1977)].

[6] Paul Ricœur, "Parole et symbole," *Revue des Sciences Religieuses* (1975) 142–161.

To name things is not just, is not first of all, to attach a label to them for ease of communication. To name is to "call" things to "come and be present" so that they can speak to us.[7] We gain a faint consciousness of this fundamental calling of language, most often forgotten, as soon as things open from inside, so to speak, for instance, when the wind ceases to be a mere meteorological phenomenon and becomes the reminder of fleeting life, when water ceases to be simply a compound of oxygen and hydrogen atoms or an element useful to quench thirst and becomes the metaphor of life or death, depending on whether it is limpid or stagnant, or when badly down at the heel shoes cease to be seen only in their material shabby condition and become the symbol of all the misery of the world.

Western rhetorical tradition has regarded the figures of speech as more or less ornamental addenda or more or less unsound deviations. This is to suppose that "content" is independent of "form," that is, as Tzvetan Todorov wrote, "two expressions, the one with, the other without image, express, as César Chesneau du Marsais (1676–1756) used to say, 'the same content of thought.'" Such a presupposition is even to be considered "one of the most persistent paradigms of Western culture."[8] In this perspective, the implicit norm of the "right" language would be the univocal language of science for which truth is identified with exactitude. The poetic treatment of language, wider that poetry properly so-called, would be but a play, a luxury, pleasant no doubt but not essential to human beings.[9] What we were just saying emphasizes, on the contrary, that *language is in its essence primarily "poetic" or symbolic,* and that by virtue of this it is the essential food enabling the subject to arise and perdure as subject: "Indeed, humans speak, but it is because the symbol has made them human."[10]

---

[7] Heidegger, *Acheminement*, 23.

[8] Tzvetan Todorov, *Théories du symbole* (Paris: Seuil, 1977) 123 and 116; [*Theories of the Symbol,* trans. Catherine Porter (Ithaca, N.Y.: Cornell, 1982)].

[9] This poetic treatment of language concerns the form of language (assonances, rhythm, and so on). "Why do you always say 'Jane and Margaret' and never 'Margaret and Jane?' Do you prefer Jane to her twin sister? Not in the least, but it sounds better this way," in Roman Jakobson, *Essais de linguistique générale* (Minuit, 1963) 218. Properly so-called poetry does nothing else than bring into play this poetical function present in all languages.

[10] Jacques Lacan, *Ecrits* (Paris: Seuil, 1966) 276.

Although the two logics of "symbol" and "sign" depend on two different principles and do not function at the same level, they are nevertheless the two poles of all human expression. Neither symbol nor sign exists in a chemically pure state. In the most poetic language and the most symbolic work of art, there is necessarily something of the sign; and in the most objective discourse of science, there is necessarily something of the symbol. But it is easy to guess that these two poles of language interact in different degrees. Let us illustrate this by four cases.

First case: *scientific discourse*. At an international convention, the paper delivered by an astrophysicist on the latest research conducted in her or his laboratory is essentially on the side of the "sign" pole. One could even feel that the symbol pole is totally eliminated because the scientist's discourse, wanting to be as "objective" as possible and omitting subjective factors of belief, ideology, preference, states of mind, aims at being a discourse "without a subject." In fact, the symbolic pole is not absent even in this case, because our lecturer would probably never have resolved to devote herself or himself to astrophysics if she or he had not been inspired more or less consciously by the desire to find a place in a meaningful universe and, in order to reach that goal, to delve into its secrets. Besides, the lecturer would not have written one line of his or her presentation without the urge, common to all of us, to be "recognized" by one's peers and possibly admired by them. Behind the scientist there is always the human being, period. Behind the facade of the most informative and neutral speech there is always a hidden "word," that of a subject having desires, even though their presence is denied, a subject who cannot not be seeking recognition. In the discourse, this word is usually perceptible, at least indirectly, in the introduction and conclusion of the presentation where the author "situates" herself or himself to a degree; more deeply, beneath the discourse itself, this word resonates through an intonation, a hesitation, a lapse, a "blank," even through the clothes adopted for the occasion and the way of standing before the audience.

Second case: the *performative act of language*. This is the case opposed to the preceding one, since here the subject is fully engaged as subject. However, the pole "sign" is discernible from the start. Indeed, if I tell you, "I promise to come and see you tomorrow," it is clear that I am transmitting information: "you" is not your neighbor, "tomorrow" is not today, and so on. But under this purely informative appearance, it is easy to sense something else. "I promise you" (like "I swear to you," "I forgive you") used in the first person and in the present tense belongs to what linguists call the class of the "performatives." Indeed, here we are dealing with a "language act" in the strongest sense of the word "act" because one realizes what one says by saying it. What is realized is a *performance*. The performance consists in this: the situation between my interlocutor and me is not the same after as before: I am now committed to this person. It is possible that I shall not keep my word; in this case, people will say that the language act was "unfortunate," but not that it was "false." The performatives are not of the order of the true or false, but of the fortunate or unfortunate. Even in this case, there was a performance, that is the creation of a new relation between two partners. This would not happen if the third person was used: "She promised to go and see her tomorrow" describes a performance but is not a performance. In the performative, the pole "symbol," that of the communication between subjects as such, is dominant.

This is easy to understand if I tell someone, "I command you to close the door." Behind the transmission of information (there is a door here which should be closed), that is, the "locutionary" dimension of language, there is, according to the vocabulary of John Langshaw Austin, an *illocutionary* dimension of relation between places (relation of superior to subordinate), a relation that is either changed or reinforced by the language act itself; language is truly "performative."[11]

Third case: *making conversation*. "It's beautiful this morning," I said to a colleague upon arriving at my office. In appearance, this statement is purely informative. If my colleague, who for her part had also had ample time since she got up to notice that the sky was blue, did not retort, "Do you take me for an idiot?" it is because she understood very well that it was my way of saying, "Hello! you're here and so am

---

[11] According to John Langshaw Austin, *How to Do Things with Words* (Oxford: Clarendon, 1962), every language act has three dimensions mixed in various proportions: the "locutionary" designates the content of what is said; the "illocutionary," the relation between the positions established between subjects as such by the simple fact of the communication; as to the "perlocutionary," it indicates the effects produced by the language act at the level of the feelings, ideas, and actions of the person addressed. In the preceding example, this effect might be a feeling of irritation, a submissive behavior, and so on.

I. What about recognizing one another for starters?" Here the pole of symbolic recognition is obviously primary. As we say in common parlance, "We make conversation." For what is said is something else than what is uttered. Such is precisely symbol. As human beings, our days are replete with it.

Fourth case: *the work of art*. Let us take as an example Van Gogh's painting of the peasant woman's shoes. Obviously, the symbolic function is dominant in this painting, as it is in every work of art in any field (poetry, music, sculpture). Van Gogh's intention when he painted this subject was not to instruct us; for this a simple illustration or a sketch would have been sufficient. Here, every sort of utilitarian purpose is banished. As Heidegger writes on this subject, this painting "does not communicate any knowledge whatsoever"; it does not serve "to illustrate better" what shoes as a mere product are; it has nothing in common with a simple "imitation or copy of reality." It shows "what the pair of shoes is in truth."[12] Thanks to Van Gogh's pictorial technique and unique sensibility, these shabby shoes have become the bearers of all the misery of the rural world a century ago, and even of the world at large; this is why they "speak" to the viewer of today. For,

"in the dark intimacy of the hollow of the shoe is written the fatigue of the steps of labor. . . . Through these shoes pass the silent appeal of the earth, its tacit gift of maturing grain, the mute anxiety over the scarcity of bread, the silent joy of having once again overcome need, the anguish of an imminent birth, the shiver before a menacing death. This product belongs to the earth and it is sheltered in the world of the peasant woman. [And when she takes them off in the evening or automatically puts them on at dawn,] she knows all this without having any need to observe or consider anything: [all this is indeed] gathered together [in her shoes; through them, the peasant woman is] welded to her world."[13]

In a word, inasmuch as all this is "tied together" *(sym-ballein)*, "the work is symbol."[14]

---

[12] Heidegger, *Chemins qui ne mènent nulle part,* trans. W. Brokmeier, Idées (Paris: Gallimard, 1962) pp. 47 and 36.

[13] Ibid., 34–35.

[14] Ibid., 16.

In the final analysis, no shoe *is* more a shoe than these shoes: the symbolic work causes things to accede to their truth. But here, this truth is no longer the mere exactitude of the scientific type in which the mind is supposed to faithfully correspond to the real. This truth belongs to the symbolic order. It is on the same plane as those tales or poems about which one says they are "truer than life" because they express a reality concerning the "mystery" of human existence (love, happiness, suffering, death, and so on) which cannot be better expressed than through metaphors. Here, the "manner" is a question of content, not form: then "it speaks to us."

Are we dealing here with a pure symbol from which our pole of sign would be absent? No, because in order for this painting to exercise its aesthetic function, one must know at a minimum what shoes are. An indigenous inhabitant of Amazonia, completely ignorant of our culture, would not "see" the painting as painting; she or he would perceive it only as a strange object to be interpreted imaginarily. There are other things to be known besides: one must know what a "painting" is and, further, a painting which is a work of "art," that is, "framed" and "exhibited"; know who Van Gogh is; know that he rejected academic subjects in order to represent "ugly" things, and so on. From this viewpoint the Romantic theory of "art for art's sake" is only a chimera because the pole of "sign" is always present to some degree. It is even this pole which predominates when this painting is reproduced in a dictionary as an informative example illustrating the evolution of painting throughout the centuries or analyzed during a class in an art school.

Of course, all gradations between the two poles concretely exist in human communication. To say "This ink is blue" is to deliver a piece of information, but it is also to place oneself to some degree in relation to others: that of a subject who wants to appear sensible and not crazy, since she or he sees clearly that this ink is not black. To ask someone "What time is it?" is to request information, but it is also to implicitly oblige the person to answer. If the person turns her back on you instead of answering, she has denied you as a subject; in certain cases ("You could at least answer!") this negation is lived as a sort of symbolic murder whose wound can remain in you all your life. The same expression, "Lamb of God," analyzed in a class of biblical exegesis or heard by chance in the street does not have the same scope at all in both cases: in the first, the pole of "knowledge" is predominant; in the second, the pole of "recognition" (of Christianity or liturgy).

Similarly, to tell my table neighbor "This cabbage is bad" can be a mere transmission of my taste in food, whereas the same words addressed by an angry child to her mother have the evident symbolic meaning of "I don't like you anymore."

Because its consequences are so decisive, we have had to insist above all on the fact that symbol depends on a principle of functioning different from that of sign. But this insistence, as we have just seen, does not minimize the importance of the "sign," that is, finally, of what pertains to critical reason. Like our body, our mind needs two legs to walk straight: sign and symbol. Left to itself, the latter would drift into all sorts of fantasies. Hence the necessity of critical discourse. The rediscovery of symbol in our day is fortunate in view of the dangerous excesses, not to say downright harmful effects, of the "totalitarianism" of critical reason, notably in its variant, ideological scientism, which claims it controls everything. Human beings also need to sing. But this being said, scientific discourse and critical reason retain all their rights; without them, the fixation on symbols risks producing other deviations, emotionalistic or esoteric-mystical, that are no less dangerous, as current events sometimes demonstrate.

THE ACT OF SYMBOLIZATION

We have said with insistence that even though it is understandable that a symbol may go astray into the "insignificant" or the "unreal," it is no less a serious danger. For symbol or, better still, language in its symbolic polarity is eminently effective. This point is of capital importance, as we shall see in the third part of this book, for the theological understanding of the efficacy of sacraments. For the time being, let us confine ourselves to showing this efficacy. We shall first analyze what happens in the act of symbolization; then we shall apply this analysis to sacramental symbolization.

Analysis

Let us start with a very simple example which is nothing but a transposition of the ancient "symbol" analyzed above (pp. 69–74). We are at the end of the Second World War. A group of resisters secretly contacts two agents who do not know each other but are to cooperate in an operation of sabotage. Each of them is given half a bank note irregularly cut in half. At the appointed place, day, and hour, the two, discreetly producing their half-bill, recognize each other by joining the two pieces. This act of symbolization can be divided into four "moments."

(a) Symbolization is an act and not an idea. This act consists in fitting together, joining, splicing two (or more if there are more partners) elements which at the same time belong to one entity (here the bill; in our preceding examples it was the English language, Christianity, and so on), yet are distinct. *Only differences can be symbolized.* This point, as will be seen, is important theologically in order to avoid confusion between Christ and the church in the sacraments, which however are the "symbolization" of their indissoluble union.

(b) Each of the elements of a symbol is relevant *only in its relation to the other* (or to the others if they are more than two). For instance, half of the bank note, say a hundred-dollar bill, is worth not fifty dollars but zero. Besides, we have seen why, when taken by itself independently of its relation to the whole, a symbol regresses toward the imaginary: someone who would not know that half a bill refers to the other half and, beyond, to the monetary system would see only pretty colorful designs that could mean one thousand things at the whim of one's imagination.

(c) The monetary *value* of the bill *does not matter* for the symbol to function: a ten- or fifty-dollar one would have done as well. The performance of the symbol, as we have seen, has no connection with its "value."

(1) Neither its commercial value: two simple pieces of wood symbolize Christianity as well as an ivory crucifix adorned with precious gems; a simple silver ring symbolizes the union of woman and man celebrated in marriage as well as a diamond one.

(2) Nor its use value: in a situation of extreme food shortage, the sharing of one's meager ration with a neighbor who has nothing is a symbolic gesture of equal (or even greater) significance than in other circumstances giving this neighbor the abundant remains of a festive meal. In order to symbolize the messianic banquet, there is no need to eat a large host or to drink a full swallow of wine.

(3) Nor its aesthetic value: the flag may be dirty and torn without ceasing to represent the homeland; the paschal candle may appear in proportion or on the contrary out of proportion with the building where it is placed: either way it is the symbol of the risen Christ.

(4) Nor its cognitive value: the fact of knowing nothing precise about the history of the Empire State Building does not prevent it from symbolizing New York; the Kyrie from a Mass composed by Mozart can perfectly well symbolize Christianity and, more exactly, its liturgy to people who are ignorant of the meaning of these two Greek words.

(5) Nor its emotional value: a sharpened flint does not need to arouse in me any great enthusiasm in order to serve as a symbol of prehistoric humanity; Gregorian chant may not move many hearers at all without ceasing to be for them also the symbol of the Latin liturgy and the liturgical world of old.

Symbol does not belong to the realm of value or utility. In this way, it is given free of charge.

(d) Finally, for our two resisters the act of symbolization is *simultaneously a "revealer" and an "agent."* By symbolizing, they reveal to one another their identity as secret agents, and at the same time they find themselves bound together in the mission entrusted to them, bound to such a degree that they are going to accomplish it at the peril of both their lives. The revelation of identity is supremely efficacious; it creates a bond or relation that causes the situation to be other than before. Such is precisely one of the characteristics of the symbol: it effects only by revealing; conversely, it reveals only by effecting.

Sacramental Symbolization

We can again take up the four "moments" which we have just analyzed to propose a theological reading of the sacraments.

THE SYMBOLIZATION OF CHRIST AND THE CHURCH

Like the act of symbolization, sacraments belong to the order of "doing"; they are not "ideas" (we shall come back to this in the next chapter about rite). This "doing" is symbolic; it aims at properly joining Christ and the church (and more widely, God and humanity) and within the church the members among themselves as "daughters and sons" and "sisters and brothers" in Christ. Because only differences can be symbolized, such a symbolization is possible only inasmuch as Christ and the church are rigorously *differentiated:* Christ is irreducible to a simple code word for the church (he is "being raised," that is, he continues to raise for himself a body of humanity of which the church is the primary locus only because he is first raised by God); conversely, the church exists only in its obedience to Christ, its Lord; it cannot substitute itself for God. The first function of the sacraments is to manifest the vacant place of Christ, his "absence," as at Emmaus. In every instance when we shall consider the sacrament as the symbolization of Christ and the church, we shall not proceed to concoct an I-don't-know-what mixture which would more or less identify Christ and the church; on the contrary, we shall presuppose their difference.

In the same way Christ and the church should not be identified, sacramental symbolization indicates that the church and Christ have relevance only in their mutual relation, even if this relation is not a simple inverse symmetry. On the one hand, the church would lose its identity if it remained constantly attached to Christ, its Lord: it exists only by receiving itself from him. On the other hand, although it is neither the church nor the faith of Christians which made Jesus "the Christ" (it is God who did that), still "the fact of being Christ" or the "Christicity" of Jesus would be reduced to nothing if there were no one claiming to belong to him as "the Christ of God." It is in this sense that the being-Christ of Jesus, although depending essentially on God, is not separable from the church. The function of the sacraments is precisely to symbolize this indissoluble "marriage" (see Eph 5:33): *one can never speak of the one without the other.*

The same approach is valid from another angle. By isolating one element of the Christian liturgy, by cutting it not only from the faith of the church but even more simply from the whole of the celebration to which it belongs, one risks attributing to it totally *imaginary* significations. Thus, the "consecration," too often cut off from the whole of the Eucharistic Prayer, as well as from the Liturgy of the Word, even from the church assembly, risks being seen as the more or less "magical" moment when in some way Jesus suddenly "falls" from heaven onto the altar. Similarly, when the priest is understood in isolation, that is, when he is cut off from the community for whose service he was sent or the mission of evangelization which is his "foremost task,"[15] his person is imaginarily exalted to the point of being placed almost above the angels.

GRATUITOUSNESS AND GRACIOUSNESS

The symbol precedes value; in this sense, it is "gratuitous." This latter term is one of the aspects of the signification of "grace." The goal of the sacraments is to establish between humanity and God a communication which theology calls "grace." So the symbol seems the fitting approach to the sacraments; and it has a twofold theological interest.

---

[15] Decree on the Ministry and Life of Priests, no. 4, in Vatican Council II, *The Basic Sixteen Documents: Constitutions, Decrees, Declarations,* rev. trans. in inclusive language, ed. Austin Flannery (Northport, N.Y.: Costello, 1996) 323.

• *Beyond the Useful and the Useless*

First of all, the properly Christian "success" of a celebration is not linked with the various types of "value" which we have enumerated. Of course, because every human being is a symbolic whole, she or he is not cut up into slices when attending Mass. Unconscious and conscious motivations are necessarily mixed and it is normal that Mass-goers expect a solid biblical and theological reflection, reasonably enjoyable musical and visual aesthetics, a stimulating feeling of belonging. If these were lacking, it is probable that few Christians would "make it." It remains that if one wants to increase and deepen one's biblical and theological knowledge, enjoy sacred music, and boost one's moral by exchanging with other Christians views on the theoretical or practical difficulties one encounters in Christian life, there are other venues than the liturgy for this: a class in theology, a concert, a meeting of reflection on and sharing of life are more effective in fulfilling these needs.

The liturgy has another, fundamental aim: the communication of the gratuitous gift of God, entrance into the mystery of Christ's passover. And this communication, this entrance can be perfectly achieved without justice being done to the "values" named above. If those values—no doubt indispensable for a balanced Christian life (see the tripod, p. 65)—are given priority, there can result for the liturgy various *deviations:* didacticism which gives priority to theological reflection; aestheticism whose criterion of "success" is the quality of the decor or else the "moving" character of the music; moralism which judges that a Mass is "the real thing" inasmuch as it mobilizes energies in order to transform the world, especially through powerful testimonies. Each of these three deviations corresponds to one of the three poles of our diagram of Christian identity (p. 28). Moreover, these deviations foster a grave error, that of believing that the properly Christian quality of the celebration depends on its human qualities. Let us repeat that we are not minimizing the theological, aesthetic, and moral demands of the celebrations, but we simply want to rightly situate their "apex." This apex is of the order of grace: The body of Christ—Amen. And grace is lost sight of if the liturgy is celebrated for the values or usefulness we just mentioned.

• *Grace: Given Free of Charge*

The fact is that—such is the second interest of the use of symbol as an approach to the sacraments—this grace, like the symbol, is outside the field of "value" or "usefulness." The two adjectives "gratuitous" and "gracious" indicate this clearly: as *gratuitous*, grace is not something due, it depends on the generosity of God, who alone takes the initiative; as *gracious*, grace pertains to beauty, to this way of being pleasing which cannot be calculated and therefore is given free of charge. One of the most beautiful biblical images of grace is that of the *manna* in the desert. According to the text of Exodus 16, the manna presents at least three characteristics.

First, its name is not a name; it is a sort of "anti-name," so to speak, since it is a question, *Man hu?*, which means "What is it?" This mystery is compounded by the way the manna is described: "When the layer of dew lifted, there on the surface of the wilderness was a fine flaky substance, as fine as frost on the ground." What is there is an object so fragile that it has all the traits of the inconsistency of an "anti-object," of a "sign" rather than a "thing." Lastly, this mysterious food has nothing to do with calculation or value; it appears literally as given free of charge, always free of charge, since it defies the laws of calculation ("those who gathered much had nothing over, and those who gathered little had no shortage"). It also defies the laws of capitalization and stockpiling: those who, disobeying Moses' order, tried to store some for the morrow saw that "it bred worms and became foul." A later text, from the book of Wisdom, accentuates these traits by interpreting the manna as "food of angels . . . providing every pleasure and suited to every taste." While manifesting to all the "sweetness" of God toward God's children (that of honey as in Exod 16:31), this sweetness took a specific taste for each person, "ministering to the desire of the one who took it," and "was changed to suit everyone's liking" (Wis 16:20-21).

Understood in the same way as the manna, the grace of the sacraments has no value that can be calculated or capitalized upon. It is not a commodity in the market of values and usefulness. Its name, "grace," indicates that it is not an "object" to be received. It is true that grammar will always demand that it be in the position of object. One will always meet sentences of this type: "God (subject) gives grace (object)," whatever the way one understands grace (gift of God, communication of the divine self, covenant, and so on). But even though one cannot do without grammar, one can learn to be distrustful of the constructions it puts together. "To think" on both the theological and philosophical planes, is precisely to learn not to be duped by language, that is, not to identify reality with the discourse about it. For two and a half millennia since the ancient Greeks, philosophers have not ceased wondering what the verb "to be" really is, a verb used or at least understood in all human discourses. Be that as it may, the work of theological thought concerning grace consists in critically distancing itself from the representation, however unavoidable, of an "object" to be received. For, even though strongly spiritualized, as is right, this object remains placed in the domain of "value."

Both our anthropological approach through symbol and our theological reading of the manna place us outside the domain of value. The grace of the sacraments must be regarded less as "something" (as spiritualized as it might be) than as a process of "receiving oneself" as daughter or son, as sister or brother in Christ through the Spirit. Such is precisely the efficacy called symbolic. But we shall have to develop this point. We shall do so at the end of this chapter.

SIMULTANEOUSLY "REVEALER" AND "AGENT"

As a preliminary remark, let us recall that theological discourse deals with faith and can in no way deduce the mystery of God revealed in Jesus Christ from any anthropological analysis or philosophical reflection. Therefore, it is not a matter of explaining here the mystery of sacraments by the use of symbol. Simply, theologians attempt to show that faith, which is not rational, is nevertheless reasonable; for this, they use the tools of analysis and reflection at their disposal. Our approach through symbol—like those using the comparisons of instrument or cause—can be but one way of getting nearer to the mystery; still, this approach enables us to understand better what the church believes.

Let us take the example of the doxology ending the Eucharistic Prayer: "Through him, with him, in him . . . all glory and honor. . . ."[16] This praise of the triune God, which is addressed to the Father through Christ "in the unity of the Holy Spirit," is accompanied by a gesture of the priest, who raises the bread and the cup of wine which have become the sacrament of the body and blood of Christ. If it is true that "one presides" but "all celebrate," it is the entire assembly (the church) which through the priest is the subject expressing to God this praise in word and gesture.[17]

---

[16] "Doxology" comes from the Greek *doxa* which here means "glory." This is the name given to the liturgical formulas of praise to God. For instance, "Glory be to the Father and to the Son and to the Holy Spirit."

[17] See chapter 2, pp. 31–34.

Such a ritual moment is both revealer and agent. Indeed, we have here a vertical and very expressive symbolic gesture of junction ("sym-bol") between heaven and earth. This symbolic gesture encompasses the raising to God of the bread and wine, recognized by faith to be the body and blood of Christ, and the words which, made visible by this gesture,[18] also ascend to God in praise. Such a rite is rich in meaning. It is first a *revealer* of Christian identity. For what is being a Christian if not recognizing oneself as coming "from" God and being "for" God in Christ as daughter or son in the one Son and, at the same time, as sister or brother in Christ, the universal Brother (see Heb 2), as the Our Father also shows? Only, this identity is not expressed here by mode of discourse, as in the Creed; it is symbolically expressed by the body (the common body of the church through the individual body of the presider).

This mediation of the gesture, which gives a body to the word, shows clearly that one must realize what is being expressed. This is why the gesture and the word are not only revealers of this identity as daughters and sons, as sisters and brothers; they claim to be its agents, that is, to effect it. This is already true of our simple statements of belief. If I say to someone, "Jesus is Christ" or "The gospel is my light," I not only describe my inner belief to this person, I take my position as a Christian and by so doing confer effectiveness on my Christian identity. To return to our approach to language, let us say that here, in spite of appearances, the symbolic pole of communication has priority over the descriptive pole of information. There is something performative here, if only because such formulas presuppose an "I declare to you that for me. . . ." or even an "I swear to you that for me. . . ."

This is truer still of the ritual gesture and word we are analyzing. And this for two reasons: first, because here we are undeniably in the domain of symbol; second, because the symbol is bearer of the convictions of the church's faith—the faith of today, since ritual gesture and word are the act of a common "we," and the faith of yesterday, since this ancient formula came to us from tradition and not from the convictions of any one individual. According to the faith of Christians, such a rite is or claims to be (if we adopt the viewpoint of an outside

---

[18] Let us remind the readers that for Augustine, a sacrament is *"like a visible word."*

observer) so forcefully operative that its symbolic efficacy can be understood from two angles. From the participants' angle, the fact of giving thanks to God in this manner, of rendering to God "God's grace," which is Christ Jesus given as a sacrament, confers effectiveness on their identity of daughters and sons, of sisters and brothers in him. By making these gestures again and again, Christians "realize" little by little what to be Jesus' disciples really means. From God's angle, the fact that human beings recognize themselves as coming from God and being for God in Christ confers a historical-eschatological effectiveness on God's fatherhood. Such affirmations are tenable only in faith. Outside of faith, one can see only a "pretense" or an "intentionality" of the gesture aiming at insuring that things will really be so: Who can judge the truth of this gesture in the inner heart of this or that person? Individual "fiction" is obviously always possible. But what is important here on the plane of theological discourse is that intentionality opens a path to understanding faith.

SYMBOLIC EFFICACY

Our first chapter already suggested that language is efficacious. But after our study of symbol and the symbolic dimension of language, we are now better equipped to understand the full scope of this statement.

The Bread of the Word

Not only is language efficacious but *it is what is most efficacious.* However, let us hasten to specify that what is meant is a *symbolic* efficacy. By now it is clear: such an efficacy does not designate, as in science or technology, a transformation of the world but a transformation of subjects, a "work" that is produced in them and allows them to accede to another way of being. Any symbolic efficacy belongs to the order of language. The young child, from the age of five or six months, gradually succeeds in recognizing itself in the mirror reflecting its image only, as we have said, because another person has named it by its first name.[19] The thousand gestures and words of love of which it has been the object from birth (and even before birth) enable it to accede to full status as a subject and, later on, to speak in a sensible manner. Whoever is not loved or, for various complex psychological reasons, feels that she or he is not loved is unable to love. This is the

[19] See chapter 1, "Language as Mediation," the stage of the mirror according to Lacan, pp. 10–13.

tragedy experienced by many delinquents. Whoever has not received the benefit of the forgiveness or the faithfulness of another person can neither forgive wrongs nor be faithful to any commitment. Love, forgiveness, faithfulness are fundamental realities that allow persons to support one another as persons. No one can live as a subject without words of love and thankfulness, whether expressed or, as is most often the case, implicit. For the aged woman whose husband and old friends have died and who never sees any member of her family life is not a "life"; if she does not feel somehow recognized and loved by someone, beginning with a nurse, she can only let herself die, slowly, sinking into delirium, or rapidly. Without this bread of words (words that can be expressed as well by gestures and looks as by being actually spoken) human beings can only die: this is true of the anorexic child, the suicidal adolescent, the adult whom nobody takes into account. Sometimes it is enough to say a few words to someone for that person to feel alive again. On the other hand, it is sometimes also enough to refuse to answer someone for that person to feel negated and to suffer a wound that perhaps will never heal. Some words save; some words kill. Symbolic efficacy in any case touches *the subject to the quick.*

Speech is really the hearty "bread" which keeps human subjects going. This bespeaks its efficacy. It is the most important efficacy one can think of because it is the condition of the very possibility of arising and perduring as a subject. One can see that the subject *as such* exists only in its relation to other subjects *as such.*[20] Although this efficacy makes use of the pole of "sign," that is, the pole of knowledge, of transmission of information, of "saying something about something," it uses primarily the pole of "symbol," that is, the pole of recognition, of communication, of "saying something to someone." As we have seen when considering the third case, "making conversation," at times the content of what is said does not matter; the important thing is to communicate, therefore to be recognized as occupying a truly human place under the sun.

The Sacraments of the Word

If things are as we have just said, a way to understanding the sacraments of faith opens before us. Let us not forget, as we have seen in

[20] This point will be developed later on in ch. 6, when the relation of the "I" and the "you" in the symbolic exchange is discussed.

chapter 3, that every sacrament is a sacrament of the word—the live word brought to us by the Holy Spirit. The discourse on the bread of life (John 6), on which we have already dwelt, shows this clearly: the "bread that came down from heaven," with which Jesus identifies himself, refers to the manna of the desert, itself presented in the Bible as a figure of the word of God (Deut 6:3; Matt 4:4). Because it does not belong to the domain of value, the manna is particularly suited to this figurative interpretation of the word. The same is true of all human words; their fruitfulness is due to the fact that they are outside the domain of calculation. In this domain, "to calculate" is to stockpile "arguments" capable of confounding others, "getting" them, "catching" them in the nets of a rigorous logic—a way of "using" them and treating them as "objects" to be manipulated. Certainly, there is also in life a time for critical dialogue guided by logical reason. But what causes subjects to communicate among themselves belongs to another order: the accumulation of value-arguments destined to "trick" others destroys the word in the same way the manna rotted when stored for the morrow.

Human speech is "substantial bread" which feeds the subject only inasmuch as it gives itself to the other without calculating simply because she or he is "the other similar to me," worthy of recognition and trust. The fruitfulness of the communication is dependent on this gracious attitude of a speech which gives itself without any profit. In this non-market, the law is *the loser is the winner*; as in the multiplication of the loaves, the more one gives, the more one is left with. The proverb says it well, "Share your bread, it decreases; share your love, it increases." Many of Jesus' parables are built on the opposition between the regime of value that can be calculated and the regime of grace: the workmen of the first hour, the elder son, the wise bridesmaids are dislodged from their position founded on distributive justice in order to enter that of a God "rich in grace" toward the latecomers, the prodigal son, the foolish bridesmaids. To live as a disciple of Jesus requires that one gives, not everything in quantity, but from one's all. It is in this sense that "love is the fulfilling of the law" (Rom 13:10). Jesus' enigmatic word in Luke 19:26, "I tell you, to all those who have, more will be given; but from those who have nothing, even what they have will be taken away" ("even what they seem to have will be taken away," says Luke in 8:18, thus somewhat softening the paradox), finds its meaning in the logic of grace. In a word, it is by losing themselves that human beings find themselves. Such is the law that rules all symbolic, that is to say, properly human exchanges, in opposition to market transactions; such is the law that rules the relation to a God of grace and mercy.

It is no more possible to manipulate God through the sacraments than through the Scriptures. In both cases, it is *always as word* that God is encountered. The efficacy of the sacraments has nothing of a guarantee. As we shall develop in chapter 6 when speaking of symbolic exchange, the self-*gift* God offers through the sacraments does not depend on the personal faith of the subjects: God gives freely through the power of the Spirit; but the fruitfulness of this gift in those who receive it, that is, the *reception* they give to this gift *as* grace, depends on their faith.

All this comes down to saying that the efficacy of the sacraments must be understood in the mode of the symbolic efficacy of the word. One is reminded of the fable by La Fontaine titled "The Farmer and His Children." The story is well known: a rich farmer, about to die, advises his children not to sell the land they are inheriting because "a treasure is hidden there." After their father's death, the sons so thoroughly plow the fields that there is no part of them "where they do not work again and again." But they find no treasure. However, La Fontaine concludes, there was indeed a treasure: the work that causes the earth to be fruitful. One can compare the "treasure" of the sacraments to this eminently symbolic, though fully real, treasure. In this perspective, there is no value-object to be found in the field of the sacrament because one does not get one's hands on God. Grace cannot be capitalized lest it destroy itself. Those who believe they can rest on "the graces" received in the past find themselves back at square one. The "treasure" of the sacrament is found in the *"work" of plowing, of turning, of "converting" to the gospel the symbolic field that Christians are*. This work is effected by the rite, or more exactly, the word of God taking on a ritual form and reaching them in its aliveness through the Spirit.

Such a work of conversion on the part of believers consists in realizing what baptism has caused them to be: a little more daughters and sons of God and sisters and brothers for others in Christ, the one Son and the universal Brother. Thus, according to Bonaventure's beautiful formula, communicants "do not transform Christ into themselves but are themselves, as it were, propelled into his mystical body."[21] In this

---

[21] Bonaventure, *Breviloquium*, pt. 6: *Les remèdes sacramentels*, ch. 9, no. 6 (Editions Franciscaines, 1967) 107.

perspective, grace is less a value-object to be received than a symbolic *receiving oneself:* receiving oneself from God in Christ, through the work of the Spirit, as daughters and sons, as sisters and brothers. It is easy to see why sacraments like the Eucharist and reconciliation are to be celebrated again and again: such a work of conversion has to be always begun again. Any who believe they are finally there are back where they started.

Return to Our Original Question

Such a symbolic itinerary of theological reflection is not the contrary of the classical way of "cause" and "instrument." To resume the terminology of the overture, it does not take place, like our second model, the subjectivist, in the camp opposite the first, the objectivist. Contrary things, as we have said, are in the same genus, on the same terrain. Our symbolic way supposes a change of terrain. Our approach itself is different. We believe that this sort of approach is able to satisfy the request formulated in the overture: to give us an understanding of the faith that enables us to see that the sacramental mystery is simultaneously a revealer and an agent of Christian identity. In its primarily symbolic dimension, language discharges this twofold function simultaneously. Furthermore, the symbol, like grace, is outside the value system. For these two reasons, the symbolic route seems to us to supply an approach much more akin to the sacraments than that of instrumentality employed by the Scholastics of the twelfth century, and still dominant in our own day.

This appears so plainly evident to us that one has to wonder how it is possible that the theologians of the past did not explore this avenue. The answer is clear enough: if they did not do it, it was certainly not for lack of philosophical and theological acumen. When one remembers the awesome intellectual work accomplished in the twelfth and thirteenth centuries, in logic as well as in grammar, in physics as well as in metaphysics, there is only one possible answer: because they were part of a cultural age other than ours, the thinkers of those centuries could not ask certain questions that we ask today. If today we can think differently, it is not because we are more clever than they but because we have available to us tools of analysis and reflection which only the modern ethos at a certain stage of its evolution could supply. This is to say that it would be wrong to discard our predecessors' approach. It was not "bad"; it was probably the best one could do at the time. In any case, in such a domain as this, one cannot produce something new without having ruminated for a long time and assimilated the old. The cultural mutations in which we are living compel us to produce the new from the old. The result is not a "better" theology; the result is "another" theology, connected with this profound cultural difference, which, however, unites us to Thomas Aquinas as much as it separates us from him.

Chapter 5

The Language of Rite

Every sacrament is a rite; but the rite does not become a sacrament unless it is in-dwelt by the word of God and converted by the Holy Spirit. The second clause underscores that it is the word which constitutes the sacrament; the first clause, that the word happens in the sacrament only under the ritual mode. This is why we cannot say anything about the meaning of the sacraments without taking into account the very act of their celebration, that is to say, their ritual unfolding, their "practice." Theology, especially in this domain, requires an anthropology, as Marie-Dominique Chenu so powerfully emphasized. In an article entitled "For a Sacramental Anthropology," he wrote:

"Sacramental anthropology: this expression attains its whole importance not as an illustration of a sacramental reality previously known but as a co-essential aspect of the sacrament. We can engage the sacrament only in consubstantiality with human beings. The two words 'sacramental' and 'anthropology' cannot be dissociated either on the plane of methods—which would already be precious—but constitutively."[1]

And further along, the author stated what he called the "principle" of sacramental theology: "the radical connaturality of the sensible in the sacramental economy," since matter is "the first component of the sacrament."[2] As will be seen, these statements entail properly theological consequences.

AN ORIGINAL LANGUAGE GAME

Christians expect much from liturgical celebrations. How not to rejoice in this? But they probably expect too much in certain respects:

[1] Marie-Dominique Chenu, "Pour une anthropologie sacramentelle," *Maison-Dieu* 119 (1974) 85–100. The quote is from page 87.
[2] Ibid.

festivity, to break away from the daily routine; prayer, to compensate for the hyperactivity of the work week, if not that of the weekend leisure; theology, to clarify the many questions they wonder about; heartwarming words, even powerful testimonies, to raise their spirits; silence, to rest from the stress of the week; a feeling of belonging to a community or a locus for relationships, to counteract the anonymity of our cities; and so on. These multiple demands of benefits, spiritual and theological as well as psychological and social, are normal since a genuinely Christian mode of life is realized only in the most human, the most daily, the most bodily. However, the liturgy collapses under the weight of these expectations, many of which are contradictory anyhow. How can both silence and festivity be honored? How can the warmth of "horizontal" relationships be combined with a ritual mode whose dimension is primarily "vertical"? How can the needs of those who are sensible to the "sacred," even hieratic character of the liturgy be satisfied simultaneously with the needs of those who favor spontaneity, even improvisation?

Although it is true that the specifically Christian liturgy can be diversified according to different modes and respond to quite different sensibilities, it remains that because it is a ritual process, it cannot allow itself total liberty. For there are *laws of rite*. To ignore them or to want to circumvent them is to expose oneself to unfortunate repercussions. When one wants to force an institution, in this case the liturgical institution, to produce what it is not made for, that institution takes its revenge. One may believe that one has expelled one demon, but it comes back with seven others, and the situation is more compromised than before (Matt 12:45). Rituality allows and fosters certain things; it prohibits certain other things. It is prudent to know what are its unavoidable constraints. We are now going to analyze these laws of ritual language.

Beforehand though, we must make clear the very nature of this language which belongs to another order than the language of science or theology or mysticism. Let us take an example. A political analyst, studying the failed putsch in Moscow in August 1991, tries to understand its reasons (economic, political, and so on) in as rigorous a manner as possible: her or his discourse aims at being truthful through exactness. A Muscovite "lambda," a direct witness of the event, explaining to some foreign visitors what happened, speaks a different language; of course this person also tries to be as objective as possible, but eager to share with her inquirers the joy of the victory won by democracy, she "hermeneutically" reconstructs the event inasmuch as she is involved in the meaning which the event has had for her. A poet or a singer can in turn address the same event; but now it is to make it "sing" in resonance with the millions of human beings who yearn for democracy. Each of the three intends to express the truth when speaking of the same event. But the truth is not treated in the same way; it is in the order of exactness for the political scientist; in the order of testimony for the witness; in the order of metaphor for the poet or the singer. We are faced with three different *language games*, each of which cannot be translated into either of the other two languages. For instance, to want to retell the poet's song in scientific language is inevitably to say something other than what it says: if need be, metaphor can be explained in analytical language, but then it loses its own power of expression.

The same is true in the domain of faith. The rigorously structured language of the theological discourse can partly explain what happens in the liturgy (this is what we are doing here). But it cannot replace it: it is one thing to speak about the liturgy, it is another to live it. The same is true also of the language of a witness in the context of a small group sharing the way they live their Christian lives in order to become truer disciples of Christ, and true also of the language dealing with the mystical. It is clear that one cannot follow the spiritual itinerary of John of the Cross if one reads it in the same frame of mind one has at a meeting of Pax Christi; no more than one can enter into the language of rituality in the same frame of mind. Therefore, the first condition for "hearing" what transpires in the liturgy is to enter into the type of language it employs.

SOME LAWS OF RITUAL LANGUAGE

An Action-Language

One of the major characteristics of rituality is surely that it aims at being *operative*. In contrast to scientific discourses, which pertain to "-logy," that is, structured discourse (biology, sociology, musicology, theology, and so on), the liturgy pertains to "-urgy," a term that comes from the Greek *ergon*, designating precisely "action" or "work," in contradistinction to *logos*. Terms like "metallurgy" and "chemurgy" designate an activity, a work. However, liturgical action belongs to the symbolic not the technical order: it aims at establishing communication between the participants and God and as a consequence among themselves.

The first liturgical law concerns the way of proceeding: "do not say what you are doing; do what you are saying." It is useless to explain at length that "we are full of joy." Let the singing itself express this joy; let it make this joy. A beautiful and long homily on baptism as being buried with Christ into death (see Rom 6) can be contradicted afterwards by the mere fact that the priest is content with pouring a few drops of water that hardly touch the top of the child's head! It is good to remind people that the Eucharist is a meal; but then let the priest not do the opposite by consuming in its entirety the host that has just been broken to signify the sharing! That the readings from the Scriptures be proclaimed in the assembly as the living "word of God" is important; but why not begin by showing a minimum of respect for the book since it carries the "word of God"; let not the latter be debased by being "proclaimed"(?) from a mere sheet of paper or a missalette; the book should have a respectable volume worthy of the word. And so on and so forth.

For us Westerners, always bent upon mastering the world by dint of ideas, it is difficult to accept this type of language, more behavioral (and pragmatic) than mental (and semantic).[3] We are prone to explaining symbols rather than letting them do their work. But to explain a symbol is to demonstrate that it does not function as a symbol. The liturgy risks swerving into an explanatory or moralizing "-logy"; it grows verbose and does not give the rites their chance to function because it drowns them in a flow of words. One must not, however, ignore the extent of the progress accomplished; but the task must be continued.

The attention given to the proper use of liturgical symbols is not based on a mere concern for aesthetics, but on a theological motivation. That the liturgy is seen as the place not for discourse on God but for reception of God's action corresponds in depth to what the Bible understands by "word of God"; this is not an abstract word, such as the Greek *logos*, but a word which is *action and event*. It is by God's word that God creates the world (Gen 1). When that word comes to the prophets, it invades them to the point of working violence on them (Amos 7:15; Jer 20:7ff.; and so on); it is the messenger that God sends (Isa 9:8; Ps 107:20). The liturgy is the means by which this "per-

---

[3] "Pragmatic" qualifies what has to do with action, therefore practice; "semantic" qualifies what has to do with meaning, therefore ideas or representations.

formance" of the divine word is symbolically given to be seen and lived by. In the liturgy, the word is made not only of words but of materials, gestures, postures, objects; the words seek not only to be there but to be "seen" and "touched"; the word aims at becoming a gesture, at being inscribed on everyone's body (baptism) or placed inside everyone's body (eucharistic communion). This intentionality is not accidental in the liturgy; actually, it is essential to it. As such, it is for the believer the expression of the dynamic nature of the word of God. In the last analysis, are the sacraments anything else than the unfolding, down to the today of each generation and each person, of this efficacious character of the word as word of God?

A Symbolic Language

We have spoken at length about symbol. We have emphasized in particular that the effect of symbol is not of the technical order (work on the world in view of its transformation) but precisely of the symbolic order (work in the participants through the work effected in their relation to one another and to God). Furthermore, among the various characteristics of the symbol, we have singled out *spareness*. This is the one point which we shall consider here.

Because its performance does not depend on its "value," the symbol is discreet: a little water is sufficient to symbolize the immersion into death with Christ in baptism; a little bread and wine are sufficient, from the symbolic viewpoint, to call people to the Eucharist or to represent the whole of creation and human work contained in it. In this, the symbol shows it is not the real. Or rather it is the real and it is not the real at the same time. It is not, since it only represents it; it is, since it represents it, that is, makes it present by a few fragments.

The *festivity* of Christian celebrations must also preserve this spareness of the symbol. Of course, being the living memorial of Jesus the Christ's victory over all forms of death, these celebrations must be joyfully festive. But this festivity must also remain discreet, lest it insult the immense pain of millions of women and men who throughout the world continue to live in despair. In any case, it must not become a popular holiday during which, under pretense of "festive sharing between sisters and brothers," the eucharistic cup is passed around as people do when they celebrate by drinking together. An excessive desire to celebrate for the sake of celebrating risks obfuscating the mystery which is celebrated and to prevent the "passage," the "passover," which the participants must share through, with, and in Christ.

Because it represents the real, the symbol *places it at a distance*. This is why the sign of peace, for instance, must remain relatively discreet. It is not supposed to replace the real, which must be lived all week long. Consequently, for this gesture to be true, there is no need for prolonged demonstrations of affection with every participant, the imaginary substratum of which can be suspect (seductive warmth; bad guilt feeling which takes advantage of the cloyingly comforting context of the celebration to effect an immediate catharsis; love of the confusional sort which denies the opacity of daily life to take comfort in the facile "transparency" of a ritual moment, and so on). A relatively restrained gesture (not too restrained, with the poor excuse that "since it is symbolic it is not important")[4] toward my immediate neighbors is enough to symbolize all those with whom I must be reconciled. Effective reconciliation with them must be realized elsewhere than at this moment of the liturgy: my gesture of peace precisely expresses the task which is incumbent upon me: to realize what it symbolizes in the actual living of my daily life.

The accent placed on the spareness of the ritual symbol is not meant just to insure the proper anthropological functioning of the liturgy. It rests on a specifically theological foundation: it is the expression of the *eschatological* condition which is that of the church and of every Christian. Paul writes, "For in hope we were saved" (Rom 8:24). The "already" of the salvation given in Christ is crossed out by the "not yet," a not yet which causes the world, and believers themselves, sometimes in danger of letting themselves be crushed by the excess of evil and suffering, continue to experience themselves as not yet saved. True, the power of Christ's resurrection is at work—and for this the church gives thanks to God—but it is at work among human beings, too many of whom experience life as a "vale of tears"—and for this the church unceasingly implores God. Like the "sober drunkenness" of communion in the eucharistic cup, spoken of long ago by Ambrose, only the moderation of a little bread and wine or a little water, and not the "real" of a sumptuous banquet or a luxurious swimming pool, is adequate to symbolize the meantime, both joyous and painful, in which the world finds itself. The *reserve* of the symbol is the theological expression of this "eschatological reserve" expressed also by the eucharistic reserve. What can appear more pathetic indeed

[4] See the semantic drift of the word "symbol" in ch. 4, 70–73.

than these few fragments of bread respectfully kept in the tabernacle when compared to the resurrection of the Lord? And yet, is there a figure more appropriate to the faith which dares to confess that, in spite of absolutely everything, the opacity of our world remains secretly inhabited by the strength of an active presence, than these opaque hosts preserved as "the body of Christ"?[5]

A Language That Breaks Away from Ordinary Language

In every religion, be it polytheistic or monotheistic, be it Christian or not, one observes a break between the ritual "scene" and the "scene" of ordinary life. The place is often exclusively devoted to religious rites (temple, church); or else, if it belongs to the ordinary space of the village, it is subjected to a minimum of consecration by being temporarily off-limits (for instance, the fencing off of the sacred enclosure at the foot of Sinai before the great liturgy of God's manifestation to the people or, in African religions, the delineation of the space within which the rites of initiation will be held). The objects can be either reserved for ritual use (stole, chalice, and so on) or taken from daily utensils; in this latter case they are the object of a manipulation by gestures which disengages them from their utilitarian status. The language can be a secret language (the "luo" among the Bobos of Burkina-Fasso, at the time of initiation) or a dead language (Latin) or a language used in its ancient state (ancient Hebrew, ancient Greek, Old Slavonic), or else a living language; but in this last case, it is replete with peculiar idioms ("The Lord be with you"—"And with your spirit," "This is my body delivered for you," and so on), with repetitions ("Lord, have mercy," said three times or even three times three times), of incantations which change it into something else than everyday language. The same is true for the time of the rite, which is of a different order than that of daily life—it is the time of communication with the divinity or divinities, the time of the memorial of the beginnings in which the group is regenerated—as well as for the agents who conduct the rite: they may be readied for their life task by an investiture ceremony (priest) or by recognized charismatic powers (shaman, diviner), or they may be occasional officiants; but in this latter case, not just anyone

---

[5] It goes without saying that by writing this we have not solved all the theological problems posed by the eucharistic presence of Christ. We simply wanted to note incidentally how much this gives food for thought from the theological viewpoint.

can do anything, one must be recognized by the group as a legitimate officiant.

In Christianity, such a symbolic break must be pastorally *negotiated*, according to the place of celebration (cathedral versus multi-purpose hall), the number of participants (vast crowd versus small group), their age (children versus adults), their degree of integration into the church and faith experience (young people seeking their way versus monastics), and so on. It is clear that the difference from daily life can be stronger with a monastic community than with youths in CCD, or with a crowd in St. Patrick's than with a Pax Christi group in some room. One will have to know how to avoid both excess and lack, too much and too little.

Excess of symbolic separation gives rise to hieratic liturgies which little by little cease to speak to participants unless it is only through a nostalgic preservation of the past—with the danger of rendering the worshippers ineffective in the present. The liturgy becomes sclerotic. De-symbolized, that is, cut off from the values that are relevant to contemporaries and from their lifestyle, it runs the risk of favoring a relation with God devoid of any grasp of present history, that is, a relation ruled by the imaginary.

Against this tendency, rather prevalent in what the liturgy had become before the liturgical reform of Vatican II, the inverse temptation, *lack* of separation, arose. Historically, it is easily understandable as a reaction against the too radical break between liturgy and life or between the Christ one celebrates and the Christ who is there "at the heart of our lives." Such a temptation is even quite seductive from the properly Christian viewpoint: Is it not true that the liturgy is the "summit" of daily Christian life and that for Christians ritual worship has meaning only as an expression of the "existential" worship which is everyday life lived under the guidance of the gospel?[6] However, even when born of good intentions and a just intuition, such a temptation is dangerous. By wanting to situate the liturgy too closely in line with life, one trivializes the language, the objects, the gestures, and the space of the rite. For the eucharistic bread, one takes the most ordinary loaf and a drinking glass; of course, to avoid any trace of "clericalism," the priest keeps on his business suit or his work clothes; the language, claiming to be comprehensible by all and to appropriate the "truth of life" shared by the

[6] See above, pp. 61–62.

group, is that of everyday, even in the eucharistic prayer, which will be "improvised" in order to make priest and participants "freer"; and so on. But people do not realize that through a lack of sufficient separation from the lifestyle and language of the group, the group continues to engage in self-celebration under the cover of Jesus Christ and to impose on "God" its own ideology. One is squarely on the wrong level.

For here again, the symbolic break is important not only because it allows the rite to function by taking into account the anthropological laws that rule it but also, and first of all, because it has theological reasons. For what is a Christian celebration all about? It wants to do (first law) and to do symbolically (second law) what one states—under the mode of discourse in the confession of faith, in a group study of the gospel, or in a sharing of Christian experience—concerning Jesus as the living Lord coming to meet us on our human roads and whom, like the disciples at Emmaus, we learn to recognize in the dailiness of life. This discourse of faith—because one needs lots of faith to dare to affirm the presence of Christ or the action of the Spirit in some parents who continue to patiently welcome their drug-addicted son or in some colleague at work who imperiled her job by defending an immigrant employee unjustly treated—is in some way led to its full completion by the celebration. The celebration takes believers at their word and it puts them on the spot by urging them to verify their words by their actions, to go from discourse to body. The question is no longer to discourse on the presence of Christ but to welcome this presence by mode of *symbolic action*.

In order that there be hospitality, there must be availability. This space of availability is symbolized and created by the ritual elements. All have been taken away from their ordinary and utilitarian usage: the language is English, but it is different from that of a small group sharing the way they live their Christian lives in order to become truer disciples of Christ or a theology course; the eucharistic cup is for drinking, but it is not an ordinary glass, purely utilitarian; the altar is a table, but this is prepared in such a way as to make it something else than a desk where one works; the participants sit on chairs, but their arrangement creates a symbolic space different from that of other meetings; and so on. The liturgy is made up of these thousand symbols (for they are symbols, and the more so as one had not thought them up. All of them have this common trait, to take the participants out of what is immediately useful, to create a *space of gratuitousness*. They signify that one ceases to possess and master. Anyhow, the participants are well aware that if they listen to the gospel or the Eucharistic Prayer they know almost by heart, it is not to increase their theological baggage; if they drink from the cup, it is not "to have a good time"; if they repeat three times, "Lord, have mercy," it is not because they fear that God is deaf; if the priest wears a stole, is not to ward off the cold; and so on.

The liturgy thus creates a *symbolic disconnection* which places the assembly in another, non-utilitarian world. As a consequence, there is symbolically room for God; there is a space of gratuitousness where God can come. The believers effect with their bodies—through the arrangement of the place, the type of language and objects they use—what they say in the confession of faith: the risen Christ, the active Spirit accompany them on the road of their life and communicate with them in an ever-surprising way. Thus, the confession of the lips becomes the confession of faith in action.

A Programmed, Therefore Repeatable Language

Be it the rite of a football game or tennis match, the birthday cake and candles, a family festive meal, a signed agreement between two states or two corporations, a civil or religious marriage, and so on, in all cases, the terms "rite" and "ritual" (adjective) designate something which is done every time in an identical way (same sequence of moments with the same gestures and the same words, for instance, one sings "Happy Birthday to You," one blows out the candles on the cake). It is evident that it would be contradictory to "invent" a rite. Every rite is *received* from tradition, received from preceding generations, and in general, when it comes to the main elements of a religious ritual, received from the founder, whether she or he is historical or mythical. One does again what Moses or Jesus commanded us to do or else what the founding ancestors did first. This is why ritual language has this characteristic of being *programmed*.

This programming must also be pastorally negotiated between too much and too little. Excess leads to fixed liturgies where the tradition becomes a shackle preventing any creativity. Through an excessive respect for tradition, or rather traditions, one hinders Christian people from entering in a living manner into the paschal mystery of Christ, which is commemorated, and at the same time one reinforces the conservative tendency inherent in all rituality by the simple fact that it is programmed. Indeed, once it has sprung from the message of the founding prophet, the rite, like the incandescent lava from a volcano, tends to congeal when cooling down. It becomes fossilized under layers of sediments accumulated through generations, to the point of being a heap of disparate elements, which have progressively lost their living significance. Let it suffice to recall the multiplication of the signs of the cross the priest used to make during Mass, the repetition of exorcisms at baptism, the three or four layers of liturgical vestments—those of the subdeacon, deacon, priest, and finally those of his own function— the bishop used to don in the past for pontifical ceremonies.

Through the culture and piety of past generations, the beautiful statue of the liturgy had been so covered over with paint, crowns, precious stones, richly embroidered garments, and so on, that it had become unrecognizable: the lines of force of baptism and Eucharist were no longer perceptible. Vatican II has removed most of the riches that choked the liturgy, not to throw them with an iconoclastic gesture into the trash can of history, because most of them were the expressions of an authentic piety proper to each period. The council has, so to speak, exhibited them in a museum case, offering them to Christians' reflection or meditation and allowing them to be reused now and then in certain cases. In any event, one can see that the *conservative* nature of the liturgy is one of the major traps for Christian faith: it appropriates creativity so thoroughly, it planes its angles so smooth, by its repetitive character and by a programming that tends to forestall any surprise, that it risks taking the edge off the living word of God.

On this point, as on the point of "disconnection," the pendulum movement in the opposite direction was historically almost unavoidable. In reaction, some wanted to place the emphasis on the "truth" and on the "conscious and active" participation of the Christian people, and have favored a *deprogramming* which is no less disastrous for the liturgy. "Spontaneous" liturgical prayers were "improvised." However, on the one hand, a liturgical improvisation is good only if the improvisors have thoroughly interiorized the biblical and liturgical tradition and are thus able to render it felicitously and are not guided just by the feelings of the moment. In the same way, a pianist does not convincingly improvise some "Mozart" without having dwelt within Mozart's music for a long time. Sometimes, for lack of a sufficient rumination on the liturgical tradition, its peculiarities, its style, its images, its rhythm, one has produced liturgies, wordy, flat, and still more boring than those one wanted to revitalize. At the same time, the so-called "spontaneity" was often nothing more than a response to the ideological expectations of the group: the silent censure of a group one is obliged to address in a spontaneous fashion is probably more dreadful than the open censure of a liturgical code known to all. Moreover, the so-called spontaneity of a freedom recaptured through a more or less systematic deprogramming ends up in many cases by being the imposition of the leader's ideology. Each one of the members is then forced in an underhanded manner to adjust to this ideology under pain of feeling excommunicated. This shows that (1) pure freedom in this domain breeds a sort of dictatorship, in any case a situation in which the participants are finally less free than in the framework of a programmed liturgy within which they can at least "breathe" and in some measure distance themselves from the rite; (2) when, under pretense of "equality" in Christian "mutual love," power is not clearly, therefore, institutionally, distributed, it is automatically liable to be manipulated (unconsciously probably) by a few. In a word, along this line there are many possible perversions whose concrete effects are the opposite of what was sought.

Obviously, we have no intention to actively promote a hard programming, whose harmful effects were mentioned above. Pastoral negotiation must take into account the place of the celebration, the number of those attending, their age, their cultural sensibility, and so on. In this negotiation, the amount of programming must be sufficient on two levels. First, it must leave to the rite its function of *protection* in relation to the personal involvement of the participants: it is one of the positive effects of ritual programming to allow the participants to be carried by this programming, that is, not to be constrained all the time to actively carry or support the rite by a participation at the level of the consciousness and intelligence. We have said it before, rituality does not function at that level; people are not put on the spot to totally and constantly involve themselves in it; if this were the case, rituality would soon become exhausting from the psycho-social viewpoint. Why should we feel guilty letting the liturgy fulfill its supporting role? A rite is wholesome only if there is an amount of previsibility sufficient to avoid the anguish of "What's coming next? What else are they going to invent for us to do?" There is need for a basic and relatively stable structure concerning the order of the successive rites, as well as enough landmarks in the words, the postures, the movements to allow participants to find their bearings. The best text of the Eucharistic Prayer as to both theological content and literary form can fail to work for lack of these landmarks: more or less confusedly, participants feel that "this is not the Eucharistic Prayer of the church."

It is clear that ritual programming carries such serious *risks* of routine, formalism, legalism, and so on for the Christian faith that one must constantly see to re-evangelizing it from the inside and keeping it supple enough to be "re-symbolized" with the culture of the present assembly and thus apt to lead it to the heart of the mystery of Christ being celebrated.

These risks must not obscure what is at issue in ritual programming from the specifically theological viewpoint. Let us mention the two main points in question, the christological and the ecclesiological. In the first place, the programming of the Christian liturgy expresses that it is indeed Jesus of Nazareth who is the Lord. We take bread and wine *as* he did and *because* he did, and we repeat the words he said (of course, as recorded by tradition). Instead of using words which to us would be clearer, more eloquent, more effective, instead of using material which to us would be more appropriate for a festive meal in our present culture, we conform to what he said and did.[7] Here is a symbol! And what a symbol! Here again, the symbol works better as a symbol if we have not previously intellectualized it as a "problem." In this eminently symbolic act, we *let* Jesus of Nazareth be our Lord. Here again, we **symbolically do** what we proclaim under the mode of discourse in the confession of faith. Here again we live this *in act*. There is probably no higher way, anthropologically speaking, to realize what the words of faith mean than to symbolically give them a body in these ritual acts in which, referring to Jesus of Nazareth as the unique Lord to whom we conform, we execute his very command. At that moment we live what the theological discourse aims at expressing when it states that the Eucharist is a sacrament "instituted by Jesus Christ," which means that the Lord Jesus is at once its author and its actor.[8]

[7] This does not decide in advance what solution should be given to the problems inherent in cultural differences, for instance, the problem of the bread and wine for the Eucharist in Africa or Asia.

[8] For the theologians of the Middle Ages, to say that Jesus Christ is the *institutor* of the sacraments is to say that he is their *auctor*, a term to be understood in the strong sense of "creator" and "agent." This does not mean that Jesus would have either predetermined the number of the sacraments (it is only in the twelfth century that the number seven was fixed) or furnished them with "matter" and "form." Jesus was not acting as a clairvoyant who would have equipped his disciples with the whole juridical, disciplinary, and

In the second place, the programming of the sacraments, implying that identical elements are used in different church communities, theologically manifests that their celebration is Christian only because it is of the church. This in no way prevents their particularization according to cultures and times: this particularization is even necessary if we remember that the fullness of the church is realized in local churches, as Vatican II reminded us.[9] In other words, for a baptism and a Eucharist to be authentically of the church, they must bear the mark of the local church with its own cultural sensibility. But there is a vast difference between particularization and particularism; the latter is reductive in the sense that it no longer manifests communion with other churches or groups of churches, a communion of which the ordained minister is the symbolic bearer. Every sacrament contests the ideological walls within which a group would want to shut it in because every sacrament is the witness of the *empty place,* that of Christ who presides over it and that of the universal church since it is always the universal church which celebrates its Lord within a local community. Thus, the programming demonstrates that the liturgy and especially the sacraments have in some way an *impregnable* character. Liturgy and sacraments do not belong to any one community. They require that a reference be made to the universal church. We cannot be content with a prayer limited to the church of the young, the church of the workers, or the church of charismatic groups.

A Language That Assigns Positions

Rite assigns positions. This means that, unlike the life of faith and the moral life which are more or less in conformity with the gospel (one could say that they are "analogical"), ritual practice does not accept the more or less. One is a catechumen or not, one is baptized or not, and one cannot make a half-communion. One could say that ritual practice is of the binary order or that it is "indexical" because like an index it *shows everyone's position.*

---

ritual apparatus they would need throughout the centuries. What is meant is that it is always the living Christ who, through the Spirit, is acting through the sacraments. To say that the sacraments have been instituted by Christ is nothing else than to recognize in the sacraments *saving acts of God,* acts in which the church, through the priest, exercises only a ministerial role.

[9] See pp. 37–38.

Its possible risks are easily guessed. For instance, requests for the baptism of young children or church weddings often do not proceed from a life of faith but from interior guilt or social pressure. This rite of passage is requested so that oneself or one's children may be well positioned as Christians, officially and legitimately registered as such (see the last chapter, pp. 179–182). Those charged with pastoral duties often have the painful impression that these persons ask for the shell without its vital content, the marks of belonging without the commitment of one's life which would give meaning to these marks, the circumcision of the flesh without the circumcision of the heart.

Despite these risks, connected with the very way rituality functions, especially in the rites of passage, the positioning effected by the liturgy carries authentic theological riches. We could cite at least three. First, to be baptized is to be marked as a Christian and therefore differentiated from a Jew or Muslim, a Buddhist or Hindu. What sort of dialogue could Christians engage in with these or with persons declaring themselves atheists if they did not stand firm in the particularity of their faith? "Difference" is not an obstacle to communication, on the contrary, it is the condition for communication and its possible fruitfulness. When one is like everyone else, one cannot witness to anything. Second, the difference inscribed on the body of every person through Christian initiation is so important that, far from imprisoning one into a clan or cultural group, as some other rites of initiation do, it opens onto the universal: by their baptism, Christians do not become members of a ghetto, but the sisters and brothers of all humans in Jesus Christ. In the third place, the fact of being positioned in the church as catechumen, baptized, confirmed, married, single, recognized lay minister, ordained minister (deacon, priest, bishop) has two consequences: (1) it makes it possible—which is sociologically indispensable—to know who does what and in what capacity, and (2) it allows persons to place themselves on the particular path of life they have adopted in response to God's calling in order to live the holiness to which the gospel summons them and to assume their own responsibilities in the church's mission.

EVANGELIZING THE RITE

Rite is capable of the best and the worst. The *best:* this is what we have sought to demonstrate in the preceding analysis. At the minimum, this analysis contests the frequent dualistic reflex which places authentic "faith" on the side of the word and ethical life, and "religion" on the side of rites. It is true that faith, when it comes to dwell in religion, may affect it with a strongly critical exponent. But faith itself cannot arise except under a "religious" form, therefore institutional, therefore doctrinal, moral, ritual, and so on. Furthermore, the "word of God" does not fall directly from the clouds. It too comes to us mediated in a body of scriptures (the Bible). Now, because it was produced in a culture very different from our own, the Bible resists every immediate appropriation and needs to be regulated by an ecclesial tradition lest it reveals to everyone only what she or he wants to find in it, as is proved by the multitude of sects that have flourished since the beginning of the church. To oppose "prophethood" to "priesthood," "word" to "rite," "life" to the "sacristy," and so on is merely an ideological delusion. One becomes a Christian only by entering an institution, and the modes of Christian behavior which may appear the most "personal" (meditative prayer, for example) or the most "authentic" (concern for others) are always the expression of an apprenticeship interiorized for a long time and of habits inculcated by institutional and highly ritualized processes. By wanting to free oneself from these institutional mediations, one falls victim to an imaginary dream of immediacy whose harmful results are easily seen.

Nevertheless, rite is simultaneously capable of the *worst*. On top of its obvious risks of routine, it is heavy with ambiguity in the psychological order (obsessional neurosis finds in it a favorable terrain), in the social order (it can function as a shell emptied of its faith content when only the "container" matters, that is, the social marks of belonging to a given religion and, through it, to a culture or a social milieu), in the political order (the manipulation of religious ceremonies by the established powers), in the spiritual order (substitution, more or less magical, of the efficacy of the rite for the word and its ethical demands), and so on. To remain genuinely Christian, rite must be unceasingly *evangelized*.

Two points are to be mentioned here. The first one is properly theological. Rite must be *inhabited by the word of God and the Spirit*. The whole content of the present book shows the importance of this task. It is needless to develop its elements here. Let us simply recall the relation that any celebration and reception of a sacrament must have to the Scriptures on the one hand and ethical practice on the other. Without reference to the other two poles of Christian existence, chances are that the sacraments will function more or less magically.

The second point, on which we shall insist more strongly here, is of the *cultural* order. There is a condition, not sufficient in itself of course but necessary for the evangelization of Christian rites: we must honor certain values of our post-modern society. We are thinking in particular of the values of democracy dear to our contemporaries; they are increasingly uncomfortable with liturgies in which power remains quasi exclusively in the hands of clerics (or of some laypersons, at times more clerical than the clerics themselves). In spite of efforts made during the last twenty years or so and the fruits they have produced, there remains much to be done for a better sharing of power in the liturgy; in any event this sharing is required in the sacraments of initiation, rightly revalorized today, and in the responsibilities that they call every baptized person to assume. We are thinking also—a thing not unrelated to the preceding—of critical suspicion, so characteristic of contemporary culture. People no longer accept faith simply as a heritage; they want to see for themselves, to understand, to verify the cogency of what they are taught; as a result our contemporaries suspect liturgical mystery to be only a mystification if they cannot satisfy themselves with a minimum of understanding. Certainly, as we have seen, the liturgy is not meant first of all to be "understood." But it remains that liturgical language is often formulated in an almost esoteric way, which causes many persons to withdraw, whereas Christians formerly had more trust in the clergy, believed to have the key to what their actions meant. How are we to honor at the same time the laws of ritual language and today's culture? It would be too long to go into explanations at this point, but is seems clear that here is a field where we must continue to work. In my personal opinion, this is one more step which we should take in liturgical reform.

THEOLOGICAL SUMMARY

At the beginning of our study we asked, "Why do we need all this ritual apparatus in the religion of the adoration of God 'in spirit and truth' (John 4:24)?" The question is the more urgent as we perceive more clearly, through the analysis of rituality, the amplitude and depth of the deviations and manipulation, psychological and social as well as political and spiritual to which sacramental rites can give rise. These snares are unavoidable inasmuch as the sacraments employ what is most human, therefore also most ambiguous in humanity with its individual desires and its most archaic or least conscious social representations.

But are not all these things the "flesh" which Christ assumed to save it? On the basis of faith in the incarnation of God in Jesus, Christians confess that they go to God not in spite of the heavy ambiguity of their humanity but *at the very core* of it; not in spite of their bodies—of desire, of tradition, of culture, of universe, as we have seen above—but in their very bodies which through faith in Christ have become "temples of the Holy Spirit" (1 Cor 6:19; 3:16); therefore, not in spite of historical and social mediations but within them.

The sacraments, which inscribe the faith in the body of the participants, symbolically give a role to play to all these modalities of the human being as "speaking body": the body of desire is given a role through the "enjoyment" of the complaint or the jubilation, of the cry or the silence, of the prostration or the hands lifted to the heavens; the body of tradition is given a role through the repetition of texts, gestures, materials that came from the apostolic tradition; the body of culture is given a role through the constant "we" of the liturgical prayer; the body of nature is given a role through the play of light and darkness, the play of seasons which punctuate the liturgical year, the play of death and life in the baptismal water, the play of food and drink in the Eucharist, and so on.

The title given to this book, *The Word of God at the Mercy of the Body*, seems to us fully justified by all that we have just explained concerning the ritual nature of the sacraments. Among the various mediations of the faith, the sacraments are the highest figure of the impossibility for the faith to be lived in what is most spiritual in it—as adoration of the Father "in spirit and truth"—outside the most "bodily" and most "religious." The sacraments thus serve as a *buffer* which repels every temptation Christians might have to ignore body, history, society in order to enter without any mediation into communication with God. The sacraments speak in their way, which is a symbolic way, therefore a way that needs only discreet, even banal gestures in order to express realities as full of significance as peace with others or the reception of the pure gift of God in communion, as "just as you did it to one of the least . . . of my family, you did it to me" (Matt 25:40). The sacraments state that the word of God wants to enter our bodies, that is, our lives, and that for anyone in-dwelt by the Spirit the road of the God of Jesus Christ necessarily uses the human road.

Third Part

Functioning of the Structure: Symbolic Exchange

In the first part of this book we have established the structure of Christian identity with the aid of the model Scriptures/Sacrament/Ethics. In the second part, we have dwelt on the originality of the element sacrament, that is, on the way it functions symbolically and ritually. We are now able to shed light on the question: How can we understand the dynamic relation of exchange between God and believers in the sacraments? To do this, we shall start again from the structure established in the first part. At the time, we considered it as if it rested on a flat surface. We are now going to set it in motion and study its *process of functioning*. We shall do this on the basis of a theoretical model which is that of exchange between persons, a model we shall set up in chapter 6. In chapter 7, we shall apply this model to the Eucharistic Prayer.

Symbolic Exchange

In this chapter, we shall first establish the notion of symbolic exchange on the anthropological level, then show how this notion is of interest to theology in order to understand the relation between God and humankind.

ANTHROPOLOGICAL STAKES

In chapter 4, we have seen that language has two major functions which we have called the function of "sign" and the function of "symbol." Both are indispensable and are always present, in different degrees, in human speech. There is no more a pure symbol, in art for instance, than there is a pure sign, in a scientist's presentation for instance. However, these two functions depend on two different principles: the sign pertains to "value" (material value, knowledge value, moral value, and so on), whereas the symbol stands outside the value system.

What is true of the exchange of words is true also of the exchange of goods on the economic plane. Simply, instead of speaking of "sign" and "symbol," we shall speak of *market exchange* and *symbolic exchange*. Market exchange, whether through barter or money, has to do with value: a bushel of apples is bartered for a length of fabric or paid for with a sum of money. There exist traditional societies, for instance in Melanesia, whose system of exchange is (or rather was) not that of market exchange but of symbolic exchange.[1] Such a system is "a total social fact," which (1) is used at all levels of the social hierarchy,

---

[1] Readers need to remember that in this context "traditional" has no pejorative connotations; these societies are fully human. Their cultures are different from that of our own Western society which is technical and scientific; nevertheless, they live in cultures which are fully human, so human that in our day there is the temptation to idealize them in opposition to that on which our modern life is based, judged too cold and bureaucratic.

the summit as well as the lowest echelon, (2) concerns both individuals and the groups themselves in their dealings either within the tribe or with the neighboring tribes (which in Melanesia live on other islands), and (3) applies to all domains: exchange of wives through the marriage system, exchange of polite gestures, banquets, honors, services, but also—and this is what astonishes us most, Westerners that we are—exchange of consumer goods.[2]

By simplifying a little, one can describe the logic that rules symbolic exchange as follows: subject A having gathered coconuts, donates the harvest to subject B who, having made some pottery containers, gives them to subject C who at the end of a day spent fishing gives the fish to subject D, and so on. Neither A nor B nor C nor D . . . calculate "for how much" they have harvested or fabricated goods and "how much" they have a right to in exchange.

Each one gives without counting; we have here a logic of *gratuitousness* or "gift." But we must immediately add that it is a "*necessary gratuitousness*" or an "obligatory gift." No one is free to give or not to give just as no one is free to accept or refuse what the other gives you. For to refuse to receive, as well as to refuse to give, is not only to short-circuit the economic system but still more to lose face or cause the one who offers you something to lose face. It is to place oneself socially and symbolically outside the circuit, to incur excommunication by the group and make it impossible for oneself to live in it as a subject.

The fact that one gives thus, without counting, simply to be recognized, to avoid dishonor for oneself, one's family, one's clan, one's tribe, allows us to understand why, in traditional societies, one may spend everything one owns in a few days simply to celebrate, on the occasion of a wedding, a funeral, the arrival of a famous guest, even when this means that one will have to go hungry afterwards. This is not due to an "infantile" logic, as many Westerners have thought until recently. It is a logic, in the fullest and most noble sense of the term. But it is a logic that obeys another *principle* than the one which rules today's Western societies. It is precisely a symbolic logic in which what is important is less "having" than "being": a logic according to which, as for the Merovingian chieftain whom Georges Duby speaks

[2] Here we are referring especially to Marcel Mauss, *The Gift: Forms and Functions of Exchange in Archaic Societies,* trans. Ian Cunnison, World Economic History (1924; reprint, New York: Norton, 1967).

about,[3] a treasure is not "capital" but "an ornament," a cause of pride for the whole people; a logic according to which the poorest person can take to the grave her or his most precious objects; a logic according to which every person must hold her or his place with honor, albeit the lowliest place.

The relation of symbolic exchange to market exchange is the same as the relation of symbol to sign: in both cases, there are two different principles of functioning, although there is in every exchange a mixture of both in various proportions.

(a) Market exchange and symbolic exchange depend upon *two different principles*. The barter system is no more the prolongation of symbolic exchange than symbol is the prolongation of sign, of which it would be an "ornate" variant. Symbolic exchange obeys a logic of another order: in it the "subjects exchange themselves," in contrast to market exchange where values are what is exchanged. The important thing is less what one gives or receives than *the very fact of exchanging* and thus, through the objects exchanged, to be *recognized as a subject, as a full member of the group*. This is the same type of symbolic logic, *outside the realm of value,* as in our Western gift-giving (see chapter 4).

Two differences, however, exist between the two. First, a gift is an exchange between two persons (A offers a gift and B responds with a counter-gift of thanksgiving toward A). In contrast, in societies practicing generalized symbolic exchange, all the members of the group enter the circuit: A gives to B who gives to C, and so on, which makes the exchange the economic basis of the circulation of goods. Second, although the symbolic exchange of traditional societies, being free of all calculation, belongs to the domain of gratuitousness and generosity, it also and simultaneously belongs to the domain of necessary obligation since, as we have noted, no one can evade it without losing oneself. Our Western languages have no words to describe this sort of exchange. We are hindered by the language barrier, as Marcel Mauss rightly observed, so that we are constrained to use words with contradictory

---

[3] Georges Duby, "Les attitudes mentales," in *Guerriers et paysans: VIIe-XIIe siècle, premier essor de l'économie européenne,* Bibliothèque des histoires (Paris: Gallimard, 1973); [*The Early Growth of the European Economy: Warriors and Peasants from the Seventh to the Twelfth Century,* trans. Howard B. Clarke, World Economic History (Ithaca, N.Y.: Cornell, 1974)].

meanings.[4] The gratuitousness in question depends on the logic of a system and therefore has no moral value.

(b) Our two types of exchange depend on two different principles. Nonetheless, they are the *two poles* of all exchanges. A pure system of symbolic exchange concerning consumer goods does not exist any more than a pure symbol in language. In the cultures fundamentally ruled by symbolic exchange, market exchange also has a place. Thus, the Melanesians call them by two different terms: *gimwali* designates the carefully limited and relatively brief moment when they can indulge in a "very persistent haggling" during fairs; *kula* designates the whole system of exchange.[5]

(c) One can expect to find all concrete possible combinations between these two kinds of exchange, depending on the type of society and the period. The two extremes are represented by the societies we just mentioned, where symbolic exchange is the rule in the whole of social and economic life, and by our present Western society where everything is dominated by a market economy and where transactions are a matter of written or electronic transmission, making it unnecessary for the exchanging subjects to contact one another. Between the two extremes one could find on the side of symbolic exchange many traditional populations of today, African or Native American, for instance, which are squeezed, in an often dramatic way, between the anvil of their cultural reflexes with respect to symbolic exchange and the hammer of the market laws imposed on them by the West. On the side of market exchange one could find societies, as in the Arab souks, which, while ruled by the market, continue to give the greatest importance to bargaining, that is, to the symbolic contest between two subjects for whom the outcome of the exchange is a matter of dignity and honor.

(d) The technological, scientific, and economic logic of the system that rules our society—Western, (post-)modern—is that of value. Practically choked by the "ever more" of growth, production, and consumption, symbolic exchange can operate only in the margins of the system, as is the case for presents.[6] The rebellion of the sixties can be regarded as an exemplary expression of social protest against this crushing of the symbolic by the reign of value.

[4] Mauss, *Sociologie et anthropologie,* 267.

[5] Ibid., 176.

[6] And even these are sometimes taken over by the logic of the system, as can be seen in many television games or advertisements or in wedding registries.

Is this to say that symbolic exchange has ceased to have any place in our lives? This would be a gross error. First, because, even though relegated to the margins of the system, it still manifests its constant presence, as we just said about presents. And especially second, since the death of symbolic exchange would be the death of subjects and therefore of human society, simply because, as we developed at length in the first part, there is no human subject who is not taken into the order of language and who can arise elsewhere than within the realm of symbolic exchange. The gift is a significant example, no doubt, but only one example of symbolic exchange; for its part, communication through speech is not only an example, albeit an outstanding one, but much more: it is the space where symbolic exchange has its origins, its literally "fundamental" locus.

The important point to understand is that market exchange, like every value exchange, is binary: product X is exchanged for value Y, in kind or money, regardless of who engages in the transaction. Symbolic exchange is structured in a *ternary* way, as shown by the example of the gift. Besides the gift and the return-gift, there is here the *reception* of the gift *as* gift and not as anything else. When A offers a gift to B, the heart of the matter resides in the reception of the object by B as a gift, which is verified in the return-gift of an expression of gratitude from B toward A. One can visualize market exchange by a diagram:

Gift  Return-gift

and that of symbolic exchange also by a diagram:

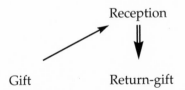

Reception

Gift   Return-gift

"*Gift*" and "*reception*" are in position of contradiction. The one who gives has less than before, the one who receives has more. This is equally valid on the plane of exchange by speech, exchange that linguistically positions an I and a YOU, this YOU being the opposite of the I since it represents the linguistic other of the I, the reversible of the I. "Reversible of the I" means that "I" says "you" only to someone who can answer by using the same personal pronoun "I." This is why, if YOU is the most completely opposite of the I, it is at the same time the most similar. Linguistically, "you" designates "the other similar to me." One can sense the interest of this observation for thinking about difference, for example, between God and human beings. Whereas in the physical order the more two things are opposed the more they are different, *in the symbolic order the more two subjects recognize their similitude the more they are different*. In other words, in the symbolic order difference is to be understood not on the spatial register of distance but on the register of *otherness* (therefore of similitude).

As to the double arrow going from "reception" to "return-gift," it indicates an *implication,* therefore an obligation. This means that there is "reception" (of the gift as gift) only by the obligatory implication of a return-gift. In other words, the return-gift is the mark of the reception. As the polite locution "I am obliged to you" indicates, every gift creates an obligation. If there is not a minimum of gratitude, B does not receive the gift offered by A, B seizes a value-object.

The same is true of exchange by speech. Not to answer the words addressed to you by the return-gift of listening, look, facial expression, is equivalent to not receiving the words as words. It is possible to perfectly hear the sounds of the words without receiving the meaning those words convey. The teenagers who, full of "hatred" for their father and mother, pretend to be deaf or turn their backs when addressed by them know very well they are inflicting on them a symbolic wound. Let us repeat: "symbolic" does not mean "unreal" or "insignificant." On the contrary, it means what touches persons as persons at the most real of their identity, what touches them to the quick. Hence the retort, which the parents often find impossible to keep back, "You could at least answer us!" There are refusals to receive which speak louder than words and can inflict mortal wounds on people. Cruel (or blessed) efficacy of speech!

Basically, daily conversations are nothing but symbolic exchange. Every word addressed to another person is a gift which is received in the measure in which the addressee answers the first person by the return-gift, if not of a spoken response, at least of a body language that shows listening and attention. And since all properly human, that is, signifying acts are encompassed by language and, as a consequence, undergirded by speech, we must recognize that *the subject constantly lives in and from symbolic exchange*. This is not the "privilege" of any society, even though certain traditional societies are built around it, especially in economic matters. That every exchange between *subjects* is symbolic means (1) that no really human exchange can be reduced to its utilitarian (otherwise necessary) purpose, that is, to its economic, cognitive, affective value, and (2) that what is vital to the subject *as subject* is not due to the value of what is exchanged but to the *very fact of exchanging,* that is, to the fact of recognizing another person as a partner and being recognized by this person.

THEOLOGICAL PERTINENCE

The sacraments are the ecclesial mediations of the exchange between humanity and God. It is interesting for several reasons to theologically think of them according to the model of symbolic exchange which we have delineated.

(a) First, we have here an approach to problems relatively *akin to grace* since in both cases we are beyond value; more akin in any case than the classical approach which, even when strongly purified by analogy, remains fundamentally dependent on the productionist scheme.

(b) Then, since the original space of symbolic exchange is language, more exactly communication by speech between subjects, we are led to understand the efficacy of the sacraments in relation to the *efficacy of speech*. We have shown in chapter 4 that (1) there is nothing more efficacious than this relation of subject to subject through speech, (2) this efficacy is not of the order of value or calculation since to seek to trick the other is to destroy communication, and (3) this process is constantly in a state of incompleteness, of a "way that sets everything on its way" (Heidegger), which means that, as in the fable of "The Farmer and His Children," the "treasure" is less an object to be received than the work of converting the field that we are, a work by which we learn to receive ourselves from others and thus to "realize" ourselves as subjects. In the same chapter, we proposed a theological reading of these reflections applied to the sacraments.

(c) The joining of the three "moments" or "positions" of symbolic exchange has several theological advantages.

(1) First, it shows that the *gift* owes nothing to the return-gift. In the sacraments, the position of gift is occupied by God's gratuitous action. Under this aspect of gratuitousness, God's grace is not something due and its measure is not that of human merit. Grace comes from God's pure initiative, that of love.

(2) Then, the *reception* of God's grace *as* grace, and not as anything else, requires (relation of implication) the *return-gift* of faith, love, conversion of heart, witness by one's life. We have said it before: in the sacraments, God alone, and not faith (no more than the other subjective conditions of the authentically Christian life), is the measure of the gift. In other words, the "validity" of the sacrament depends on God, its "fecundity" depends on the believing subject. Taking advantage of the trusting words someone addressed to you to deceive that person proves that the words were not received for what they were but that they were trapped (register of value) and perverted. Such words are authentically received only inasmuch as they lead their beneficiaries to spread in their turn trust and life around them. Likewise, taking advantage of someone who has offered you a gift to get "still more" out of the giver is equivalent to stealing a value-object. The gift is received as such only if it elicits the return-gift of gratitude, thanksgiving, increase of love.

It follows, as theologians have so frequently repeated since Augustine, that one can take part in a sacrament without receiving the reality of that sacrament (grace). This does not mean that the presence of Christ in the Eucharist depends on the subject's disposition since it is God who, through the Holy Spirit, realizes it. This means that, for lack of a personal disposition of faith and love, the human subject would not receive this presence *as presence* but as something else which may possibly be verging on representations of a magical nature. Christ's presence is not an available object to be seized with the hand. To want to take advantage of it by receiving communion as often as possible is to deny what is at stake. Like the manna, God's gift decays as a gift as soon as one claims to "use" it. Obviously, the same goes for the other sacraments. Thus, the offer of God's sacramental forgiveness through the ministry of the priest is not connected with the human subjects' disposition, but it is not received *as forgiveness* if they do not repent of their sins. Their relation to God is no truer after receiving the sacrament than before—rather the contrary.[7] In such a case, sinners can at best be freed from what, according to the disciplinary viewpoint, was keeping them in the margins of the church as institution. But one can be a full member of this institu-

---

[7] In the same way one can receive communion to "bring judgment against [oneself]," as Paul says (1 Cor 11:29), one can misuse sacramental absolution.

tional church without being, for all that, in communion with God. "The habit does not make the monastic."

(d) The same joining of gift, reception, and return-gift enables us to clearly distinguish two dimensions of grace: gratuitousness and graciousness.

(1) God's grace is gratuitous, that is to say, it is not necessitated by anything and it is God who has the initiative. Under this aspect it occupies the position of gift in our diagram.

But if one considers grace only under this aspect, one isolates the first term from the structure of exchange and causes it to function *imaginarily*. Indeed, if this were the case, a human being would be "alienated" from God. Too much generosity alienates. To overwhelm someone with gifts so gratuitous that one takes away from the other even the possibility of giving in return is to treat that person as an object because, by denying her or him the possibility of being a subject of duty, one deprives her or him from the dignity of subject, period. Every gift obligates, we have said above. True, the code of good manners in all cultures allows the giver to partially "disobligate" the person to whom one offers a gift by saying, "It's nothing. By giving you pleasure, I please myself. . . ." But only partially, because the recognition of another as a subject entails the recognition of this person as obligated. In contrast to necessity, obligation belongs to ethical relation.

(2) This is why the category of gratuitousness must be allied with that of *graciousness*. What is given without necessary reason, therefore "for nothing," is gratuitous; what is given without regard to value, therefore "given free of charge," outside any calculation, is gracious. Under this aspect, grace occupies not only the position of the gift given by God, but also that of the return-gift given by the believing subject. The gratitude of the latter toward God is gracious if what was received was really the gratuitous gift of God and not anything else: the believer responds to love by love and not by calculation. In this case believing subjects would debase their relation with God by reducing it to bargaining, which would be to negate the gift of God as grace.

Therefore, it belongs to the circuit of grace to elicit the gracious response of human freedom. It is not one of the least advantages of our diagram of symbolic exchange to make clear that there is no competition between God's grace and human freedom and responsibility. When it is understood in the twofold dimension we have just elucidated, grace never reaches its essence of grace as fully as when it invites humans to this gracious return-gift, which is always inspired by love.

Among the many possible consequences of this reflection, we can note that the paradigm of the sacraments must never be, whether explicitly or implicitly, the baptism of infants, but that of adults. The former is too often the case, it seems. Of course, infant baptism expresses in an unsurpassed manner the gratuitousness of God's grace coming to meet everyone, without taking account of their merit or lack of merit. This sort of baptism expresses an important truth: to enter into the new covenant in Christ, age is no more a limit than race, social status, or sex (Gal 3:26-28). Nevertheless, too strong an insistence on this gratuitousness of grace, so well demonstrated by infant baptism, runs the risk of reinforcing a scheme which is already much too prevalent in the minds of many: that of competition between God and humanity. This comes down to stating that the more powerless human beings are, the more strongly grace is affirmed. This is visible in Augustine for whom "the gratuitousness of grace is opposed to its universal diffusion," which means that this gratuitousness would be the better attested if fewer human beings were saved.[8] But such a scheme, which seems to have in fact been part and parcel of Augustine's never examined presuppositions, treats grace as a value-product—share your belongings, they decrease—whereas in the order of symbolic relation, and particularly of love, which alone is fitting when it comes to grace, the more one gives, the more one receives—share your love, it increases. If there is someone in the New Testament who has spoken (and with what force!) about grace, it is Paul. But he never speaks of grace in relation to little children, only to adults: it is in the nature of gratuitous justification by faith to elicit the free gracious response expressed by thanksgiving and by a life lived under "the law of the Spirit" (Rom 8:2; on this subject see the whole letter to the Romans).

(e) Lastly, if symbolic exchange is part of what allows the young human to become and perdure as a subject, it is constitutive of the fact of being human; it is irreducible to a simple "experience" from which, by analogy, one could approach the mystery of communication between God and humanity. This means that the relation of believers with God is not only *as* in symbolic exchange but is inscribed *in* this type of exchange that structures the subject. Again, the theological takes "place" in the anthropological.

[8] Charles Baumgartner, *Le péché originel,* Le mystère chrétien: Théologie dogmatique 5 (Paris: Desclée, 1969) 96.

In the last analysis, the development of the present chapter on symbolic exchange brings nothing fundamentally new or different to the reflections we have proposed on language in preceding chapters. But it allows us (1) to reinforce those reflections on some points from another angle; (2) to emphasize new elements which previous analyses could establish only with more difficulty, and (3) to supply a theoretical model whose theological pertinence can be verified in relation to each sacrament. And it is the pertinence of this model that we shall now verify in the next chapter on the Eucharist.

Chapter 7

Symbolic Exchange Between Humanity and God: The Eucharistic Prayer

Symbolic exchange between humanity and God is especially visible in the Eucharistic Prayer. We are going to verify this with Eucharistic Prayer 2 which, being very concise, has the advantage of giving us almost the pure framework of this type of prayer, a framework which, with some minor differences, is also present in more developed prayers like numbers 3 and 4.[1]

An important preliminary remark is in order. Our reflection does not bear on the different parts which constitute the Eucharistic Prayer, parts whose technical names we want to list, in their order of appearance, for readers: opening dialogue, thanksgiving (preface), Sanctus, first epiclesis (called epiclesis on the gifts, or sometimes epiclesis of consecration), narrative of the institution, anamnesis, second epiclesis (called epiclesis on the assembly or epiclesis of communion), intercession for the church on earth (see, according to Eucharistic Prayer 4, "all who seek you with a sincere heart") and then for the dead, eschatological prayer, doxology. We are going to work not on these different parts, but on the "gear wheels" by which they mesh, therefore the *mechanism* which causes them to function "eucharistically." It is this mechanism which constitutes the eucharistic process.

NARRATIVE ANALYSIS

Narrative analysis is based on the fact that any written text, like any oral discourse, starts from a negative situation of lack and stops (at least if the text or the discourse is coherent) when this lack is filled. It is filled when object X (which can be a material object, a moral consolation, the relationship with a person, and so on) needed by subject B ("receiving subject") is transmitted to this subject by subject A (who is

---

[1] All quotations from the Eucharistic Prayers in this chapter are taken from the Roman Missal, translated by the International Committee on English in the Liturgy, 1973.

called "operating subject"). This results in the following general diagram which we shall take as a guide:

$$\text{Operating Subject} \implies \text{Object} \longrightarrow \text{Receiving Subject}$$

The lack to be filled which underlies the whole text of our Eucharistic Prayer is indicated by the initial dialogue, "Let us give thanks to the Lord our God." Such is the *program* (we shall call it "principal narrative program" or "NP") which undergirds the whole. "We" as a collective operating subject (the church) must attribute to God, the receiving subject, an "object" which is called "grace" or "glory." The writing of this program is of the simplest:

$$\text{We [us]} \implies \text{Grace/Glory} \longrightarrow \text{God}$$

Our text stops, in fact, when the program is accomplished, as shown by the final prayer of praise (doxology), "Through him, with him, in him . . . all glory and honor is yours."

The fulfilling of this program by the "we" of the ecclesial assembly is a *performance*, which requires *competence* for it to be realized. The whole of the text, between the initial dialogue and the final doxology, indicates precisely how we acquire such competence. This is done in three steps, which constitute the narrative sub-programs, called NP 1, NP 2, and NP 3.

(a) *NP 1* covers the initial thanksgiving (preface) and the Sanctus. The church gives thanks ("eucharist") to God for God's "beloved Son, Jesus Christ," God's living Word through whom "the universe" was created and who is "the Savior . . . sent to redeem us." The Eucharist of the church has for a twofold theme creation and especially the salvific mission of Jesus the Son, that is, a summary of salvation history. In all cases the Eucharist is polarized by the sending of Jesus, the Christ. In our text, it is entirely focused on him. But in other texts, it is either more developed into a summary of the main phases of salvation (creation, transgression, covenants, mission of the prophets, then of the Son, Jesus; thus Eucharistic Prayer 4)[2] or, on the contrary, cen-

---

[2] After having addressed a vibrant praise to God for having "created all things to fill your creatures with every blessing," a praise which leads to the

tered on one aspect of the mystery of Christ according to the feast and biblical texts of the day: the manifestation to the Magi, the encounter with the Samaritan woman, and so on.

Whatever the case, two theological principles rule the initial thanksgiving of the church. On the one hand, it has no other object than the Scriptures, or rather than what God has done for humankind according to the Scriptures, so that even when this thanksgiving has the mystery of Christ for its sole object, in the background the Old Testament is always presupposed. On the other hand, the thanksgiving always culminates in the paschal mystery of Christ, so that even if only one aspect of Jesus' work is mentioned, this aspect is relevant only inasmuch as it is understood as one of the many facets of the whole paschal mystery. Since in any hypothesis this sequence culminates in the gift of the Son, Jesus, that is, of his historical body (born of the Virgin Mary, dead on the cross) and of his glorious body (risen), one can synthesize NP 1 in the following manner:

$$\text{God} \implies \text{Historical \& glorious} \longrightarrow \text{We [us]}$$
$$\text{(Father \& Holy Spirit)} \quad \text{body of Christ}$$

The fact that the text continues after the praise of the Sanctus demonstrates that the principal program, in spite of appearances, is not fulfilled: to give thanks in a properly Christian way demands other conditions, especially the reception of the gift, which up to now has been spoken of exclusively in the past tense. This is done by the second program.

NP 2 covers the epiclesis on the gifts, which, after a few words that form a link ("Lord, you are holy indeed. . . ."), follows the Sanctus; the narrative of the institution; and the anamnesis, which is its development ("Do this in memory of me"—"In memory of his death . . . ."). The object which is transmitted to "us" ["we"] in this program by God (the Holy Spirit "sent" by the Father in order to transform the bread and wine into the body and blood of Christ) is the same as in NP 1; it is Jesus Christ. But there is a twofold difference: the same is given in

Sanctus, Eucharistic Prayer 4 enumerates the main steps of salvation history after the Sanctus. In this case, NP 1 extends beyond the Sanctus to the end of this sequence.

another way as a "present," under the mode of food and drink and no longer under the historical mode; and he is given in the present and no longer in the past. The whole of this sequence, to which we shall return, can be schematized in the following way:

$$\text{God} \Longrightarrow \text{Ecclesial body} \longrightarrow \text{We [us]}$$
$$\text{(Father \& Holy Spirit)} \qquad \text{of Christ}$$

Here again, the fact that NP 2 ends with thanksgiving ("we offer you. . . . We thank you for counting us worthy to stand in your presence and serve you") does not mean that the properly Christian performance of thanksgiving to God is realized, since the text continues. There is still something needed: that "we" become ecclesially what we are going to receive eucharistically. This is the task of the last program.

NP 3 covers the remainder of the prayer, that is, the second epiclesis (the request for the Spirit to come on those who are going to communion so that they may "be brought together in unity by the Holy Spirit") and the final eschatological prayer (that one day with the Virgin Mary and all the saints, the participants may "share eternal life"). Between the two there is a twofold intercession: the first one for the church on earth (pope, bishops, priests, and all the people of God) is in direct line with the epiclesis preceding it (the "already" of salvation attested by the church here below); the second, for the dead, orients us toward the eschatological prayer that follows (the "not yet" of salvation standing in expectation of its ultimate fulfillment). The object transmitted in this last narrative program looks to the future, but a future eschatologically understood, that is, stretched between two poles: the already, implicit in the fact that the church, receiving through the Spirit the eucharistic body of Christ, becomes the ecclesial body of the same Christ; and the not yet, implicit in the hope that what is still in the state of gestation will be completed in the fullness of the reign. By distinguishing the two eschatological dimensions of this section, one can write NP 3 as follows:

$$\text{NP 3a: God} \Longrightarrow \text{Ecclesial body} \longrightarrow \text{We [us]}$$
$$\text{\& Holy Spirit} \qquad \text{of Christ}$$

$$\text{NP 3b: God} \Longrightarrow \text{Eternal Life} \longrightarrow \text{We [us]}$$
$$\text{(Perfected Reign)}$$

This very simple analysis shows that to give thanks to God in a Christian manner is not a "natural" matter but demands a complete itinerary. Itinerary of conversion in the strongest sense of the word since the fulfillment of such a thanksgiving by human beings (operating subjects of the principal NP) needs nothing less than the action of God (the Father and the Holy Spirit, co-operating subjects of the three sub-programs) giving the Son to humankind under a triple mode (historical, eucharistic, and ecclesial) which itself corresponds to the triple dimension of time (past, present, and future). The realization by human beings of the performance of thanksgiving demands that *God give them the competence.* The itinerary that the Eucharistic Prayer makes us travel is thus exemplary of the way of conversion which Christians are called to walk throughout their lives.

THE STATUS OF THE NARRATIVE OF INSTITUTION, THE ANAMNESIS, AND THE EPICLESIS

Before utilizing our narrative analysis according to the process of symbolic exchange, we must dwell on these three central parts of the Eucharistic Prayer.

The Story of the Institution

The literary status of this part is absolutely obvious: whereas the rest of the Eucharistic Prayer is a *discourse,* that is, a language act in the present tense ("'it is right to give you thanks' because you have done this and that. . . ."; "we ask you to send your Spirit. . . .") in which an I (or rather a collective WE, that of the church) addresses a YOU (that is, God), the story of the institution is a *narrative* in the past tense with the pronoun HE, this HE which always represents an absent person ("Before he was given up to death, he took bread. . . ."). This narrative, inserted in a discourse of prayer, abruptly ruptures the literary genre of the whole text. But what appears incoherent from the strictly literary point of view is heavy with theological significance inasmuch as the narrative of the church about Jesus (about what Jesus did at the Last Supper) functions in fact at the core of the liturgical action as a *discourse of the Lord addressed to the church,* which we are going to verify.

Our story contains two quotations from Jesus' words, on the bread and on the wine. Now, according to the dictionary "cite" has as a first meaning "to call upon officially to appear (as before a court)"; a witness is cited. The second meaning, "to quote by way of example, authority, or proof," must be understood in connection with the first, at least if one remembers that the quotation from a text has a greater weight if the quoted person is recognized as an "authority" in the matter.[3] To cite is therefore first of all to bring someone forward as an authorized witness. There is no lack of cases in which what matters is less the content of the quote than the presentation of the *auctoritas* (authority) itself: "St. Augustine has said that . . . ." or "St. Thomas has written that . . . ." In this way, the authors can deem themselves dispensed from thinking for themselves, protected as they are by these prestigious names, and readers are expected to immediately assent to the proposition after a mere look at the "authority" who formulated it.

We may observe that the second citation, which ends with "Do this in memory of me," addressed to the disciples two thousand years ago, is immediately followed by a "we remember" said by the church "in memory of his death . . . ."[4] This sudden passage from a citation referring to a faraway past to its being used in the present, in the discourse of the Eucharistic Prayer, shows that *by citing Jesus at the Last Supper, the church sees itself in fact cited by him, its Lord, cited to act.* This is so true that throughout the eucharistic liturgy it translates into action the four technical verbs of the Last Supper: "to take" = the presentation of the gifts, "to pronounce the blessing" = the Eucharistic Prayer, "to break" = the breaking of the bread, "to give" = the communion. This story is central for the church; it is the effective norm of its actions. Thus, the church "executes" the story as a simple literary document on the last hours of Jesus (a simple storytelling of the past) in order to make it reach its true status: that of a *discourse of the Lord Jesus obliging the church to obey.*

We have here, as was suggested when the programming of rituality was spoken of (in chapter 5), the confession of faith in the action of the church: the church is the church only in the measure in which it recognizes itself as dependent on Jesus, its only Lord, a recognition which it expresses to the highest degree when it says and does what

---

[3] The definitions of "cite" are taken from *Webster's Ninth New Collegiate Dictionary* (Springfield, Mass.: Merriam-Webster, 1989).

[4] In order to simplify, we omit the acclamation of the assembly ("We proclaim your death, Lord Jesus"). This is not to say that this acclamation is unimportant, but it changes nothing in the nature of the problem which we pose here: the "in memory of his death" pronounced by the presider is only the repetition of the acclamation of the assembly.

he himself said and did two millennia ago. It cannot "narrate" Jesus as Christ and Lord without being itself taken in the present into what it narrates in the past. The church holds its identity by constantly receiving itself from him.

The Discourse of Anamnesis

What appears only as in the negative of a picture in the story of institution, that is, the *fundamental dependence* of the church on its Lord, is manifested as in a positive in the prayer of anamnesis. For it is made up of a phrase ("in memory of . . . ."), then of the principal sentence with a verb in the present, "we offer you."[5] The way for the church to hold a memorial of Jesus' death and resurrection is to offer in the present what "re-presents" him (makes him present in a new way, that is, the sacramental way): the reason for which he gave his life and for which God raised him from the dead.

We find ourselves in a singularly paradoxical situation: whereas the whole sequence (NP 2) is concerned with the present *reception,* by the church, of Christ under the sacramental mode, here the church, instead of appropriating the gift as a value object, opens its hands since it *offers* it. This paradox brings us back to Christian identity. Because, as was forcefully emphasized above, the gratuitous and gracious gift of God is not in the order of value-objects, the church can appropriate it only by letting go of it, take it only by giving it back, giving it back with thanksgiving or, better still, giving back to God the very Grace of God, that is, Christ Jesus who continues to give himself up to the church in sacrament.

Consequently, since this ritual act of offering constitutes the properly Christian mode of the reception of God's gift, it is not the final return-gift of the church. Otherwise, it would be enough to go to Mass to fulfill one's duty toward God. But the fact that this offering is not the

---

[5] This is valid not only for the prayer we have chosen, but also for the other eucharistic prayers. Let us take this opportunity to mention that this structure of the anamnesis, with its principal words, "we offer you," is found not only in the anaphora of Hippolytus (beginning of 3rd c.), which is the source of Eucharistic Prayer 2, but also in most of the Eastern anaphoras dating from the 4th and 5th centuries, whether Syrian or Egyptian. We are in the presence of a long and solid tradition. See the synoptic chart presented by Louis-Marie Chauvet in AGAPE ASSOCIATION, *L'eucharistie, de Jésus aux chrétiens d'aujourd'hui* (Droguet-Ardent, 1981) 346–351.

final return-gift of the church does not mean that it has no connection with it. This offering is a symbolic act (see the first two characteristics of ritual language, pp. 99–103) which prefigures the gift and commits the church to presenting it. In other words, the *sacramental* offering of the body and blood of Christ is the ritual mediation which symbolically shows what the return-gift is: the *existential* offering of one's own life. This is what the second epiclesis demonstrates.

The Discourse of Epiclesis

The "we offer you" of the anamnesis must be understood in two senses, *objective and subjective*. In the objective sense, it designates the offering of Christ-in-sacrament by the church. In the subjective sense, it designates the offering of the church "through, with, and in" Christ. Again, for the same reason that the "object" (the "anti-object" as we said when speaking of the manna in chapter 4) is not in the order of value, the first sense cannot go without the second.

Already from the anthropological viewpoint, we understand that to offer (a present for example) is to let go of something; and to let go is in some way to place oneself in a state of offering. It is impossible to offer a gratuitous gift without offering oneself.

This is eminently valid on the theological plane, but for an additional reason. There is but one Christ, both "head" and "body"—which Augustine calls the "total Christ."[6] One cannot offer one without the other since they are indissociable. Moreover, the head cannot be offered without the body being offered in it since the body is subordinate to and dependent on the head. If it is true, as Augustine explains, that the offering or historical "sacrifice" of Christ on the cross is the "sacrament, that is, the visible sign" of his invisible sacrifice—that of his love for God and humankind lived to the point of accepting death in martyrdom—it is no less true, still in the logic of Augustine, that this offering was also the "sacrament" of the offering of the whole of humanity by and in him or, as Yves de Montcheuil wrote in the past, "the sacrament of the sacrifice accomplished by the total Christ."[7] All this being so, we understand the force of Augus-

[6] On this theme, see especially Jean-Marie-Roger Tillard, *Flesh of the Church, Flesh of Christ: At the Source of the Ecclesiology of Communion*, trans. Madeleine Beaumont (Collegeville: The Liturgical Press, 2001).

[7] On this point, see the superb texts of Yves de Montcheuil, *Mélanges théologiques*, Théologie 9 (Paris: Aubier, 1946), in ch. 2; the quotation is on p. 53.

tine's formula, "This is the sacrifice of Christians: we, being many, are one body in Christ. And this is also the sacrifice which the church continually celebrates in the sacrament of the altar, known to the faithful, in which the church teaches that it itself is offered in the offering it makes to God."[8]

The church cannot offer Christ-in-sacrament without being itself offered through and in him. As Jean-Marie Tillard writes on this subject, "The eucharistic sacrifice is the sacrament of the sacrifice of the ecclesial body *as such*, that is, *inseparably*, of the sacrifice of Christ as head surrounding the sacrifice of its members, and of the sacrifice of the members incorporated into that of their head. . . ."[9] Thus, the church conforms itself not only to his command ("do this in memory of me") but to his very person. This conformation is such that, following Paul ("one bread, one body," 1 Cor 10:17), Augustine symbolically plays on this same term of "body" to make it resonate on three registers: the historical and glorious body; the sacramental (eucharistic) body; the ecclesial body. By offering the eucharistic body of Christ, the church symbolizes ("teaches" Augustine said above, that is, "manifests") what it must become, his ecclesial body. This is exactly what our second epiclesis expresses: that the holy Spirit may come over the assembly so that, through the church's participation in the eucharistic body, it may become the ecclesial body of Christ.

In a more concrete way, this means that eucharistic communion demands that the church and individual Christians give to the risen Christ a body of humanity and history, a body which may keep his presence in the middle of the world by keeping his memory alive. And this is before all a matter of ethical practice. Tradition, medieval and modern as well as patristic, has never stopped saying that the supreme goal of the Eucharist (its "ultimate grace") is the gift of charity between sisters and brothers and unity; charity and unity within today's church, but also within the whole of humanity which is in the process of becoming the body of Christ. This is what "to become one body in Christ" means. And this is at work essentially in the ethical sphere of mutual love as a response to the love of God which precedes it, of the "living-in-grace." Obviously, the "love" we are speaking about here has little in

---

[8] Augustine, *City of God*, 10.6, in Philip Schaff, ed., *A Select Library of the Nicene and Post-Nicene Fathers*, 14 vols. (1886–1890; reprint, Grand Rapids, Mich.: Eerdmans, 1980–1983) 2:182–183. [Adapted by the editor.]

[9] Tillard, *Flesh of the Church*, 44. Emphasis, the author's.

common with the bourgeois virtue of the "good soul"; similarly, the living-in-grace must not be identified with a naive transparency. The terms we use here designate concrete realities which must be lived not "above" the ambiguities of social relationships but at their core. What is at stake is everything that pertains to justice, sharing, reconciliation, forgiveness, all at the collective level of economic, political, and cultural relations between nations and races as well as at the level of interpersonal relationships. This shows the importance of the ethical implications of the Eucharist and their possible effects on our world.

Furthermore, the fact that this ethical practice is mentioned at the end of the Eucharistic Prayer (and not at the beginning, contrary to an all too frequent tendency of some Christians), and particularly after the section devoted to the gift of the eucharistic body, means that its proper character comes not from its degree of generosity but from its nature of *response* to the prevenient gift and commitment of God. This same dependence on the sacrament enables us to liturgically reread it as a "spiritual sacrifice," a notion whose frequency in the New Testament we have pointed out (chapter 3, pp. 61–62).

"Look with favor on your Church's offering, and see the Victim whose death has reconciled us to yourself. Grant that we, who are nourished by his body and blood, may be filled with his Holy Spirit, and become one body, one spirit in Christ."

This epiclesis of communion from Eucharistic Prayer 3 admirably expresses what we just developed: it is in the "sacrifice of the church"—a sacrifice which consists in our becoming "one body in Christ," as Augustine says—that the "sacramental sacrifice of Christ" gains its full truth. In other words, Mass would be barren if it did not enjoin on Christians the obligation of "becoming what they receive." What do they receive? The sacramental body of Christ. Consequently, what are they to become? His ecclesial body in and for the world. Such is the *final return-gift* (NP 3) which is implied in the reception (NP 2) of the gift of God (NP 1). The reception of grace as grace (and not as something else which would be more or less magical) never goes without a task; it implies the ethical return-gift of justice and mercy.

THE RELATION CHRIST/CHURCH IN THE EUCHARIST
Let us leave aside for a moment the text of the Eucharistic Prayer and go a little deeper into what we just said, in order to look at the

relation Christ/church in the Eucharist as it appears (a) in the theological tradition of the "threefold body" of Christ, (b) in Paul (1 Cor 11), and (c) in today's rites of communion.

The Threefold Body of Christ

It was common for theological tradition to distinguish a threefold body of Christ: (1) his historical and glorious body; (2) his eucharistic body which was called "mystical body" up to the end of the twelfth century because it is "his body in mystery," that is to say, in sacrament; (3) his ecclesial body, growing throughout history. In the perspective of the Fathers of the Church, the accent was not placed on the relation of the second with the first: the church did not know any controversy on the presence of Christ in the Eucharist before the ninth century; up to that time, it was serenely professed, apparently without problem. The accent was placed on the relation of the second body with the third, the ecclesial body: for the Fathers, the ecclesial body was the "truth" of the eucharistic body. This was particularly clear in Augustine, as can be verified from what has been said above.

But in the middle of the eleventh century a certain Berengar, a schoolmaster in Tours, France, in reaction against the ultra-realistic representations of the eucharistic presence of Christ, widespread in his time, came to deny the reality of the eucharistic presence. This heresy caused a real trauma in the memory of the church. The upshot was that from then on the accent was placed on the relation of the second body to the first in order to steadfastly affirm the "real presence." About this, Henri de Lubac says that from the end of the twelfth century on a "deadly dichotomy" between the eucharistic body and the ecclesial body became firmly rooted. At the same time symbolism became "something artificial and accessory . . . the essential bond that joined eucharistic worship to the unity of the church disappeared." Thus, "the ultimate reality of the sacrament," that is to say, the unity of the ecclesial body, "that which formerly was its reality and its truth par excellence, is ejected from the sacrament itself." It does remain its finality; but from then on, it does not belong to its "intrinsic symbolism." Consequently, "it will be possible to ignore this symbolism without impairing the integrity of the sacrament."[10] One can easily

---

[10] Henri de Lubac, "Du symbole à la dialectique," in *Corpus mysticum: L'eucharistie et l'Église au Moyen Age, étude historique*, Théologie 3 (Paris: Aubier, 1944) see complete chapter, especially pp. 280–283.

foresee the consequence: to better forestall the risk of heresy regarding the "real presence," theologians tend to cut it from the church. The "real presence" becomes isolated from the liturgical context in which it arises and from the ecclesial context for which it arises. According to this viewpoint, the risk is (1) seeing the real presence in an imaginary way, as we previously explained, (2) enclosing it in a metaphysics of "substance" which ignores the supreme importance of its relation to humanity (the "for you" of Jesus' words at the Last Supper, a "for" which clearly indicates that what is meant is a "presence," therefore a relation and not the simple, bare fact of "being there"), and (3) reinforcing individualistic tendencies which effectively will continue to grow.

The Lord's Supper According to Paul

The whole point of our approach through symbol aims at denouncing this so-called realism produced by the "deadly dichotomy." More concretely, it is sufficient to refer to Paul or to the present rites of communion to expose the too narrow character of this dichotomy. The text of Paul on "the Lord's Supper" in 1 Cor 11:17-34 is well-known. Let us simply study the structure of this text:

(a) In a first part (vv. 17-22), Paul castigates the Corinthians, whose assemblies are in contradiction to the meal of the Lord. This meal supposes sharing and communion between members, whereas, on the contrary, "each of you goes ahead with your own supper, and one goes hungry and another becomes drunk." Such behavior can only "humiliate those who have nothing" and thus "show contempt for the church of God" (vv. 21-22). Here we have an ecclesiological problem made concrete by an ethical behavior in total discordance with the Lord's meal.

(b) One would expect Paul to oppose to this conduct a word of Jesus that would be on the same ethical level, for instance, "Love one another. . . ." But no; instead, Paul has recourse to a sacramental argument (vv. 23-37). He inserts a liturgical piece, well known to his congregation, a story already well polished by having been used by communities in their liturgies: the story of the Last Supper. He reminds them that he "handed on" this story as he "received [it] from the Lord" (let us understand: from a tradition going back to the Lord). The rabbinic pair "to receive/to transmit" indicates that it is a question of a tradition which one reports with all faithfulness and which no one can take the liberty of changing.

(c) The third part (vv. 27-34) is a consequence of what precedes. Introduced by a "therefore" (v. 27), it culminates in v. 29, "For all who eat and drink without discerning the body, eat and drink judgment against themselves." The Corinthians do not discern the "body" of the Lord. The expression surely does not apply to the sole eucharistic body; otherwise, Paul's argumentation would fall flat. Furthermore, the Corinthians' problem did not concern their faith in the Lord's presence in the Eucharist; this sort of problem will not arise, as we have said, before the ninth century. The expression "to discern the body" responds to the first two parts of our text: "You are deluded; furthermore, it is an absolute contradiction on your part to claim you discern in truth the *eucharistic* body of the Lord without at the same time discerning his *ecclesial* body and, as a consequence, without adopting a conduct of sharing that would be in harmony with the unity this eucharistic body signifies." So saying, Paul does nothing more than amplify the formula he had written in the preceding chapter: "Because there is one bread, we who are many are one body, for we all partake of the one bread" (1 Cor 10:17).

It is exactly this intrinsic relation between the Eucharist and the church, expressed by the Pauline formula "body of Christ," that the Eucharistic Prayer develops in NP 2 and NP 3. This theme has been greatly exploited by the tradition of the church, so greatly that in the early church it received an institutional form, the "ex-communication" applied to Christians gravely unfaithful to their baptism; it was a deprivation of eucharistic communion. The ecclesiology of that period is fundamentally sacramental: to be cut off from the Eucharist is to be cut off from the church, not from the church as institution since the sinners remained baptized persons, but from the church as communion ("communion of the saints") since they were the dead members of Christ's body. Through the penance imposed by the church, God called these members to come back to life. Because the theologians of the thirteenth century were assiduous readers of the Scriptures and the Fathers, they were not ignorant of this theme. But for the reasons mentioned above, their attention became too narrowly focused on the question of transubstantiation. Thus, they were instrumental in giving to this theme a secondary place instead of the preeminent first place which the earlier tradition had granted it.

The Rites of Communion

Our present day rites of communion are also indebted to the Pauline theology of Eucharist which we just recalled. After the Our Father, three symbolic gestures or movements succeed one another. Each one of them expresses simultaneously a relation to Christ and a relation to sisters and brothers, but the emphasis is different. They can be represented by the following table:

	Relation to Christ	Relation to the church
Gesture of peace	+	++
Breaking of the bread	++	++
Going to communion	++	+

The first rite, that of the sign of peace, turns the participants first toward one another; but it is in the name of Christ that they do so, as the priest's words used in the Mass in France indicate, "Brothers, in the charity of Christ, give peace to one another." The third rite, that of going to communion turns us first toward Christ: it is he who is received at communion, not the sisters and brothers, but one cannot do this in truth without being in communion with others as the first gesture shows. Between the two, the rite of the breaking of the bread takes place; it symbolizes simultaneously and at the same level the relation of each communicant to Christ and to the church. What is broken is indeed the body of Christ; but this body of Christ is given through bread, that is, something essentially both nourishing and convivial, indicating that there is a eucharistic body of the Lord only in view of his ecclesial body. In patristic, especially in Augustinian language, the latter is really the "truth" of the former.

The ritual sequence of these three acts is imbued with the theology previously discussed: one cannot truly receive the eucharistic body of Christ without being in communion with his ecclesial body. The Eucharist is really the *symbol* of the indissoluble "marriage" of Christ and the church (see Eph 5); it is impossible to say the one without saying the other. As a direct consequence, it is impossible to give a firm foundation to the realism of the presence of Christ in the Eucharist while omitting to take into account the relational "for" in Jesus' words, therefore, the relation to the church. Conversely, it is impossible to confuse the two, which would be theologically disastrous (the church made up of sinners cannot be identified with its Lord) and anthropologically inconsistent (we have shown that only different realities can be "sym-bolized"). In the course of a session at which I was the moderator, a priest asked me a question, "Last Sunday, while pronouncing the words, 'This is my body,' I made a gesture designating the assembly. What do you think of it?" I immediately answered, "Congratulations! but never do it again!" One understands why. This priest's intention was no doubt a good one: he wanted to have the Christians understand Augustine's "Be what you see and receive what you are"; but he was creating a most dangerous theological confusion between the body of the risen Christ and the church, and he was forgetting what the "sym-bol" is.

SYMBOLIC EXCHANGE IN THE EUCHARISTIC PRAYER

The clearer and deeper theological explanations we just gave concerning the results of our narrative analysis of the Eucharistic Prayer enable us to enter without difficulty into the process of symbolic exchange between humanity (the church) and God, who is the key to its eucharistic nature.

The Eucharistic Process

Using the model shown previously, we are in a position to illustrate the result in the following manner before commenting on it:

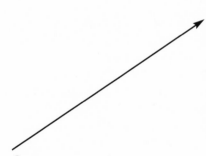

2. RECEPTION
   a. Moment "Sacrament"
   b. Sacramental body of Christ
   c. Present
   d. "Here is the time to give thanks to our Father" (reception under the mode of offering or "rendering")

1. GIFT
   a. Moment "Scriptures"
   b. Historical and glorious of Christ

   c. Past

   d. "Here is the time when God (a) shows mercy to our earth"

3. RETURN-GIFT
   a. Moment "Ethics"
   b. Ecclesial body of Christ
      • right now
      • forever
   c. Eschatological future:
      • already
      • not yet
   d. "Here is the time to live in grace with our sisters and brothers"

The "a" of the three positions repeats the three major elements of Christian identity. The "b" corresponds to the threefold body of Christ we just spoke about. The "c" marks the temporality with, as far as the future is concerned, its eschatological tension, characteristic in Christianity, the already and the not yet. As to the "d," it is formulated from a hymn from the Liturgy of the Hours in French: "Let us take the hand which God extends to us" (Didier Rimaud).

(a) Everything starts with God's gift, this gift described in our foundational writings and presented in a synthetic way in NP 1. This is nothing but a (more or less) brief summary of salvation history, from the creation to the sending of the Son, Jesus; here we have called it the moment *Scriptures*. This moment is itself condensed in the event Jesus-Christ announced by these same Scriptures, according to the Christian reading since the apostolic age. All this is narrated in the past tense in Eucharistic Prayer 2 and expresses the gratuitous initiative of God who through benevolence wanted to overcome the sin committed by humans in order to lead them to this communion of life with God, projected since "before the foundation of the world" (Eph 1:4). In the first part of the Eucharistic Prayer, the church gives thanks to God for this past history, where, in a decisive way, God "has shown favor to our earth."

(b) This past gift concerns human beings of every generation. And this is exactly what the moment *Sacrament* signifies by marking the actualization of this past gift: we receive in the present and as a present the same Jesus Christ as that of the past, but under a new mode which he himself left us as a memorial, that is, his glorious body still bearing the wounds of his death, therefore marked by his history, handed on to us under the eucharistic mode. But this reception is paradoxically effected in an act of dispossession and offering. We have noted above the motive of such a dispossession: no one grasps grace; it is taken only by rendering thanks. The sacramental time of giving thanks to our Father is the time of the reception of "another" history into the history which is ours.

(c) But there is no reception of a gift without a return-gift. This corresponds to our NP 3. It is the moment *Ethics,* that of responsibility, in which Christians are called "to become what they have received" according to the beautiful formula of a prayer after communion. The reception in sacrament of Christ dead and risen demands this ethics of *agapē,* that is, of love lived in justice, mercy, sharing. This ethics, founded on the very love of God which the Spirit causes to dwell in believers (Rom 5:5), gives to Christ, through the church, his present "body" of humanity in its process of growth "to the measure of the full stature of Christ" (Eph 4:13). Without this return-gift of the living-in-grace with one's sisters and brothers, eucharistic communion, though "valid," would be fruitless: to receive communion in those conditions would yield no profit; rather it would be a misapprehension of God's gift, even a case when it could be said that Christians "eat and drink judgment against themselves" (1 Cor 11:29).

Widening of the Perspective

The process of exchange with God which was just analyzed can unfold much beyond the Eucharistic Prayer itself. It can be extended to every sacramental celebration, as well as to Christian identity itself.

SACRAMENTAL CELEBRATIONS

Every sacramental celebration follows the model we have just delineated. It opens with a sort of preliminary to the process, and this is the fashioning of the church assembly by the entrance rites, of a common "we" realized in the name of the Other, Jesus, the Christ. A sacrament is always a church act. It is within this ecclesial matrix that the three moments analyzed above take place: reading of the Scriptures as the living word of God attesting God's gift in the past; sacramental gesture of reception of this gift in the present; rite of sending into mission indicating the ethics of responsibility which is incumbent on all in order to "veri-fy" in their own daily lives what has just been celebrated and received. It is easy to apply this model to every sacrament.

CHRISTIAN IDENTITY

If every sacramental celebration thus implements the same process of gift/reception/return-gift, a process concretely corresponding to the figure Scriptures/Sacrament/Ethics, this cannot be by pure chance. In fact, such a process can be understood as the very process of Christian identity. In other words, *every sacrament shows us how to see and live what transforms our human existence into a properly Christian existence.*

Obviously, as we were careful to point out in the introduction to chapter 2, this "pattern" is not "one size fits all." In real life, the way one accedes to faith does not necessarily begin with the discovery of the Scriptures; the initial call can as well happen through a liturgical experience or the encounter with a person whose life and actions witness to the gospel. God's ways are innumerable.

Nonetheless, this first call becomes properly Christian only inasmuch as the witness one has encountered leads, directly or indirectly, to the One whom the Scriptures reveal when they are read in a Christian manner. The point of departure is always necessarily the recognition of God's gift in the person of Jesus, the Christ, what we call the moment "Scriptures." But this gift from the past, has to be received in the present; this is what the moment "Sacrament"—in this case baptism— figures and effects. It is hardly necessary to specify that, as the medieval theologians as well as the Fathers all taught, the reception of the gift does not have to be existentially connected to the very moment of baptism. Exceptions apart, it happens long before as the catechumens gradually convert their hearts and their lives to the gospel. Still, it remains dependent on baptism, on the intention of receiving baptism, which constitutes its structural and sacramental moment.[11] But baptism is not the last word. Although in it God offers the divine self as a gift of grace independently of the receiving subject's dispositions, this gift is received as such, that is, is fruitful, only if the subject takes to heart the obligatory implication of a return-gift. This return-gift corresponds to the moment "Ethics": the moment of an effective conversion of heart and a conformation of life to what the sacrament symbolizes.

Function of the Moment Sacrament

If one extends the preceding scheme, apart from the functioning of the Eucharistic Prayer, to all the sacramental celebrations and to the process that gives Christians their identity, one clearly perceives what the function of the sacramental celebrations in Christian life is. They are a *point of passage:* nothing but this, but all this.

(a) "Nothing but this": the sacraments are neither a point of departure—since it is the reference to the Scriptures or rather to Christ announced through them which plays this role—nor a point of ar-

---

[11] This is a most classic doctrine. For Thomas Aquinas, adults who present themselves for baptism are normally justified by God before receiving the sacrament provided they intended to receive it: "Baptism has a certain efficacy for the remission of people's sins, even before they actually receive it." However, "sometimes grace is bestowed and sin is remitted in the actual reception of baptism." There is the same reasoning, in the same passage, on the subject of the relation between the forgiveness of sins and absolution. *Summa Contra Gentiles, Book 4*, literally trans. English Dominicans (New York: Benziger Brothers, 1929) ch. 72; p. 161 [quotation adapted by the editor].

rival—since this is the part of ethical behavior. They simply have a function of transit, as has already been suggested in chapter 3. What is written in the Book—that the letter is dead if, through the Spirit, it does not reach the body, that is to say, ethical behavior—is symbolized by the sacrament. For, in the sacraments, the believers' bodies absorb the word heard in the Scriptures in order to transform it into life. The staging of the body in the rite (personal body within the ecclesia body) shows what that passage is and how it should always lead from the Book to the living of life.

(b) "But all this": this point of passage is not left to everyone's free choice. Certainly, the reception in the present of God's gift, made in the past and attested by the Scriptures, is not limited to the sacraments. But as was mentioned about baptism, it is not independent from them. *There is only one structure of the covenant.* In this structure, the sacraments of the church have their own function: to offer believers God's gift in the present. Even though in fact multiple obstacles—psychological, sociological, cultural, or institutional—can prevent their reception, it remains that by right the passage through the sacraments belongs to the unique structure of the covenant. As intimate and personal as it may be, conversion is never reducible to pure interiority; it is always-already structurally mediated by the church and oriented toward the sacrament.

Besides, it is this "passage" which makes it possible for daily life to become a "liturgy," a "spiritual sacrifice" to the glory of God. As was said before, what makes the ethics of daily life be liturgy and sacrifice is not its degree of generosity but really the fact that it is lived as a response to God's gift, which is primary. The function of the sacraments is to propose this gift. For if the sacraments are the revelatory expression of the "already-here" of God's grace in daily life and therefore the summit of Christian life, they are also simultaneously the operating expression of the gratuitous gift of God and the source of what makes daily life a properly Christian life, that is to say, a "spiritual offering" to the glory of God.

CHRISTIAN IDENTITY AND JEWISH IDENTITY

In this chapter, we have constantly spoken of Christian identity. In order to better understand its singularity, it is interesting to compare it with that of Judaism. The similarities are such that the Christian difference appears more clearly: the material is the same, but the treatment (the "form") is quite different.

One Process of Identity

Let us go back to the study we have done of the rite of the offering of the firstfruits described in Deut 26:1-11 (pp. 56–59). According to the diagram of symbolic exchange, that text functions in the following way:

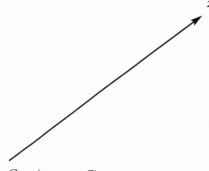

2. RECEPTION (SECTION B-B')
   a. Moment "Sacrament"
   b. Ritual B-B' framing the memorial (C)
   c. Present (twofold "I" in the present in B and in B')
   d. Reception of God's gift (the land) under mode of offering or "rendering (grace)"

1. GIFT (SECTION C)
   a. Moment "Scriptures"
   b. Memorial of history of the origins (Egypt, Exodus, gift of the land)
   c. Past (in "We")
   d. God showed mercy to Israel

3. RETURN-GIFT (SECTION A')
   a. Moment "Ethics"
   b. Sharing with those who have nothing (Levites and immigrants)
   c. Future (in collective "you")
   d. "To live-in-grace" with others

The process of symbolic exchange is of the same type as for Christians. Deuteronomy never ceases to repeat that the land of Canaan is a gratuitous gift from God. That gift, made in the past to the ancestors (section C), God continues to make to each generation. This is why every year Israel ritually symbolizes the present reception of this gift: "Today I declare to the LORD your God that I have come into the land that the LORD swore to our ancestors to give us" (v. 3). To receive this land *as a gift*, Israel makes of it a symbolic offering: "So now I bring the first of the fruit of the ground that you, O LORD, have given me" (v. 10). For the land is not reducible to a value-object whose owner would be Israel; Israel is only its steward. What is given the people is not a rough piece of land, a mere thing, but a land made special by gratuitousness: the land is at once a "thing" and a "sign." Here is why the reception of Canaan as a gift requires the return-gift of the sharing with the Levites and immigrants. The text says approximately, "You will be toward the ones who have nothing as I, God, have been toward

148

you when you had nothing" or "The ritual symbolic gesture of offering by which you receive the land *as* a gift in every generation is the figure of the existential gesture of sharing with the needy which you are called to practice in your life." The ritual offering does not constitute the final return-gift for Israel; it is the same for Christians. This oblation is the figure of an ethics of sharing; such is the return-gift which "veri-fies" what the rite symbolizes and which is the obligation implied by the reception of the land for what it is, the gift of God.

The stakes are high. Indeed, in agreement with the theology prevalent in Deuteronomy, one can express it by the following theological categorization:

Pagan regime (EGYPT)	*Transitory Regime* (DESERT, MANNA)	*Intended Regime* (CANAAN, OFFERING OF THE FIRSTFRUITS)
Conquered land	No land	Land received as gift
Earth without heaven	Heaven without earth (manna)	Earth and heaven
Attaining without expecting	Expecting without attaining	Attaining and expecting
Work without grace	Grace without work	Work and grace

For Israel the important thing is to possess a land while never forgetting, contrary to the pagans, that this land is a gift from God. Deuteronomy incessantly denounces the pagan temptation to which the people succumb. Hence the numerous warnings, "Take care that you do not forget the LORD"; "Do not say to yourself, 'My power and the might of my own hand have gotten me this wealth'" (Deut 6:12 and 8:17, among many other places). Against this temptation, the remembrance of the desert and the manna, pure gift from heaven which the people gathered without work, was of the utmost importance. However, this regime in the desert was a transitory one: God wanted to lead God's own into a land where they could settle and which they would make fruitful.

One can visualize the import of this "theological categorization" by the following diagram (called a "semiotic square"): the diagonals A-B and C-D represent the axes of contradiction (possession—non-possession; dispossession—non-dispossession). The sides A-C and D-B indicate the contrary terms ("dispossession" is the contrary of "possession" but not its contradictory, which is "non-dispossession." Similarly, in a system of colors, "red" can be the contrary of "white," whereas the contradictory of "white" is "non-white"). As for the double lateral arrows, they indicate an implication ("dispossession" implies "non-possession," as "red" implies "non-white").

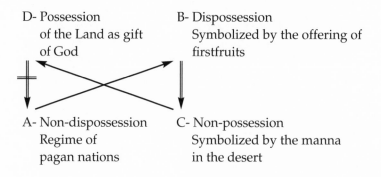

D- Possession
of the Land as gift
of God

B- Dispossession
Symbolized by the offering of
firstfruits

A- Non-dispossession
Regime of
pagan nations

C- Non-possession
Symbolized by the manna
in the desert

The diagram is to be read in the direction of a double loop: A-B-C-D. We start from the pagan regime (A) in which humans ignore or forget God and consequently think themselves the owners of the land reduced to a mere thing. In order to live like Israel, in faithfulness to the covenant, the people must adopt the contrary attitude (B); this is symbolized by the offering of the firstfruits as an act of dispossession and therefore of recognition of the land as a gift from God. But this act of dispossession is possible only if (obligatory implication) every generation of Israel remembers its origins and especially the time of the desert where the people were in a condition of non-possession, which the manna (C) eminently symbolizes. Thus, it is in virtue of the reversal of the pagan (A) state of affairs by the offering of the firstfruits (B), which implies the memory of the manna (C), that Israel can authentically enter into possession of the object God gives it, that is, the land of Canaan (D). Israel can possess it, but it is always as if not possessing it; Israel can grow all sorts of fruits, but these fruits are always received as a gift from God. For "one does not live by bread alone, but by every word that comes from the mouth of the LORD" (Deut. 8:3; cf. Matt 4:4). It is clear that the offering of the firstfruits involves nothing less than Israel's very identity.

One can cross out the path of logical implication going from possession (D) to non-dispossession (A). For it is precisely to spare Israel from falling into the pagan temptation that the offering of the firstfruits and the memorial of origins, especially of the journey through the desert, take place. But this is the ideal; concretely, the people will never cease to betray the covenant, therefore their identity; but God will not cease to restore this covenant to the point of making it "new" by writing God's word in the heart of the people and giving them a share in God's spirit (Jer 31; Ezek 36). It is this new and definitive covenant which will be sealed in the self-donation of God in Jesus.

A Different Treatment

The process of Jewish identity in its relation of exchange with the one God is therefore "materially" the same as that of Christian identity. Then where is the difference? This does not appear in our diagram of symbolic exchange since the "mechanism" is the same. To see the difference one must focus on *the "object" that is transmitted:* God's gift, no longer under the mode of a land stamped with the seal of the Law, but as the Fathers of the church have often commented, under the mode of the One prefigured by the land, Jesus the Christ, marked by the Father with the seal of the Spirit (see John 6:27; Acts 10:38). In both testaments, the object is gratuitous; this is why the symbolic logic of its reception is the same: one receives such an "object" ("anti-object") only by giving thanks. But the second testament has this new trait, that its object is the very Grace of God or better still, God revealing God fully as grace in the gift of self as Son in Jesus, a gift actualized by the Spirit, as the prayers of epiclesis in the sacramental celebrations demonstrate. This is why, in the wake of the liturgy, a long theological tradition has rightly perceived in the gift of the Spirit the grace par excellence given to humanity.

The difference between the two objects, both thoroughly gratuitous, is not only in the order of intensity, as if on a graduated scale the second were higher (even much higher) than the first. This difference must be understood as "radical" in the etymological meaning of the word, that is, as pertaining to the very root of the transmitted object, and thus to the relation between God and humanity. If indeed through the resurrection of Jesus "what God promised to our ancestors he has fulfilled for us" (Acts 13:32-33), if therefore the Spirit of God, the object of the promise of a new covenant (Jer 31:31-34; Ezek 36:24-28), is now given, as the story of Pentecost means to attest, then in order to enter into a communion of life with God, Christians no longer need to pull themselves up by their own bootstraps, that is, by the fulfillment of the works of the Law but to welcome in their daily lives the very gift of God, that is, the Spirit of the risen One. By the same token, their human lives are sanctified. They become a "spiritual worship" (Rom 12:1), a "spiritual sacrifice" (1 Pet 2:5) offered in thanksgiving to the glory of God, as we have developed in chapter 3.

This introduces a fundamental difference between Judaism and Christianity, but a difference at the core of two structures so close to one another that there was need of Paul's energy, often mixed with anger ("You foolish Galatians!" [Gal 3:1]), to establish it and in this way avoid a break in the early church (see Acts 15). The Christian difference is never as clearly perceived as in its nearness to Jewish identity. Then it probably finds its most appropriate qualification: the difference is eschatological.

Fourth Part

Sacramental Mystery and Trinitarian Mystery

The sacraments are acts of the church; God communicates with humankind through their mediation. This communication is traditionally called by the beautiful name of "grace." Thus, these acts which are fully human, so human, so laden with psychological, social, institutional ambiguities that at times one would wish to be free of them in order to have direct access to God in a worship "in spirit and truth" (John 4:23)—but we know this is an illusion coming from the empire of the imaginary—constitute, according to Christian faith, the concrete mediation of God's communication at its most divine.

This paradox of the most divine given within the most human has often appeared in the preceding pages of this book. In fact, it is a sort of challenge that undergirds the whole work. However, the fundamental ground on which it rests has not yet been the object of a specific study. This ground is found nowhere but in God as God was revealed as Tri-unity in Jesus, the Christ. This is what this part would like to show in its one chapter.

Chapter 8

The Sacraments of Christ's Passover in the Spirit

In the last analysis, the claim that encounter of and communication with the living God are done through traditional and fully human materials—gestures, postures, words—which the church assumes in the name of Christ and calls "sacraments," does not hold good unless, *the very being of God* can in some way be conceived of as "human" in its very divinity. This means that the discourse affirming "sacramental grace" can be held with assurance only if it is in harmony with a properly "theo-logical" discourse giving food for thought concerning the "humanity" of the divine God. In Christianity, such a discourse is necessarily rooted in christology, which no less necessarily opens onto a trinitarian discourse. In any case, how could we construct a sacramental theology without relying on such a christological discourse woven with trinitarian references since in its various liturgical rites the church constantly proclaims that the grace God communicates to humans comes from the Father through the Son and in the Spirit?

CLASSICAL SACRAMENTAL THEOLOGY'S
POINT OF DEPARTURE: THE INCARNATION

In Scholastic theology, the treatise on the sacraments directly followed the treatise on christology, itself centered on the mystery of the incarnation of the Word in the human being Jesus: the mystery of the hypostatic union.[1] In this perspective, the sacraments were regarded as the prolongation down to us of the "holy humanity" of Christ.

Such a point of departure has the advantage of immediately underscoring that every sacrament is a gesture of Christ, itself shown through the gesture of the church. However, it also had a grave disadvantage.

---

[1] "Hypostasis" has become approximately equivalent to our word "person." The term "hypostatic union" designates the assumption of human nature by the person of the Word in Jesus.

In the Scholastic approach, the dominant question about the hypostatic union was "*How* could God (the assumption being that one knows a priori what God is) become a human being?" In the same way, the dominant question of sacramental theology was "*How* can God communicate with us through the purely human means or instruments that the sacraments of the church are?" The presupposition was that one knew in advance all about God and one applied this representation to Christ through the concept of his divine nature. Thus, once the question of the hypostatic union was elucidated, the question of the sacraments, which are the prolongation of the redeeming incarnation, was solved.[2]

Now, is this the correct way of posing the question? Rather than "*How* can God (it being understood that *we know who God is*) do such and such?" would it not be more in keeping with biblical revelation and especially with the "scandal of the cross" to ask "*Of what God* are we speaking when we say that we have seen God in Jesus? Who is God for us that we are able to say this about God and therefore are able to say that God communicates with us, that God comes to us as 'body of Christ' in the fully human mediations of the sacraments?" No response to such a question can be given except by having recourse to the full revelation of God that happened in Jesus' history and, more precisely, in his death on the cross. Our point of departure, then, is assigned to us: the paschal mystery, that is, the cross of the risen One.

OUR POINT OF DEPARTURE:
THE PASCHAL MYSTERY OF CHRIST

The Ancient Tradition

It is perfectly in accordance with the ancient tradition to take as our point of departure the death and resurrection of Jesus.

FIRST, THE TRADITION OF THE NEW TESTAMENT

At the heart of the testimonies in the New Testament, we find not the incarnation as such but the death and resurrection of Jesus. This is true of (a) the primitive *kerygma*, that is, the first announcement of

---

[2] The parallelism between the two was not complete, however; Thomas Aquinas specifies that the humanity of Christ is the "conjoined instrument" of his divinity (as is the hand to the painter's mind), whereas the sacraments are its "disjunct instrument" (as is the brush to the painter's hand.)

Christ, according to the earliest attestations in the New Testament, (b) the earliest *confessions of faith* (for instance, 1 Cor 15:3-5), and (c) the history of the *redaction of the [synoptic] gospels:* the gospels of the infancy, written at a later date, are replete with paschal references. The mystery of the incarnation of God as Son in Jesus is certainly not without importance, but it is understood the other way around, from the resurrection from the dead. We should therefore not be surprised that for the Fathers of the church, as Wolfhart Pannenberg writes, "We can say that all christological ideas have had soteriological motives."[3]

THEN, THE LITURGICAL TRADITION OF THE ANCIENT CHURCH

(a) The progressive organization of the liturgical year is a good example for our topic: In the beginning, the sole feast that was celebrated by the Christian communities was the weekly passover of the Lord, every Sunday. It is later, at least in some churches,[4] that the yearly Christian passover appeared with its long vigil which developed the three facets of the Sunday passover: the death, resurrection, and parousia of the Lord. In the course of the third century, the joy marking the end of the paschal vigil was extended into a "fifty-day period of rejoicing" regarded as one great Sunday spread over fifty days. Not until the fourth century did the feast of Pentecost acquire the status of the completion of the fifty days, parallel to the Sunday of the resurrection. At the same, the feast of the Ascension appeared on the fortieth day, arrived at by counting days according to the chronology of Acts.[5] Likewise, the feast of Christmas-Epiphany arose only in

---

[3] Wolfhart Pannenberg, *Esquisse d'une christologie* (Paris: Cerf, 1971) 38; [*Jesus, God and Man,* 2nd ed., trans. Lewis L. Wilkins and Duane A. Priebe (Philadelphia: Westminster, 1977).

[4] Thus, the yearly paschal vigil seems not to have been known in Rome before the pontificate of Soter, ca. 165.

[5] Antoine Chavasse, in *L'Église en prière: Introduction à la liturgie,* ed. Aimé Georges Martimort (Paris: Desclée, 1961) 694, thus summarizes this processus: "At the beginning, the liturgical year unfolded the uniform course of the weeks which brought back, every eighth day, the celebration of the Eucharist and the commemoration of the death and resurrection of Christ. From the second century on, against the background of the weekly cycle, one can see arise the celebration of the passion and resurrection on the exact day which one deems to be the anniversary of the event. At least from the beginning of the third century, the celebration is followed by 'Fifty Days,' but it is especially from the fourth century on that the fiftieth day (Pentecost) is particularly solemnized."

the fourth century (ca. 330 in Rome), probably partly under the influence of the Council of Nicaea (325), which had just solemnly proclaimed the full divinity of the Son.

This fact constitutes a true theological locus which it behooves us to ponder. Was there not enough material, from the beginning, in the gospels and Acts to organize a liturgical year: Advent, Christmas, Epiphany, Baptism of the Lord, Lent, Holy Thursday, Good Friday, Holy Saturday, Easter Sunday, Ascension on the fortieth day, Pentecost on the fiftieth, parousia at the end of the liturgical year? For three centuries this did not occur. In the beginning, people were even content with the sole paschal celebration of every Sunday. For what reason, if not because the liturgy does not celebrate the various "anniversaries" of Jesus' destiny and because the liturgical year is not a sort of immense socio-drama in which one would somehow mime the events that have punctuated this destiny? Christianity is lived under the regime of memorial, not of anniversary or mime. The unique object of the Christian memorial is Christ's passover in its undivided unity of death and resurrection. This is why, as Irénée Henri Dalmais writes, "during the first Christian centuries, Easter is the feast, not only the feast par excellence, the feast of feasts, as the Martyrology says today, but the only feast, beside which there could be no other."[6]

What makes Christmas, for instance, a truly Christian feast is not that it celebrates the anniversary of Jesus' birth but the memorial of the coming of the *Lord* Jesus (a pascal title) into humanity.[7] Consequently, this coming is lived as an event "today," sung by the church at Evening Prayer II of this day, "Christ the Lord is born today; today, the Savior has appeared."[8] This explains why in the course of this same feast the Eastern churches continue to associate his "manifestation" in the flesh[9] with his manifestation to the Magi and even with his first public manifestation as "Beloved Son" at the time of his bap-

[6] Irénée Henri Dalmais, in ibid., 218.

[7] Hence the liturgical name of this feast, *Natale Domini Nostri Iesu Christi* (the Nativity of our Lord Jesus Christ).

[8] *The Liturgy of the Hours*, trans. International Commission on English in the Liturgy, 1975.

[9] The meaning of the Latin word *natale* (from which Noel comes) is rather close to that of the Greek *epiphania:* in both cases, it is a question of the "manifestation" or glorification of the emperor as he inaugurates his reign or of a helpful deity whose statue was carried throughout the city.

tism and, further, with the first manifestation of his "glory" by the miracle at Cana.[10] Be that as it may, we are faced with a true paradox: the liturgical year can be understood in a genuinely Christian way only if one forgets what it has gradually become and instead reflects on what it was at its birth: the weekly celebration of the whole paschal mystery of Christ.

(b) The *anamnesis* of the Eucharistic Prayer orients us in a similar direction: although it seems it developed by following the second article of the Creed, it does not allude to the incarnation as such; everything is centered on the paschal mystery. The fact is the more striking in the fourth and fifth centuries, marked by both the great trinitarian controversies and the formation of the eucharistic prayers in the several liturgical families which take their definitive form at that time. In the very same period when theological struggles keep the church on the battle line of the hypostatic union, the liturgy serenely continues to celebrate the memorial of Christ's passover without ever mentioning the incarnation. As in the previous tradition, as in the New Testament, the incarnation is understandable only within the passover of the Crucified.

A Paschal Mystery Demanding to Be Understood in Its Whole Extent

It is important to specify that when one speaks of the paschal mystery of Jesus, the Christ, one must not isolate either his death or his resurrection like mere separate moments. The scope of his death can be understood theologically only if it is taken as the totality of his life: he "died-for" because he unceasingly "lived-for." As to his resurrection, it cannot be reduced to a simple return to his previous state; his risen body bears the marks of the wounds of his death, therefore, all the scars of his concrete historical life. This latter is theologically pertinent to the meaning of his death as a death that saves all humans. One can, one must go further: the incarnation itself is included in the paschal mystery; but then it is understood the other way around, as in the New Testament, from the life of self-giving unto death and from the resurrection of Jesus.

---

[10] Traces of this tradition are extant in the Roman liturgy. At Evening Prayer II of Epiphany, one sings this antiphon before the Canticle of Mary: "Three mysteries mark this holy day: today the star leads the Magi to the infant Christ; today water is changed into wine for the wedding feast; today Christ wills to be baptized by John in the river Jordan to bring us salvation." *Liturgy of the Hours.*

Similarly, but this time, looking to the future, the resurrection of Jesus includes its ultimate fulfillment in the parousia: Are we not already in the eschatological "last days" (Heb 1:1)? Is not the parousia already begun? The parousia includes the ascension, which in any case is just another way of saying, according to the spatial symbolism of "being lifted up" and "being exalted," what the term "resurrection" for its part expresses according to a (spatio-) temporal symbolism of "awakening" or "standing again" after having been lying down. The parousia also includes Pentecost, which in certain respects, as we have already observed, is nothing but the "for us" of the resurrection, that is to say, the embodiment of the risen One in history through the Spirit, under the form of the new People of God, the church in its historical visibility.

We can visualize what we understand by paschal mystery, taken in its full extension, by the following diagram:

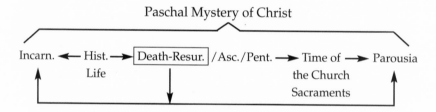

Paschal Mystery of Christ

Incarn. ←— Hist. —▸ Death-Resur. / Asc./Pent. —▸ Time of —▸ Parousia
        Life   the Church
                                          Sacraments

Consequences of This Point of Departure

According to the diagram above, the sacraments appear not as the somehow static prolongations of the incarnation as such but as the major expression, in our own history, of the embodiment (historical/ eschatological) of the risen One in the world through the Spirit, embodiment whose "fundamental sacrament" is the church visibly born at Pentecost. The sacraments are thus situated in the dynamism of a secular history reread as a holy history. The theological affirmation of sacramental grace is understood in the wake of the church's faith in the power of the risen One continually raising for himself, through the Spirit, a body of new humanity. "Before" the question of the efficacy of the sacraments we have the question of the active presence of the risen One in the world through the Spirit. This active presence is what faith is about. In this perspective, sacramental grace is nothing but one of the expressions of this faith. True, it is only one expression among others, but there is something radical about it in that, due to its eminently concrete and singular character, it is a buffer which tests or "veri-fies" the faith unceasingly threatened with drifting toward general and generous ideas on the active presence of the risen Christ.

A change of point of departure always entails consequences. In this case, the one we propose requires a representation of God different from the "simple notion" which "theism" gives of God. We must think of God as somehow *human in God's divinity*. This leads us back to the cross of Jesus (relation Father/Son) and to the Spirit (without which the relation Father/Son is theologically unthinkable). Hence the twofold journey, christological and pneumatological, that follows.

SACRAMENTAL DISCOURSE AND CHRISTOLOGICAL DISCOURSE

Although we are not able to develop here this statement as it should be done, let us say that according to the faith of Christians it is in Jesus, and ultimately in his cross (as the victorious cross), that God has been fully revealed to humanity. This means in particular that the mystery of the "crucified God" in Jesus can be understood only within the framework of trinitarian theology.[11] From among the diverse approaches to this mystery found in the New Testament, we choose those in the account of Jesus' death in Mark (and Matthew) and the meditation of Paul on the scandal of the cross in 1 Cor 1.

My God, My God, Why Have You Forsaken Me?

According to Mark and Matthew, this cry is the only word spoken by Jesus on the cross. Whereas Luke places in Jesus' mouth the psalmist's prayer representing the righteous person surrendering her or his life to God ("Father, into your hands I commend my spirit"), Mark and Matthew have Jesus utter the cry of the righteous person abandoned by God.[12] It is evident that there is here a theological intention, which is not respected by simply interpreting in a "psychologizing" way what the dying Jesus felt.[13] The early communities were

---

[11] Jürgen Moltmann has particularly accented this last point in *The Crucified God: The Cross of Christ as the Foundation and Criticism of Christian Theology*, trans. R. A. Wilson and John Bowden (New York: Harper & Row, 1974).

[12] Mark 15:34; Matt 27:46; Ps. 22:1. Luke 23:46; see Ps. 31:5.

[13] Besides, in the Gospels there is always a christological intention underlying the rare mentions of Christ's psychology.

not duped when they felt such a presentation of Jesus' death to be scandalous, as is proved by some manuscripts which transform Jesus' cry into "My spirit, my spirit, here you are abandoning me" or "My God, my God, what do you have to reproach me with?"[14] The scandalous character of Jesus' words expressing his abandonment (dereliction) by God is not eliminated because they are a prayer. However, and this point is of the utmost importance, the fact that we have here a prayer shows that it is within the framework of his relation to God that Jesus expresses his being forsaken by God.

The Son and the Father

The mystery of this relation in what is felt like abandonment is expressed by the Roman centurion at the foot of the cross, "Truly this man was God's Son!" (Mark 15:39). The centurion "saw that in this way he breathed his last." But did Jesus not die pronouncing as his sole words his abandonment by God? Did he not die by living to the end the trial of human solitude, solitude that is never experienced more acutely than in death? And in this case the more so since it was the unjust death of the sole just One, a death one would have expected the God whose cause he always defended to oppose by sending "more than twelve legions of angels" (Matt 26:53) or by allowing him—since the condemned man was his "son" (even if, especially if, one gives this term its simple meaning in the Old Testament of "elect," "protégé" of God)—to "come down from the cross" and "save himself" (Mark 15:29-32). But God remained silent. God did not intervene. God let Jesus live to the end his love for human beings (Heb 2:17). For a total solidarity with the human condition demands that death be assumed in the silence of God who does not intervene to spare anyone from it, be it the just One par excellence.

It is precisely at the moment when Jesus radically experiences the human condition that through the centurion the faith of the church

[14] Thus, Walter Kasper comments, in *Jesus, le Christ* (Paris: Cerf, 1976) 176 [*Jesus, the Christ*, trans. V. Green (New York: Paulist, 1976)]: "Already within the biblical tradition, the fact that Jesus died forsaken by God was regarded as shocking." See Xavier Léon-Dufour, "La mort rédemptrice du Christ selon le Nouveau Testament," in Xavier Léon-Dufour et al., *Mort pour nos péchés: Recherche pluridisciplinaire sur la signification rédemptrice de la mort du Christ,* Publications des Facultés universitaires Saint-Louis 4 (Brussels: Facultes Universitaires Saint-Louis, 1976) 38–42.

bursts forth: "Truly this man was God's Son!" There is mystery here. God is never better recognized than in the disfigured human being on the cross. Such is precisely the *language of the cross* on which Paul has meditated: it is in Jesus crucified, reduced to the state of a "slave" (Phil 2:7), that is, to the state which socially "is not" (1 Cor 1:28), because reduced to less than a "nobody" in humanity, that Paul confesses "paradoxically" the glory of God.[15] The proclamation of the "crucified Messiah" is thus as "scandalous for the Jews" seeking "signs" of their election through spectacular interventions of God in their favor as it is "foolish for the Greeks" seeking this "wisdom" that at last would ultimately give a reasonable explanation of the world (1 Cor 1:18-25).

God reveals God in what is most different from God. God reveals the divine self ultimately as God when God "crosses out" God in humanity. God reveals God as human in God's very divinity. This does not just mean that God is "morally" more human than humans, who so often are inhuman, but that "ontologically" it belongs to God to be the only one fully human. The relation of love alone makes one fully human because the subject gains in being in the measure in which it gives itself that the other may live or else because the subject comes to its own truth in the measure in which it has a relation (of love) with the other which lets the other be other—instead of reducing it imaginarily to the "same." "God is love" writes John while meditating on the Son's cross (1 John 4:8, 16). This is what happens in the symbolic order: the subject lives only because it is in relation with other subjects, as we have explained when speaking of language; but this relation to other subjects is not humanly fruitful if it establishes a similitude which is not sameness since it comes to being solely in the respect for the radical *otherness* of the other. Such is love: a relation to the other as "the other similar to me."

Analogically, it is in the most other of the divine self which is Jesus crucified that the glory of God is revealed: "Philip . . . . whoever has seen me has seen the Father" (John 14:9). Cannot this word be applied eminently to Jesus on the cross? Let us understand: "Whoever has seen me has seen nothing of the Father," the absence of the Father being radicalized in some way in the most other than God, that is, the Son-in-humanity; at the same time, "Whoever has seen me has

---

[15] The adverb is here taken in the etymological sense of *doxa,* "glory," manifesting itself in an oblique manner, *para.*

seen all of the Father," the very identity of God being paradoxically most visible in the crucified human being.

Many contemporary theologians, such as Jürgen Moltmann and Eberhard Jüngel from the Protestant side and Walter Kasper from the Catholic, do not hesitate to use forceful formulas on this point. Moltmann writes that the abandonment of Jesus "challenges the divinity of his God";[16] according to Jüngel, "God defines God when God identifies God with the dead Jesus";[17] Kasper declares that "the cross can only be interpreted as an expression of God renouncing to be God."[18] If things are so, it is impossible to give a "theistic" answer to the scandal of the cross. The scandalous revelation implied in it requires a theo-logy which, eminently paradoxical as it is, subverts the representations which humans more or less spontaneously have of God.

The Sacraments

The sacraments, these fully human acts believed to be the symbolic carriers of God's "grace," are precisely the expression of this humanity of the divine God. If they are, as was developed in the preceding chapters, the concrete expression of the embodiment of the theological in the anthropological, they presuppose a christology that can allow the "revolution" in the way of thinking about God just sketched.

SACRAMENTAL DISCOURSE AND PNEUMATOLOGICAL DISCOURSE

In order to assume in a coherent manner the analogy based on anthropology Father/Son, we must appeal to a third term. Indeed, in the human order in which we place ourselves here to analogically speak of God, one is never just one (there is no human subject except in a relation with another subject), not even two, but three: the communication between an "I" and a "You" (the reversible of the "I," therefore the other similar to the "I") is possible only under the third agency of the "Other," that is to say, of Law, Tradition, or Culture.

[16] Moltmann, *Crucified God*, 232.

[17] Eberhard Jüngel, *Dieu, mystère du monde* (Paris: Cerf, 1983) 224; [*God as the Mystery of the World: On the Foundation of the Theology of the Crucified One in the Dispute between Theism and Atheism*, trans. Darrell L. Guder (Grand Rapids, Mich.: Eerdmans, 1983)].

[18] Kasper, *Jésus, le Christ*, 251.

Without this agency, which is neutral and to which they are both "subjects," they could not "hear" one another. Analogically, to approach the mystery of the relation Father/Son, one needs to refer to a third term, also revealed: the Spirit.

The Paradoxes of the Spirit

GOD ENTIRELY OTHER

It is remarkable that, in contrast to the names of the Father and the Son, which are drawn from anthropology, the name of the Spirit is drawn from cosmology. Its great biblical symbols—the space between sky and earth, wind, breath, fire, water—all come from nature; and all connote an elusive reality. In contrast to the Father and the Son, the Spirit has no face. Besides, in the language which has been determining for Christian theology (Greek), its name is neuter, *to pneuma*. Reinforcing the cosmic symbolism, this neuter gender strongly suggests that the Spirit is God inasmuch as God cannot be mastered, seized, managed, and is beyond any institution, including, of course, the church. The Spirit "blows where it chooses" (John 3:8).

In the Bible, its place is, as it were, hidden. Certainly the Scriptures speak of it, but less than of God the Father or of Jesus, the Son. However, it is the Spirit which is the principle of the inspiration of the Scriptures as word of God and of their orientation toward Christ which is the key to their Christian interpretation. It is omnipresent in the Scriptures, and yet it does not have an assignable place, as though its trace is less in the letter than on the letter's underside. In a word, the Spirit is less *object* than *principle* of any Christian discourse. It is the Spirit which opens the passage where the discourse on God becomes authentically, on the one hand, "word" to God, prayer to the Father (Gal 4:6; Rom 8:15-16) and, on the other, living witness (*martyria*) rendered to God before humans. To use again the linguistic terms previously employed, one could say that the Spirit's function is less of the "locutionary" order (the content of the statements on God) than of the "illocutionary" order (the work it does concerning the truth of Christians' relation with God and with one another) and "perlocutionary" (the witness given by their lives).[19]

Thus, the Spirit expresses God above all as "different," totally other than humans, that is to say in biblical language, "holy"—this is why it

[19] See p. 80, n. 11.

is called "Holy Spirit." Without a doubt, one could apply to it what Jesus says of the reign, "[They will not] say, 'Look, here it is!' or 'There it is!' For, in fact, the kingdom of God is among you" (Luke 17:21).

However, and this is the paradox, this same Spirit, as elusive as the wind or fire, which proclaims the radical difference or holiness of God, simultaneously announces its closest proximity to human beings. For it is the Spirit, as was just noted, that allows the word of God to be deposited in a body of Scriptures; it was the Spirit also which, swooping down on the prophets and imbuing them with its ointment (see Isa 61:1) as an oil penetrates the body, turned their very existence into a living parable of the relation of God with God's people. It is the Spirit also which writes the letter of the Scriptures in the hearts of believers, that is, in their life itself, in their "body," making them, as Paul writes, a living "letter of Christ" (2 Cor 3:2-3), or which comes to "dwell" in them to make them the "temple" of the living God (1 Cor 3:16; Rom 8:9; Eph 2:19-22; 1 Pet 2:5; 1 John 2:27; 3:24, and so on). In summary, the Spirit appears as the agent of God's embodiment: it gives a body to the Word. And this of course applies first of all to Christ, as the Eucharistic Prayer expresses so well: the threefold body of Christ, historical ("conceived by the Holy Spirit"), eucharistic (first epiclesis), and ecclesial (second epiclesis), is the Spirit's work.

Such, therefore, is the Spirit's function: *to write the very difference of God in the body of humanity,* and first of all in the body of the church, which was its first visible work after the resurrection (this is why the church belongs in the third article of the Creed), and also in the body of every believer (1 Cor 6:19). The Spirit appears as the agent of God's communication with humankind in their radical difference. At the same time, as shown by the story of Pentecost, in opposition to the story of the Tower of Babel (Gen 11:1-9), the Spirit is the agent of communication among human beings in the very institution of a play of differences between them. Finally, within the Trinity itself, the Spirit is the "mysterious third one which accomplishes the difference without the least separation" (Olivier Clément).

THE SPIRIT IN ITS RELATION TO CHRIST AND THE CHURCH

If the prime "sacrament"—both revelatory and operating—between God and humans is Jesus, the Christ, its active principle is the Spirit. Being the agent of the appropriation of what is most divine in God by humans in their *most human*, the Spirit is the operator of the self-effacement of God in Christ in the flesh of humanity. When one thinks of God on the basis of a christology full of trinitarian references, God is revealed as the one who, through the Spirit, "crosses God out" in humanity, giving to the latter the possibility of becoming the "sacramental locus" where God continues to be embodied.

This sacramental locus where in some way the risen One withdraws through the Spirit in order to be "rising," that is, to raise for himself a body of new humanity, is *the church*, "body of Christ" in the process of growth "to the measure of the full stature of Christ" (Eph 4:13). In its historical visibility, the church is the promise and pledge of the transfiguration to which humankind and, in connection with it, the whole cosmos are called (Rom 8 and theme of "new heaven and new earth").

THE SPIRIT IN ITS RELATION TO THE SACRAMENTS: THE EPICLESIS

Understood in the dynamism of salvation history, the sacraments appear as the symbolic expression of the eschatological embodiment of God through the Spirit, first in Christ (the "source-sacrament" of God), then in the church (the "fundamental sacrament" of the Christ of God). The theological discourse on sacramental grace is understood as the *concrete* unfolding of what is affirmed in the preceding sentence, according to which, since Easter and Pentecost, the world is the eschatological place of God and of the body of Christ in process of growth through the Spirit.

If the Spirit directs us first of all to the difference of God and if it is the agent of the embodiment of this divine difference, the sacraments are inconceivable without the Spirit's action. "For everything that the Holy Spirit touches is sanctified," wrote Cyril of Jerusalem.[20] Hence, the capital importance of the epiclesis in the liturgy.[21] This applies as much to baptism and confirmation as to the Eucharist. In the Syrian tradition of Antioch, there is even a strict parallelism between the three epicleses (a) on the bread and wine of the Eucharist, (b) on the

---

[20] Cyril of Jerusalem, *Catéchèse mystagogique* 5.7, in *Catéchèses mystagogiques*, trans. Pierre Paris, Sources chrétiennes 126 (Paris: Cerf, 1966) 155.

[21] Yves Congar, "Le Saint-Esprit et les sacrements," in *Je crois en l'Esprit Saint*, vol. 3 (Paris: Cerf, 1980) 279–351; [*I believe in the Holy Spirit*, trans. David Smith, vol. 3: *The River of the Water of Life (Rev 22:1) Flows in the East and in the West* (New York: Seabury, 1983)].

baptismal water, and (c) on the holy chrism used for the anointing at confirmation.[22] In any case, there cannot be a Eucharist without the epiclesis, and similarly there should not be a baptism without it. Is it not of "water and Spirit" that we must be reborn (John 3:5)?[23] Besides, the nucleus of the prayer for the ordination of bishops, priests, and deacons is made up of a prayer asking for the Spirit.[24] As to the sacrament of reconciliation, Eastern Christians still keep alive the tradition according to which the forgiveness of sins is unthinkable without the Spirit (see John 20:22-23). The sacramental words for the anointing of the sick attribute the forgiveness of their sins and their "being raised up" to "the grace of the Holy Spirit." In the East, the Father "blesses" the spouses, but it is the Holy Spirit which "sanctifies and perfects" their union. For its part, the Reformed Church of France prefaces the proclamation of the word by this beautiful invocation, "Through your Holy Spirit, open our minds and hearts to your truth."

The sacramental reference to the Spirit is part of a most ancient tradition, unfortunately weakened somehow by Western theology since the thirteenth century to the benefit of a "christomonistic" tendency (Yves Congar's expression). But it is important for several reasons. First of all, a theological reason, which we have expounded above concerning the Spirit's role in the relation of God to humans. Second a catechetical reason: God's action in the sacraments is real of course, but its reality is wholly spiritual (one should say "pneumatological"), irreducible to any demonstration, opposed to any reification. Finally, a pastoral reason: when the Spirit's action is taken into account, the sacraments are introduced into a dynamic movement of opening, and this in a twofold way. First, an opening to history be-

[22] Emmanuel Patak Siman, *L'expérience de l'Esprit par l'Église dans la tradition syrienne d'Antioche,* Théologie historique 15 (Paris: Beauchesne, 1971); see especially the synoptic table of these three epicleses.

[23] Xavier Léon-Dufour, *Lecture de l'évangile selon Jean,* vol. 1, Parole de Dieu (Paris: Seuil, 1987) 292. Remarking that there is only one preposition, the author sees here "a sort of hendiadys" which should be translated by "of water which is Spirit," and he makes reference to Ezek 36:25-27.

[24] For the ordination of a bishop, "So now pour out upon this chosen one that power which is from you, the governing Spirit whom you gave to your beloved Son, Jesus Christ. . . ." For the ordination of a priest, "Renew within him the Spirit of holiness. . . ." For the ordination of a deacon, "Lord, send forth upon [the ordinand] the Holy Spirit. . . ."

cause the breath of the Spirit impels the sacraments to verify what they symbolize, by having Christians take responsibility for history, that is to say, practice the ethics of service to others. We have said above that this service is the primary locus of worship or the "spiritual sacrifice" which—provided it is energized by faith—keeps strong the communion of believers with God. Second, an opening to the church, because the Spirit, which makes the church, connects each member through the sacraments to the "body of Christ" and thus counteracts the temptation of an individualistic participation.

* * *

As a consequence, sacramental grace is the expression of the eschatological advent, through the Spirit, of God into history, of a God in whose divinity there is humanness. Through the Spirit, God becomes inscribed somewhere in humanity. But God is inscribed without being circumscribed, without ever being assigned to any one place.

It is therefore impossible to erase, in the name of the *universal* of the Spirit (who "blows where it chooses"), the *particular* of God's being written down somewhere: in this particular people, Israel; in these particular Scriptures, Judeo-Christian; in this particular human being, Jesus of Nazareth, confessed as "Christ of God"; in this particular group which claims to belong to him, the church; and finally, in these particular ritual word acts that this church effects in memory of him.

But conversely, it is impossible to enclose God's salvation within a particular institution: the Spirit knows no boundaries. The particular character of the grace given by baptism is for believers the concrete way enabling them to give thanks for the universal love of God. For how could they give thanks for this universal if they had not received from it their particular grace? At the same time, the universal character of God's love is the horizon without which they could not give thanks for the particular character of the grace they received.

Thus, in the sacraments we have the interaction of the christological pole—the particularity of the church-institution—and of the pneumatological pole—the universality of the reign of God which knows no boundaries. Consequently, from another perspective, we see the interaction of the pole of God and the pole of humanity.

Fifth Part

Pastoral Applications

We end our study on a pastoral note for two principal reasons. The first one is a theological one: the sacraments are, as we have not ceased to state, a "practice" in all senses of the term. This practice is celebratory and is the soil into which every theological discourse about the sacraments is rooted. It is also pastoral and requires from those who request the sacraments both a preliminary evangelization or re-evangelization and a subsequent follow-up. The second reason is connected with the approach to symbolism and the body, developed in the preceding chapters. There are consequences to this approach not only on the theological level but also, as will be amply shown, on the pastoral level.

This last point will appear with particular clarity in the pastoral domain we have selected, that of the request for "rites of passage." It was obviously impossible in this last section to deal with all the concrete problems which preparation for and celebration of the sacraments present for today's pastors. Therefore, we were faced with a choice, and even with a limited choice. Our choice was also motivated by two reasons. On the one hand, we can surmise that among the readers of this book many either assume pastoral responsibilities in their parishes, in their school chaplaincies, in any other church institutions, or simply have direct or indirect responsibilities as educators of the faith. All these persons are especially challenged by the problems inherent in the requests for rites of passage (infant baptism, First Communion, wedding, funeral). On the other hand, it was important to insure the coherence of this section with the overall approach of the book. And it so happens that the reflection we propose, concerning what is at work in the minds and reactions of those who request an infant baptism or a wedding as well as in the minds of the pastoral ministers does not divert us from symbolism and the body, which have been the themes of our study up to now.

Consequently, it is the pastoral management of these requests for rites of passage (in particular infant baptism and the wedding) which we have chosen as the pastoral field of our reflection.

171

Chapter 9

Managing the Request for Rites of Passage

Since the pastoral problems which we have chosen to ponder concern the rites of passage, it is fitting to begin by elucidating this notion commonly used in ethnology. The locution itself was coined by a French folklorist at the beginning of the nineteenth century, Arnold Van Gennep.[1]

THE CELEBRATION OF THE FOUR SEASONS OF LIFE

The celebration of the four cardinal moments of human life (birth, adolescence, marriage, death) seems to be universal. This fact, which cannot be a chance happening, suggests that this type of ritualization is highly significant on the anthropological level. What is going on here? The best way to answer this question is to observe what happens in traditional societies in which—because the richness and stability of the ritual processes specific to each of these seasons—it is easier than in our own society to discern what is at work.[2]

We shall consider only one characteristic of these ritual processes: that of a *passage*, as the name under which they are grouped indicates. And more exactly, of a passage from a pure fact of *nature* to an event of *culture*. In traditional cultures, this passage itself is reconfigured by a cultural idea according to which what concerns the social group but remains too exterior to it is dangerous for it. Therefore, the diverse rites of passage seek to symbolically integrate into the culture what would remain too threatening—because too foreign to the social body—if it were left in its natural state.

Thus, the biological fact of birth ceases to be felt as dangerous and becomes meaningful only through the conferring of a name on the

---

[1] Arnold Van Gennep, *Les rites de passage* (Paris, 1909); [*The rites of passage*, trans. Monika B. Vizedom and Gabrielle L. Caffee (Chicago: University of Chicago, 1960)].

[2] See ch. 6, n. 2, on p. 118.

newborn by the head of the clan. The baby has no social existence as long as it has not thus become a member of the group through the traditional rite of naming. Similarly, the biological fact of puberty regularly concerns a class of youngsters about to leave their childhood world. Hence the rites of initiation we shall speak of at the end of this chapter. Another event: up to now, a man and a woman have had their status in the society; but they are going to marry, or rather the chiefs of each lineage want them to marry. A new cell is in the process of formation. A priori, it is like a foreign object that the society must transform in order to assimilate it and enable it to find its proper function in the social body. The lengthy rites of passage in which the complex relations of exchange of women between clans and families [in patrilineal societies] are negotiated are intended to smoothly effect the passage in question (as smoothly as possible because rivalries between the husband's clan and the woman's, although symbolic, can degenerate into true confrontations). The same sort of problem arises in the case of death. Death cannot be left to its status of mere natural fact; it must receive a meaning, be socialized. The spirit of the deceased would dangerously roam around the village if she or he was not given through the funeral rites a partner status within the group of the living members. The deceased are posthumous partners of course, but partners just the same, endowed with functions which it is hoped will be beneficial, partners with whom one continues to maintain relations through a variety of sacrificial rites in order to keep their vengeance at bay and to obtain their protection.

In all cases, as can be seen, the passage from one state to another can only be progressively transacted, for one does not carelessly manipulate elements which are a priori foreign, therefore dangerous. One may also guess that the rites of passage (notably initiation, to be seen later) are prodigious systems of integration into the social group and of perpetuation of its cultural value system.

IN CONTEMPORARY CATHOLICISM

Requests for Sacramental Rites of Passage and Content of Beliefs

A fact established by multiple surveys done for twenty of thirty years deserves explanation: it is the surprising persistence, in a society largely secularized, of the request for the church's rites of passage. True, in France the requests for baptism went down by 20% in twenty years (1958–1978); thus, "the percentage of baptisms would be about 50% in 2000, whereas it was definitely above 90% in 1958." True again, the proportion of Catholic weddings compared to civil weddings had gone from 79% in 1954 to "less than 55% in 1987."[3] But this rate is still relatively high if one considers the content of the requesters' beliefs; there is "a striking dissociation between practices and beliefs."[4] A survey in 1971 showed that 80% of French people wanted to have a church burial, but according to a survey conducted three years earlier, only 35% declared they believed in "life after death." This discrepancy between practice and belief is found even among practicing Catholics: a survey in 1970 revealed that 11% of those who practice regularly and 47% of those who practice irregularly do not believe in life after death.[5] These results confirm the conclusions of the PASCO group in 1965: "One cannot deduce anything from the fact of practicing, either with respect to belief in God (theists) or with respect to belief in the divine filiation of Christ (Christians) or with respect to the belief in life after death (believers)."[6]

It is clear that the motivation and legitimization of the request lie *beneath* the content of the faith which they should presuppose according to orthodox theology. From the viewpoint of the latter, what one has to deal with in a great number of cases is a divorce between the offer of the church and the request of the faithful. Whereas the ritual of baptism, for instance, insistently proclaims that baptism is the sacrament of the faith in God the Father, Son, and Holy Spirit, revealed in the life, death, and resurrection of Jesus, numerous people who ask for the sacraments are so faraway from this faith that they have not just forgotten everything they learned in catechism but in many cases believe only in a vague deism, when they have not reached a sort of practical atheism. The least one can say is that the

[3] Jacques Maître, in Guy Michelat et al., *Les Français sont-ils encore catholiques?: Analyse d'un sondage d'opinion*, Sciences humaines et religions (Paris: Cerf, 1991) 31, 33.

[4] J. Sutter, "Opinions des Français sur leur croyances et leur comportements religieux" in *Maison-Dieu* 122 (1975) 67.

[5] Ibid., 69–71.

[6] Liliane Voyé, *Sociologie du geste religieux: De l'analyse de la pratique dominicale en Belgique a une interprétation théorique*, Questions économiques, sociales and politiques (Brussels, 1973) 225.

"system of the practice," the faith content which theoretically precedes the practice, is in disharmony, even in contradiction with the "practice of the system," the request addressed to the church for the sacraments. One gets the impression that in a great many cases "the order of the rite," as it is established by the church, practically functions as "the rite of the order"—of the established order, that is, of a mediation of conformity to the dominant value system.

Psycho-Social Clarifications

How can we understand why people persist in asking for the rites of passage while the content of the beliefs appears greatly deviant from the viewpoint of the church's institutional logic? Many different approaches are possible, depending on how one regards the phenomenon in question from the angle of sociology, psychology, rituality, history, and so on. Let us give some examples.

RITUAL LANGUAGE FUNCTIONING AS AN INDEX

We have already treated this topic in the chapter on rituality, (chapter 5) where we emphasized that ritual language "positions" (pp. 110–111). It is needless to repeat this development here. It is enough to direct attention to one point: from the simple fact of functioning as an index, rite can be valorized for itself, independently of the faith that it normally presupposes. What is important for the requesters is less the content than the "shell" itself, that is in this case, the "trademark" which confers "Christian" status and identity.

THE FIVE DIMENSIONS OF RELIGIOSITY

Religion is a complex phenomenon. The American sociologists Charles Y. Glock and Rodney Stark distinguish five dimensions in it: (a) personal experience, affective in character, which causes a strong attachment, for instance, to a "liberating" Jesus in one person or in another to a "mystical" Jesus; (b) "ideology," that is to say, articles of faith proposed by the church to its members; (c) intelligence, that is, the comprehension of what one believes and the coherence one can give to it; (d) the effects, ethical in character, produced in society and in the conduct of individuals by the faith; (e) finally, the ritual dimension: the cultic practices. These several dimensions of religiosity "do not evolve in a parallel manner."[7] The intellectual dimension can be

---

[7] Ibid., 223.

relatively strong in a "seeking" subject while her or his "ideological" acceptance of church dogmas is weak. This is also true on the socio-historical plane: the "uncultured faith" which accepts everything without trying to understand may have prevailed in the past; today one sees within a widespread religious indifference the emergence of the reverse tendency towards intellectual search among many Christians wanting "formation." This relative disjunction of the different dimensions of religiosity allows us to understand better that groups or individuals can highly valorize the ritual dimension of Christianity (notably for reasons which will be developed later on with regard to rites of passage) while paying scant attention to its "dogmatic" dimension in the sense in which the church understands it or to its intellectual aspect.

LOGIC OF COMMUNION AND LOGIC OF DIFFERENCE

As for the ritual dimension of Christianity, it is useful to distinguish the rites of passage, which, by definition, one undergoes only once in a lifetime (except in the case of remarriage) and the rites which one could term "everyday rites" or "maintenance rites" since, like Sunday practice or even the sacrament of reconciliation, they are repeated more or less frequently. Therefore, there are the rites of "only once" and the rites of "every time that": the non-repeatable rites and the repeatable ones.

These two kinds of rites are ruled by different logics from the psycho-social viewpoint. It is possible to use the distinction made by Jean Baudrillard, in his study on "the ideological genesis of needs,"[8] between the logic of communion, in which the individual's realization is possible only by and for the group, and the logic of difference, in which this same realization is the more valued as it takes place (or claims to take place) without reference to the group (see Pierre Bourdieu's strategies of "distinction").[9] The former, based on a logic of hierarchical stability, is characteristic of traditional societies of a "closed" type; the latter, based on a logic of

[8] In Jean Baudrillard, *Pour une critique de l'économie politique du signe* (Paris: Gallimard, 1972) 59–94; [*For a Critique of the Political economy of the sign*, trans. Charles Levin (St. Louis: Telos, 1981)].

[9] Pierre Bourdieu, *Distinction: A Social Critique of the Judgement of Taste*, trans. Richard Nice (Cambridge, Mass.: Harvard, 1984).

egalitarian competition, fundamentally rules a society of an "open" type like our own.

In the past, all of religious behavior, whether repeatable or not, obeyed the logic of communion, like everything else in a stable and strongly hierarchized society. But this is no longer the case in today's Western society in which the logic of differences tends to dominate. As was shown by Liliane Voyé, while the rites of passage continue to be practiced according to "a logic of communion and therefore of integration in the measure in which they are largely adopted by the whole population," Sunday observance, in contrast, is guided by the logic of difference.[10] This is easy to observe today: in any building of our cities where the majority of the families want or have wanted baptism, First Communion, a wedding (and later on the last passage through the church at the funeral), it is not rare that only one family—and not necessarily all its members—practices in a somewhat regular way. The attendance at Sunday Eucharist differentiates people from the surrounding milieu and demands a relatively high level of interiorization of the values of the church and of Vatican II. The baptism of children and the wedding continue, on the contrary, to be lived as social gestures of *conformation to the surrounding milieu*; here the "cultic" plays a primarily cultural role. One baptizes as much into "the American people" or into "the ways of the Western world" as into "the Christian mode of life" corresponding to theological criteria. In fact, the sacramental rites of passage seem to have but a "weak significance on the plane of interior identification" if judged by the theological significance normally supposed to justify the request. Thus, the psycho-social functioning of these sacramental rites appears to be the opposite of that of Sunday observance (and, in part, of the sacrament of reconciliation). All this sheds light on the question that was asked (p. 176).

A PROCESS OF AUTO-REPRODUCTION

Religious behavior belongs to that sort of social phenomena for which "there is a non-identity between what was at [their] origin and what explains their stability and reproduction." Following the American sociologist Arthur L. Stinchcombe, Voyé says that it is the effect of a "general process of auto-reproduction": certain effects B, for

---

[10] Voyé, *Sociologie du geste religieux*, 233.

instance the practice of baptism, created at the origin by certain causes A—in this case the message of Jesus, the Christ, and the ensuing discipleship in faith—after some time become themselves causes of these same effects B'; these can then subsist by their own internal social energy, independently of their original cause of production. The present logic of their reproduction is not identical to the original logic of their production (which can be understood all the better because rites, programmed by their very nature, tend toward conservatism).[11] This is valid, in Stinchcombe's opinion, for "all social practice having few negative consequences." It is all the more valid for every social practice perceived as bringing positive psychological or social benefits to a group or an individual.[12] This is precisely the case for rites of passage, as will be seen.

THE EXPECTED PSYCHOLOGICAL AND SOCIAL BENEFITS

Let us limit ourselves to the examples of baptism and the wedding: they are experienced as practices producing beneficial effects, both psychological and social. The still high rate of requests for these rites suggests that these benefits are perceived by a large percentage of people as more important than the "negative" consequences connected with them ("constraints" of the preparation, commitment to send the baptized child to catechism, and so on), which could have a dissuasive effect.

Let us try to pinpoint the principal benefits that are expected. They probably are mostly unconscious. The best way to proceed is to establish a typology, approximate of course, of the main motivations as they are sometimes explicitly expressed or, still more often, as they would be expressed if a sort of social censure had not developed with respect to what "is best not to tell the priest" (or the lay pastoral ministers) at the time of the preparatory interview. Let us note that here we leave aside "convinced" requesters who have absorbed the teachings of Vatican II relatively well and who ask for the sacrament out of faith. Their presence is certainly very important to the church. It is the others who are a problem for pastors. A simple table can suffice to present the summary typology we have announced.

[11] See ch. 5, p. 103, n. 5.
[12] Voyé, *Sociologie du geste religieux*, 213–214.

Expressed Motivation	Reference God	Function of religion
"It's always been done in my family"	The God-of-our-ancestors	Religion-Tradition
"We want the child to be like everybody"	The God-of-the-tribe	Social integration
"Like this, the child will receive good principles"	Guardian of the established order	Morality
"If anything bad should happen to the child . . . ."	The God of retribution	Insurance for the hereafter
"We want to give the child every possible chance"	The all-powerful God	Protection for the future
"We aren't dogs . . ."	Feeling of something "Sacred"	Transcendence
"This makes a beautiful celebration possible"	Reference to God's "beauty"	Festivity/esthetics
"They're so innocent at that age!"	The God of childhood, of lost innocence	Religion-nostalgia

Of course, in life, things are not as simple as the labels we use in our table to shed light on the subject: motivations are mixed in a much more complex fashion. The purpose of this table is simply to indicate the type of psychological and social advantages which the requesters expect, most often not consciously, from the baptism, the wedding, the First Communion they ask for. It is important to stress the importance of this "most often not consciously." Because of the "censure" mentioned above, most requesters no longer couch their motivations in terms judged "naive." Nevertheless, (as psychoanalysis reminds us) the least conscious is not the least influential. The request may be formulated in terms deemed "acceptable," but the unconscious motivations are still present. And in many cases they are the *most determinative:* the more the requesters live on the fringes of the church, the more they insist on obtaining their baptism or wedding.

From where does this come if not from the fact that the rites of passage trigger on the psycho-social plane *archaic mechanisms the more potent for being latent,* the more determinative for being the more diffi-cult to clarify and reason about? Let us take some examples from the table above.

To ask for baptism because "it's always been done in my family" is certainly the expression of a reference to the God-of-our-ancestors and of a certain attachment to religion. But we must look farther. Who are the parents who do not unconsciously desire to inscribe their child in their own genealogy in order that she or he may be like themselves, like their own parents, like their ancestors since "always"? It is there-fore necessary to place on the child the symbolic marks of their own identity, to do again on her on him what was done on themselves, their own parents, their ancestors. Without this symbolic marking, baptism in this case, something is not right, something which the par-ents would be hard put to clearly enunciate. But it is something they feel so strongly that *"they can't help it"* and that they will make a fuss with the priest or will "never set foot in a church again" if he refuses the baptism they want. Indeed, "it" speaks from afar; "it" speaks from the utmost depths of the unconscious when they make such a request. Although fully justified, the theological logic, showing the discrep-ancy between the sacrament of faith that the church offers and what the parents in effect ask for, is in most cases unable to convince them by itself. Even though they understand the reasonableness of this logic, it is their unconscious desire, which "has reasons unknown to reason," that in the end will win. The parents say or at least think, "No doubt you are right, but still. . . ." Their true "word" is in this "but still" or what takes its place, ellipses, sigh, heavy silence. Be-cause they cannot help it.

One can develop the same sort of reflection concerning the "we want the child to be like everybody." Despite all the good reasons they have for telling themselves that the lack of baptism is not (or is no longer) a disgrace for their child, many parents cannot resign them-selves to this lack because in their socio-cultural system not to be bap-tized is among the things that are "simply not done." It would be experienced as a debasement in their own eyes and those of their so-cial milieu. It would be to lose face, to be dishonored, to feel oneself somehow marginalized. In many cases, this archaic feeling is so strong that a non-baptism is in the category of the "unthinkable." One can imagine, especially if the parents are among the great number of people who have been deprived of an adequate religious and/or general education and do not have the vocabulary to make a clever discourse in their defense, the depth of their heartache and bitterness if the pastoral ministers deny their request because of the lack of orthodoxy in their beliefs (we shall go back to this). This happens when pastoral ministers fail to take into account the anthropological and social weight, that is, the *symbolic* weight, of their motivations.

In the case where the parents intend "to give the child every chance," a tiny bit of reflection is enough for them to admit that such a sacred rite is in no way a lightning rod which will ward off the risks of life from the child. Of course; "but still . . .": the desire to put all the chances on the child's side, to insure for her or him the protection of a beneficent power (even though the parents' representation of this power may be the vaguest) at the beginning of life's adventure, has the upper hand. In any case, most parents would feel guilty if they neglected to give their child the benefit of baptism.

Guilt: this is precisely what underlies "If anything bad should happen to the child. . . ." Here again reason, supported by theology, says clearly enough to the parents that should their child die before baptism it would not be condemned to hell. But beneath what appears to their reason as a conviction, "it" nevertheless reacts differently in their innermost heart; reconfigured by centuries of the "pastoral ministry of fear" (Jean Delumeau), an archaic guilt feeling arises, diffuse but irrepressible, and they ask religion to take it away.[13] Here again, the desire is the more powerful because its roots go down more deeply into the unconscious. It is perhaps because of the often anguished uncertainty regarding "life beyond," which like all salvation religions the church fostered, that its control over the masses primarily spread.

And then, the child that slumbers in every adult always awakens at the occasion of a baptism. Such a rite causes a nostalgic regression toward the time of childhood, the time of innocence and wonder, the time of the baby Jesus in the crib or of the good grandmother who would tell stories from the Bible so wonderfully.

No need to further develop these brief analyses. Their only goal was to show the weight of what is not said or maybe cannot be said

---

[13] From the viewpoint of psychoanalytical anthropology, every religion is a system of guilt management; see Jacques Gagey, *Freud et le christianisme: Existence chrétienne et pratique de l'inconscient*, Jésus et Jésus-Christ 16 (Paris: Desclée, 1982).

and yet is a weight hidden under the request for rites of passage. Most of the time, the locutionary (the content of the request) only masks the illocutionary, which is first of all a begging for "recognition."[14] For the requesters, securing baptism or marriage *is symbolically rooted in their body:* in the individual body of their desire and in the cultural body of their social milieu and traditions. Inasmuch as it is possible to clearly express what is at work in such behavioral patterns, it seems that two main types of benefits are expected:

(a) The first are largely psychological: management of guilt, God's protection or "blessing," memories from a childhood more or less idealized.

(b) The others are largely social: integration into family and society, feeling of belonging, strengthening identity, and so on.

As will be developed later on, in pastoral conduct with regard to requests for the baptism of little children, First Communion, weddings, even funerals, it is not possible to go along solely with the anthropological components; nevertheless, these must be taken into account. In any case, they enable us to comprehend why the request made to the church for rites of passage is still so strong, on both the psychological and statistical planes, despite the disparity existing between it and the value system (that of orthodox faith) and norms (those of the ethical and ritual practices) of the church as institution. The anthropological components facilitate understanding especially well when they are combined with some of the results of our previous analyses, such as the primary role of rituality as an "index," its ability to perdure independently of other dimensions of religion, the logic of "communion" which socially rules the rites of passage, their reproduction largely disconnected from the original conditions of their emergence, and so on.

Besides regarding the preliminary pastoral interview, it is important to observe that because the motivations enumerated above are mostly unconscious, they are present to some degree in everyone, *including therefore those who receive the requests.* Between the convictions of the duly recognized theologians and the reactions they have when faced with their own death, there is the margin, if not the chasm that yawns between the conscious and the unconscious. Profoundly Christian parents who are well able to justify the request for their child's baptism with motives firmly rooted in their life of faith are nonetheless

[14] See above, p. 80, n. 11.

also desirous that the child may be "like themselves" or are unconsciously impelled by some guilt at the thought of possibly harmful
events or by some secret wish for divine "protection." And this happens if (and especially if) their culture "forbids" them to admit to
themselves such "naive" motivations. No one is ever through with
mastering her or his "archaisms." All this should prevent the minister
engaged in the pastoral interview from dismissing with a simple
gesture of the hand the requests we have analyzed as "not serious,"
"infantile," or "merely sociological." This does not mean that the pastoral minister must simply go along with them. This is the whole crux
of the pastoral interview which prepares for the sacrament that has
been requested.

THE PASTORAL INTERVIEW
Since Vatican II, policies for the preparation for infant baptism and
marriage have been devised. These policies are extremely variable depending on the parishes and the dioceses. They go from one encounter with the priest to a series of collective meetings and/or
personal interviews with a priest or one or several laypersons over a
period of several months. Our intention here is not to analyze the "per-
formances" of these different plans, but to focus on what is at work in
the pastoral interview, whether conducted in one or several meetings,
with a priest or with laypersons.

In any case, the expression "pastoral interview" seems to be the
most judicious. *Interview,* that is to say, neither a vague exchange on
disconnected topics nor a simple dialogue, a term which immediately
connotes, in today's parlance, a symmetrical position of the participants and a certain familiarity between them. In the pastoral interview the respective status of the parties is different; and if a certain
familiarity is not excluded, it is in no way obligatory, nor is it even always desirable. The qualifier *pastoral* has the advantage of indicating
that any sort of interview regarding the preparation for a sacrament,
whether by a layperson or a priest, is an eminently pastoral act.

The pastoral ministers would be wrong to regard these interviews
as a mere appendage to their mission, whose "serious" part would be
elsewhere; they would be even more wrong to see them as a chore
("since there's no choice"). In fact, what we have here—the majority
of interviewers have (little by little) understood this—is an *important
missionary platform* destined to develop a great deal in the coming
decades. In our post-modern society, the loss of landmarks among

Catholics is such that it seems an increasing number of them feel at some given moment the need to reposition themselves: the preparation for baptism or marriage gives them this opportunity. Besides, through the avenue of the pastoral interview, one reaches especially persons between twenty-five and thirty-five, that is, a category of the active members of society with the major role of bearing the future but at the same time largely absent from church structures. Lastly, concern with welcoming "run-of-the-mill" persons is one of the conditions the church must fulfill if it is to maintain a sufficiently extensive surface of contact with society and avoid being relegated to the rank of a sect (in the sociological meaning of the word). One can see that the stakes are high.

They are high for the church and no less for the requesters themselves. Most of them find here one of the very rare opportunities offered to them, by going beyond their usual subjects of preoccupation and conversation (the car, the television, the videocamera), to bring language into the domain of meaning and thus to give it a more authentically human[15] and spiritual form. It is frequently observed that this can be experienced as a "time of grace." And why should the pastoral ministers balk in principle at a responsibility which on both the human and evangelical planes is without a doubt one of the noblest since it is a way of helping people arrive at their own truth, even if only partially, to ask themselves what importance they attach to the basic realities of life, to wonder where they have placed their "treasure," therefore also their "heart" (Luke 12:34)? Only, conducting such an interview is a difficult thing because of what is at stake on both the human and spiritual planes.

Let us remind readers that in the following reflection, for the reason already mentioned, we essentially consider the great percentage of "seasonal" or "holiday" Christians.

Communication as Interaction and Decoding
Before coming to the pastoral interview as such, it is good to list some general characteristics of every interpersonal communication. This will be done briefly; for a more detailed presentation of these complex problems, readers will consult the part of Michel Scouarnec's

---

[15] Such is indeed the fundamental function of language, as we have established in the first part.

book, which specifically treats of the pastoral approach to sacraments from this angle.[16]

It should not be forgotten that there is no communication without *interaction* between the transmitter and the receiver, reacting to what the other says by body language, tone of voice, as well as actual words, which necessarily affects the discourse transmitted from either side. According to Austin's terminology spoken of above, the locutionary is always influenced in some degree by the illocutionary and the perlocutionary. There is no pure transmitter any more than a pure receiver: the first always has something of the second and vice versa. The communication is constantly reversible.

In the pastoral interview, this interaction is determined by certain factors. Two principal ones will be mentioned here.

(a) First, there is the object which occasions the encounter and which will necessarily be discussed, what linguists call the *referent*. In this case it is the sacrament. But frequently it does not have the same meaning for the two parties: sacrament of faith for the one who welcomes; essentially socio-cultural rite for the requester (although a certain belief or even an authentic faith may be present).

(b) If the communication about the referent is jammed, it is because the *code* is not the same on both sides. Two persons who converse cannot hear one another except by sharing at the minimum the same linguistic code, for instance, the code of the English language with its sounds (its phonemes), its vocabulary, its grammar. But they can still understand the sense of the sentences without comprehending their full meaning: beneath the various interferences (blanks, extraneous noises, inner preoccupations, suitability or unsuitability of the place chosen for the meeting, and so on) which can short-circuit the communication, the cultural, social, personal code of the one is never totally identical with that of the other, which one must know how to detect in body language, intonations, omissions. The same words do not have the same meaning for both. When the pastoral ministers receiving the engaged couple speak to them of the "sacrament of marriage," they allude to many elements (personal faith, ecclesial life) which the couple are often incapable of perceiving because this sort of

---

[16] Michel Scouarnec, *Pour comprendre les sacrements: Les sacrements, événements de communication* (Editions ouvrières, 1991). Pages 187–251 give a presentation both well documented and most simple of these complex problems.

thing is not part of their language, their culture, their feelings, their usual type of relationships; it sounds "strange" to them, even foreign. The code between the participants is jammed, as we have shown above in our analysis of the motivations underlying requests for rites of passage. Whence a dialogue of the deaf which risks beginning and continuing if the pastoral ministers do not first take care of *decoding* the request made to them.

This is why it would be disastrous to first focus on the motivations of personal faith and ecclesial life which, from the church's viewpoint, the sacraments imply. In any case, it is advisable to proceed to a mutual taming as it were. On the side of the pastoral agents, this means that, first, they should seek, with proper discretion, to find out the characteristics identifying their visitors (their milieu, their occupation, and so on) as well as the principal events which marked their lives; second, they should see to it that the conditions of the interview are favorable (pleasant location, appointment at a time convenient for the applicants, and so on). Without this welcoming of the "human," a welcoming that can take time, the essential, of which we are going to speak, is in great danger of being missed.

From the Start, a Situation Fraught with Pitfalls

From the start, the situation is relatively difficult, even tense.

(a) Most often there is *insecurity* on the requesters' part. It is simply due to the effort that the obligation to take part in an encounter demanding reflection on their part represents for many people (and even, underneath, to the fact that the meeting interferes with their watching television). And it is magnified because, from what they have heard from the grapevine active in their neighborhood or place of work, they fear having to submit to a sort of examination for which they feel unprepared: Have they not forgotten the catechism they learned as children? And inasmuch as they learned from the grapevine that the topics of conversation will be God, the gospel, the church, they feel they will not have "the appropriate words," and so they fear to lose face. In addition, there arises a gnawing feeling of guilt because for years they have distanced themselves from the parish and even more from religious practice. Things even get more tangled when they know that the interviewer will not be a priest but one or more laypersons. A priest, that is symbolically clear. But a layperson? Their traditional code is jammed.

It is important that those in charge be aware of this insecurity affecting their callers at the beginning. Among other things, this allows them not to be surprised by the initial reactions they meet with: a relative mutism or hostility, the latter most often "repressed" and polite, at times rude. This hostility is generally not directed at the person, but at the institution the person symbolically represents. Sometimes there is need for a cathartic process in the course of which the persons disgorge their old rancor against the church in general or one priest in particular; it is a first clearing at the outset and things often go better afterward. In any event, it is advisable to interpret the slight hostility that is shown as a psychological parry for self-defense or reassurance in the face of a representative of the church who is supposed to judge you. This being the case, it is clear that to respond to this sort of hostility with another would derail the process from the start.

(b) The difficulties at the beginning are caused also by the discrepancy between the *offer* and the *demand*. These terms require some explaining because they belong to marketing language. But such a language is valuable here because, willy-nilly, baptism and the wedding are symbolic goods which the ecclesial institution offers on the public market and which it seeks to negotiate on the best possible terms; in certain respects, they are subject to a commercial strategy. However, these terms of "offer" and "demand" are not without drawbacks from the pastoral viewpoint. For in the eyes of faith the pastoral ministers are not simply on the side of the offer, and the others on the side of the demand. The former are also in the position of requesters in two ways: first, they desire that those they receive advance further in the logic of the ecclesial institution; second, and at a deeper level, they must never forget that they too are in search of God and in a state of continual conversion and that, consequently, they must humbly accept to be evangelized by the ones they receive. These persons, estranged as they might be from ecclesial values and norms, can be, in their own way, witnesses of God: the Holy Spirit, which blows wherever it wills, can speak through them and touch the pastoral ministers' heart. The nature of the church, its nature of "mystery" or "sacrament" of the coming reign of God, demands a critical distance from the "offer" and "demand" vocabulary. It is adopted here because it is practical and partially pertinent, but we do this only with prudence.

We saw that there is an undeniable discrepancy and at times a downright opposition between the sacrament of faith offered by the church and the request presented to it. The analyses we have proposed agree in suggesting that it is practically impossible to solve the dilemma immediately in the pastoral interview. Let us repeat that this is not for reasons of understanding or logic, but because the request arouses reactions *the more powerful for being archaic*. Not being on the same wavelength, those who ask and those who receive risk engaging in a dialogue of the deaf.

It is the duty of the welcoming ministers to take into account the full anthropological weight of what is not said. This is rarely reckoned with. Most of the time, this anthropological weight proceeds from the fact that the request belongs to the type of social behavior which cannot be called into question. It is in the cultural air they have been breathing since their childhood and it sticks to their skins. It belongs to the "world they live in" Jurgen Habermas would say or, to speak like Ludwig Wittgenstein, it is part of this "language game" which is one of the fundamental "forms" of their life. It is indispensable that the ministers be aware of the human weight inherent in the request. Otherwise, they are naive, either not understanding or forgetting that they see only the tip of the iceberg; further, they are unfair, judging the requesters unfavorably from the start, without having taken into consideration these all-important factors, this in total contradiction to the evangelical attitude of welcome they are supposed to exemplify in the name of Christ. Indeed, how can one welcome in truth persons as they are without adverting to the deepest elements of their humanity, elements that most often rule their choices and their lived experience?

(c) Almost inevitably, the situation is *objectively conflictual* at the outset of the process. Between the two parties there is a conflict of interests, at least a latent one. On the side of the requesters, the important thing is, first, to "get" their ceremony in due form on the date which suits them and if possible in the church of their choice, with all the practical difficulties this entails—to gather the family, often scattered to the four corners of the country, on a given day; to make reservations in a restaurant; and so on—and second, to mesh as felicitously as possible the religious feast and the family feast. On the side of the ecclesial institution, the important thing is, first, to help the people think, examine themselves, and progress in faith and, second, to harmonize as felicitously as possible the celebration with the participants' lived experience and level of faith. To forget the concrete interest of the requesters in order to forcefully align them with the church's interest is to block communication from the start. This is the reason why the simple fact of letting the threat of refusal hang over their heads, like Damocles' sword, until the end of the conversation or the series of meetings is most deleterious. Instead of removing this obstacle at the beginning and making them receptive to the essential, that is, the (new) contact offered them with the God of the gospel, one gets them stuck on the one question which, in the last analysis, is determinative for them, securing their baptism or wedding.

(d) Let us widen the perspective. The conflict is so objective that it is definitely *structural*. It can be represented by the following diagram:

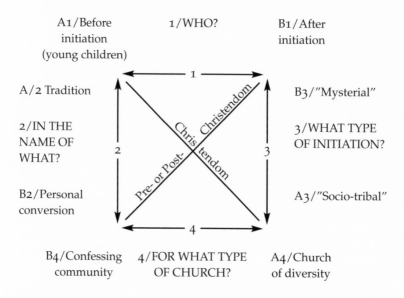

Each of the four sides answers a question (1) Whom does the church baptize? Most of all, small children (A1), baptism coming before their initiation, which takes place especially through catechesis; then, in fewer numbers, children of school age (B1), their baptism always following initiation. (2) In whose name is baptism asked for? Massively, in the name of tradition (A2); in certain cases, particularly among adults, because of a personal conversion to Christ (B2). (3) To what type of initiation does this correspond? We shall abide by the difference, often noted by ethnologists, between the initiation which all persons of the same age undergo and which we call "socio-tribal" and the "mysterial" initiation of charismatic figures, whom traditional societies need to exercise certain particular functions, such as divination or shamanism, or of those accepted into a specialized sisterhood or brotherhood. The baptism of babies (A1) by tradition (A2) ranks as a socio-tribal initiation (A3) which is considered obligatory for all throughout their school

years and lived in an almost automatic way according to steps programmed in advance: confession, communion, profession of faith, and
so on; as to baptism after initiation (B1), (theoretically) requested after a
personal conversion (B2), it corresponds to an initiation of the mysterial
type (B3) since, far from being automatic for everybody, it is offered
only to those who, having received a personal call from God, request it.
(4) These two types of initiation obviously contribute to the fashioning
of two different types of church: in the first case, a church, which sociologists call "diverse" (A4), that is, open to all without any other condition
than their submission to certain rules, especially ritual and disciplinary
ones; in the second case, a church of the "confessing" type (B4), that is,
made up of motivated and convinced persons and from the point of
view of the sociology of religions tends to exhibit some sect-like characteristics as a consequence.

The diagram has two diagonals: roughly, that of the As corresponds
to the period called Christendom, whereas that of the Bs corresponds
either to the pre-Christendom period of the first centuries or to present
day post-Christendom. The structural conflict mentioned above becomes visible: today pastoral management of the sacraments of initiation has inherited the characteristic system of the Christendom period.
But at the same time, (post) modern culture, which valorizes personal
choice, freedom, motivated commitment, places individuals on the B
diagonal. Pastoral ministers, priests or laypersons, share for a large
part these values and want to promote them in the name of the gospel,
while those who request baptism (or a wedding) are, for the reasons
enumerated above, easily satisfied with the traditional pattern. The result is a *structural dysfunctioning* because the pastoral ministers strive
to introduce the values of the B diagonal into a system which is un-
friendly to these values. The most glaring illustration of such a dysfunctioning is the importance given in our day to the sacrament of
confirmation: the trend is to invest this sacrament, received at the
threshold of adolescence, with the whole of the modern values mentioned above at the risk of valorizing it at the expense of baptism received in early childhood. This is easy enough to understand from the
viewpoint of the psychology of adolescents and the "interests" of their
educators, but it cannot be theologically accepted. Confirmation remains an "appendage" of baptism, theologically its "completion."

Here again, of course, transformation of the way Catholics approach rites (novelty yesterday, tradition tomorrow) is taking place
little by little so that a whole segment of seasonal or holiday Catholics

accept, even appreciate the pastoral efforts which are made. Nevertheless, the difficulties listed above betray the underlying structural conflict we have just analyzed.

LANDMARKS FOR THE PASTORAL INTERVIEW

Interviewers and requesters are in the same boat. By virtue of their ecclesial status, the former are entrusted with the mandate of bringing the latter safely to port. The crossing is rough, as we have said. However, there is a channel, well marked with buoys, which shows the way to reach port. We would like to delineate these buoys or beacons. On both sides of the channel, one can distinguish four pairs of them.

(a) The first pair signals that pastoral ministers must let go of a twofold tension: concerning (1) the object of the request and (2) the requesters themselves.

(1) To relax concerning the *object* of the request means that the pastoral interview must not be fixated on the question of its issue: baptism or no baptism, wedding or no wedding. We do not mean to say that the issue is unimportant. We mean to say that this importance must be relativized, that is, subordinated in any case to the modest advance toward the God of the gospel which the pastoral apparatus primarily aims at rendering possible. With few exceptions, the requesters' fear that the baptism or wedding might finally be denied them constantly risks clouding their mind. In any event, it risks making them unavailable for the essential: the welcoming of the gospel as good news for them today.

(2) Conversely, one must not be fixated on the *subjects* who make the request, that is to say, on their motivations. There are unwholesome ways of having them reveal their motivations or exerting pressure on them to say the minimum of what is "proper." What should be examined by pastoral agents is their lucidity concerning *their own interests* or their own unconscious motivations: defense of their power, their rulings, their theological knowledge, their pastoral expertise. Obviously, a minimum of duly recognized power is necessary; a set of guidelines, resulting from a consensus among pastoral ministers and made known to all, is indispensable. As for knowledge and expertise, how are they to function without them? But confronted by the more or less passive resistance of the persons they receive, pastoral ministers fear to be destabilized, to lose face. The danger then is to manage to have the requesters say the minimum of what they, the ministers, consider acceptable, even if this means in certain instances

to speak in their place by reading into their lives an "evangelical" meaning. What is in fact "negotiated" in the pastoral interview is not only an "object" but *subjects* between whom there is interaction concerning their respective places.

(b) The second pair of buoys has to do with the interviewers' attitude, "hard" or "soft."

(1) The *hard* position characterizes the one who imaginarily takes herself or himself for "the almighty parent." One believes oneself to be the law rather than its symbolic witness pointing to it. In some way, one usurps God's place, which concretely can be done in two main ways: either through a judgment bearing on orthodoxy, in which case the requesters are seen as pupils to be taught and the interview turns into a mini-course in theology, or through a judgment of orthopraxis, in which case the requesters are seen as followers to be won over and the interview turns into an exhortation to militant or charismatic commitment.

(2) Conversely, the *soft* position characterizes the "thoroughly compassionate brother or sister" who renounces her or his obligation to be the symbolic representative of the law as well as any solidarity with the ecclesial institution under pretense of being at the level of the requesters. The interview, intended by the minister to be a "dialogue" and have no connotation of "power," in fact risks being only its more or less deceitful *theatricalization*. The so-called dialogue could be unconsciously aiming at neutralizing the anxiety-ridden hazards of communication; and the power relinquished by the right hand could be slyly retrieved by the left. This strategy does not serve either party well: neither the requesters, who wonder what sort of person they are dealing with, nor the interviewer, trapped in an untenable game of hide-and-seek. By erasing their function of qualified representatives of the church too much, such interviewers are in danger of falling into demagoguery. The pastoral interview finally risks comforting the requesters in a narcissistic way by strengthening their established positions instead of confronting them with the unavoidable questioning demanded of each of us by the gospel.[17]

---

[17] One finds again in the four buoys signaled up to this point a certain number of elements which, for his part, Scouarnec (in the book cited above, pp. 219–229) classifies differently, by distinguishing in a way as interesting as pertinent three main types of pastoral strategy in this matter, depending on whether this strategy is centered on (1) the referent, (2) the transmitter, (3) the receiver.

3 (c) Third pair of buoys: those in charge of receiving the requesters must accept to witness to a paradoxical tension between two poles: (A) *attestation* and (B) *contestation*. One can present this tension in a synthetic fashion as follows:

(1) (A) Faith is the effect of a socio-cultural heritage, of a historical tradition, of a milieu to which one belongs; in this, faith does not differ from traditional pagan religions. (B) But this heritage takes its properly Christian form only if it is appropriated in a personal, even critical manner.

(2) (A) Christian initiation appears as a ritually marked figure which closes at a certain point or as a process which has a beginning and an end; here again this is a common trait of all traditional religious initiations. (B) But, no one is ever finished with becoming a Christian; from this angle, initiation into the mystery of Christ takes place throughout one's whole life. This is shown by First Communion; it is both non-repeatable, as is baptism and confirmation, and yet constantly destined to be repeated, thereby indicating that if the process is completed as to its sacramental figure, it is to be continued throughout one's life as to its signification.

(3) (A) Belonging to the church is connected with marks (reference to the Bible as word of God, confession of christological and trinitarian faith, sacraments, and so on); under this aspect, the process of identification of the Christian is the same as that of anyone in any religion of the world. (B) But, Christians are truly faithful to these necessary marks of ecclesial identity only by going constantly beyond them in order to open to the universality of the reign. To be a Christian is not to belong to a "clan"; it is to become sister and brother in Jesus Christ to every human being.

(4) (A) In the preparation for baptism or a wedding, the function of pastoral ministers is partly that of initiators who open the way because they represent the law or the religious institution which has empowered them for this task; in any religion whatsoever, such initiators are needed. (B) But, in the measure in which they never are done with their own conversion to Christ and their own faithfulness to respond to the signs of the Spirit, they must simultaneously be humble companions, ready to let themselves be evangelized by those they evangelize.

The tension between these two poles is of course uncomfortable. But it is inherent in the very nature of the church, which is both "in the world" and "not of the world" (see John 17). By insisting too much on attestation (A), one reduces faith to a cultural heritage, the church to a religious system, Christianity to a "civilization." We must recognize that many Christians seem to stay there; and numerous political officials do not wish for anything else to have the church confined to a role of maintenance and guardianship of "Christian" culture and values. Conversely, by insisting too much on contestation (B), one makes the very existence of the church impossible for lack of sufficient cultural, social, and institutional buttresses, and one becomes the victim of the mirages of a "pure" faith which exists only in the realm of the imaginary.

The pastoral interview must be supported by the pole of attestation of the faith, instead of rejecting it with contempt as too "sociological"; however, if it does take stock of the religious request expressed there, it is not to assuage it but to convert it by directing it toward the other pole. The Gospels demonstrate that such was the way Jesus proceeded. And such is the difficult tension to be maintained.

(d) It is precisely this reference to the gospel which the last pair of buoys indicates: the interviewer must first (1) *ask evangelical questions* and, (2) second, do it *in an evangelical way*. In other words, what is needed is to connect in the best possible manner, the categories of law and grace, by means of which a "Promise" is offered to the persons received. This can be applied to the three theological virtues: a good connection between faith and charity in the pastoral interview can produce hope. We are going to explain.

(1) A pastoral interview in which the minister was content to stroke the people in "the right way" would be deprived of one of its essential dimensions. The confrontation with the astonishing newness of the gospel is indeed one of the obligatory points of passage. This does not just mean that pastoral ministers must allow the persons to confront necessary transformation of their ideas about God, a transformation—as we have seen in the preceding chapter—implied by Jesus' life, death, and resurrection; indeed, the questioning of the vague theism or even deism, professed it seems by the majority, is already an important moment. But it is insufficient: Jesus did not give his life just for a new "idea" about God but for the "salvation" of human beings. The acceptance of this salvation requires the *conversion* of the heart and life. The confrontation with the good news of the gospel has the opportunity to be effective only in the measure in which the love that is revealed there opens a space of freedom; but this freedom, no one can gain it without consenting to be converted. "Repent, and believe in the good news" (Mark 1:15) is Jesus' first message. This call to

195

conversion, in view of the "freedom . . . of the children of God" (Rom 8:21; see also Gal 5:13), assuredly constitutes one of the primary tasks of pastoral ministers, a task the more necessary because many requesters are easily content to identify themselves with a system of religious or even simply moral values.

In the pastoral interview it is good to avoid "conversations" on "religious" subjects: changes in the church, the latest trip of the Pope, wars of religion, history of the sacrament of marriage, original sin, and so on. When these questions are asked, they have to be honored. But the ministers must watch lest they remain stuck there: it could be for both parties an unconscious tactic for bringing about a cheap satisfaction since "the conversation was about religion," but the confrontation with the essential, that is to say, the call to conversion, would be bypassed. In this case, the celebration of the baptism or wedding resulting from this sort of preparation risks appearing so "successful" that one cannot but ask the question, "What is success in this domain?" Far from cutting the subjects to the "quick," as one of the functions of Christian rituality demands, the celebration is so well "adapted" to their sensibility and convictions that it only reflects in their eyes and those of their families and friends the idealized image of themselves which they expect to receive from it. But then if it is true that any Christian liturgy is lived as a memorial of Christ's passover, what passage with him through death toward life is made possible for them?

To pose evangelical questions is finally to confront what is the *law* for Christians' identity: the God revealed in Jesus the Christ, in other words, the church's confession of *faith*. A pastoral interview which, claiming to place itself at the level of the requesters and consequently to show them greater respect, would avoid the confrontation with this law of faith and what it implies in the way of upsetting established convictions and would no doubt be robbed of one of its most fundamental dimensions. Besides, does it show respect for the parents or the engaged couple who come to meet the pastoral ministers whom they know to be believers—and even believers qualified enough to have been charged with a mission by the church—to spare them stumbling against the church's confession of faith? Do not the requesters expect, even if they fear it, such a challenge? Furthermore, does it show respect for them to judge them unworthy to taste the "new wine" (John 2) of the gospel because it would be too strong for them? Surely, it is necessary to adapt speech, questions, manner to the people being received. But to adapt, as we have already remarked (pp. 52–54) does not mean that the new and heady wine of the gospel must be diluted with water to the point of becoming a flavorless beverage. What sort of conversion can be expected in this case? What is meant is that the quantity they seem able to tolerate must be measured in order to avoid either the euphoric effects of a short-lived enthusiasm or the dysphoric effects of disgust. Although all must be able to feel or sense the astonishingly new taste of the good news, it is evident that the ability to absorb is not the same for a twenty-year-old deist as for a forty-year-old Christian who is an active member of the church.

(2) But this confrontation with the law of faith which is the gospel must be effected in an *evangelical way*. And the law of the gospel is a law of grace and mercy. Lest the truth which is Christ be debased, witnesses to the truth must adopt the manner of Christ, that is, that of *love* understood as charity. The attitude of the ministers must be one of "graciousness." This attitude has nothing to do with some imaginary transparency or availability which would be only theatricalization, an attitude the more dangerous as it is less conscious: the body, thus the desire, resists.

The "gracious" attitude we are speaking of is fundamentally respect for the other as other. Which means that it forbids the unethical attempt to "rope in" the other persons (this would be to treat them as objects), even in the name of a "good cause." This gracious attitude is first of all one of attentive listening to what is said but also to what remains impossible for them to say. Second, this graciousness speaks words which, as far as possible, want to free the graciousness of the participants so that an authentic communication may occur. In this perspective, it is not a question of making a religious or theological speech but of involving oneself, *in the first person,* therefore at one's own risk, in words saying how the gospel nourishes one's personal life and the life of others (reference to the present community but also to the church of the past); how staking one's life on the gospel is effectively, for oneself and for others, a path of freedom and happiness. Words of a *witness*. Not of a witness who has prepared her or his piece (what a trap here also!) but who, as the interview progresses, consents to speak of herself or himself without any other support than the Holy Spirit, which speaks as much through silences, awkward language, intonations, hesitations as through lucid enunciations. However, a witness's word never amounts to a proof. Because it is always the expression of an interpretation in which believing subjects risk their own selves, it does not win consent by being evident. But this is precisely its opportunity: by remaining open to contestation, it is an invitation to the others to risk expressing in their turn a different experience. A confrontation, a debate can be the result. But then the two parties are really in communication and by each speaking the truth about themselves, can advance toward the truth which is above both.

This is the decisive moment in the pastoral interview. This can be truly the *moment of grace*. Of course, for such a moment to happen, it is indispensable to speak first of all and sometimes at length of many things, eventually important anyway: family, work, society, religion, and so on. How can people meet one another if they have not first become accustomed to and comfortable with one another? Moreover, a moment of grace can take a relatively short time in comparison with the whole interview or the series of meetings; when it happens does not matter. It is this moment which works as a catalyst for the rest; it is this moment which will mark with its trace (its "seal," Paul or John would have said) the heart and life of the persons encountered.

(e) Then, at least one can hope, a *promise* for the future is open to them. Confronted by the faith of the church and by the call to conversion addressed by the Spirit but confronted with love, they will have met neither Christians so bent on being at their level that they had nothing to tell them nor narrow-minded representatives of the law who would have loaded them with heavy burdens of demands and would have negotiated their "wares" to the profit of a church intent on gaining the maximum of benefits to further spread its influence. They will have simply met witnesses to the faith, in solidarity with the grandeur and weakness of the ecclesial institution which they represent. As in John's story of the call of the first disciples, these witnesses will have known how to help them ask the vital question, "What are you looking for?" and find an answer in the form of a question, "Rabbi, where are you staying?" and they will have given no other answer than the invitation, "Come and see" (John 1:35-39).

Chances are relatively slim that the relationship between the requesters and the church will rapidly change if one takes into account the complexity of psychological and social factors which are entangled in this affair. But one can deem well-founded the *hope* that the preparation for a baptism or wedding will have been for the former the opportunity to truly take a step toward the gospel, a step which later on will lead them on a road which God alone knows. Be that as it may, the pastoral ministers will have accomplished their mission to "plant" and "water," as Paul says; the rest, that is, the growth, is God's work (1 Cor 3:6-8).

Obviously, after having committed oneself in a personal testimony, one cannot relinquish one's concern over the difference between the person's faith and that of the church, over the desire to see them grow into active and responsible Christians, or over the kind of celebration that will follow. Here again one will simply have stopped being tense, having subordinated everything to the *only* truly essential question from the viewpoint of the mission: How can we help these persons hear and receive the word of Christ as the good news for them today?

CONCLUSION

In this process, pastoral ministers have, it seems, three steps or three thresholds to travel through.

(a) the first one concerns the acceptance of this pastoral task as a *particularly important and urgent mission for today's church*. Along with participation in catechesis, the preparation for baptisms and weddings is one of the main sources of the renewal of Christian communities everywhere, cities, suburbs, rural areas. We have little doubt that this source will become more important in our "post-modern" society in which so many people feel the need to rediscover landmarks and to reposition themselves on the religious plane. This requires that dioceses, parishes, services, chaplaincies develop a true concern and strategy in this field. The development of the adult catechumenate—which could be more substantial if more persons and more contributions of competent skill could be engaged in this work—gives a rather clear sign of it. In our kind of society, it is a whole *"catechumenal" dimension of the church* that should be developed as one of the major "strategic" axes of its mission.[18]

---

[18] We are placing the adjective "catechumenal" in quotation marks because we mean catechumenate not only in its proper sense (preparation for all or one of the three sacraments of initiation) but in a wider sense, questionable it is true. What we mean is in some way a "re-initiation" of all those adults who, having "had it all" on the sacramental plane, start again practically from zero when they are thirty, forty, fifty years of age. Would not it be a good thing to offer them the sacrament of reconciliation toward the end of their journey of rediscovery of the faith and of the church? By the same token, one would

(b) The second is the acceptance of *confronting* the persons received with the gospel, the church's confession of faith, or the pastoral rulings which the pastoral team has devised for itself for this or that sort of case. This requires a certain position of authority. But this authority owes its legitimacy only to the status (at least unofficial at the lowest level) which is given to the persons in charge of receiving the requests. This point is not always clearly evident in laypersons who prefer to remain "like everybody else" and not feel too tied up with the ecclesial institution. However, the recognition of this status is psychologically very desirable in order to avoid certain deviations or abdications previously described. Besides, on the social plane it is indispensable that the people know who they are dealing with.

(c) The third is the most difficult: in a certain way, one is never through negotiating it. Indeed, if it is necessary to confront the persons with what is the law for Christian faith and for the church, if at times one must take shelter behind the local rulings, one must at all costs *avoid falling into rigorism*. Rules are of course necessary, but they are only means. The end is no other than the God of the gospel toward whom a way must be opened. In this perspective, it is important to constantly remember that the reign of God is wider than the church as institution and that the Holy Spirit is bound neither by sacraments nor—still less—by the discipline devised for their preparation, as indispensable as it may be. All this puts pastoral ministers on the spot concerning their own conversion. For in this domain, as in all the other sectors of the mission, what counts above all is an inner attitude, a *spiritual potential:* that through which the Holy Spirit enables pastoral ministers to discern and welcome that part of the reign that comes to them or can come to them through persons who may be relatively distant from the ecclesial institution. The Spirit's subtlety is not on the side of rigorism; it is rather on the side of this practical sixth sense, so precious in pastoral care, a sense to which the medieval theologians assigned the first place among the cardinal virtues and which they named "prudence."

---

recover the original signification of this sacramental gesture as a reimmersion (a "dry" one) into the baptism which these persons have denied or, more simply, ignored.

Index

Eucharist
    celebrated by all, presided by one,
        32–33
    four technical verbs in institution
        and celebration of, 25, 134
    synonymous with church in early
        Christianity, 36, 141
    See also Church; Sunday
Eucharistic Prayer Number 2,
    129–133
eucharistic presence
    and eucharistic reserve, 102–103
    named "real presence" in the
        eleventh century, 139–140
    not contested before the ninth
        century, 139
evangelization
    preceding reception of sacra-
        ments, 51
    structured by sacraments, 52

faith
    assent to a loss, 39–40
    healthy when "tripod" is bal-
        anced, 41
    renunciation of immediacy, 25
    respect for God's difference, 40–41
    seeking understanding, ix–x
firstfruits, offering of. *See under* Jew-
    ish worship

God
    "Crucified," 161, n.11
    entirely other, 165
    inscribed but not circumscribed,
        169
    somehow human, 156, 161, 163,
        164, 169
grace
    given free of charge, 87–88
    gracious and gratuitous, 86, 87, 125
    outside the field of market value
        and usefulness, 88

Heidegger, 12–13, 77, 78, 81
    See also Van Gogh

imaginary, danger to symbol when
    isolated, 15, 16, 71, 85
    See also Lacan
immediacy,
    in the relation of Christian with
        Christ, 38
    in the relation of subject with real-
        ity, 4
    temptation of, 39
    See also faith; mediation
incarnation
    in New Testament, understood
        within the passover of the Cru-
        cified, 159
    point of departure of Scholastic
        sacramental theology, 155–156
institution, story of, 133–135

Jesus
    abandoned on the cross, 161–164
        (see also centurion at the cross)
    and Jewish worship, 59–61
Jewish identity, 147–152
Jewish worship
    memorial of Passover, 54–56
    offering of firstfruits, 56–57,
        148–151

Lacan, 10, 11, 15
    See also mirror, stage of; imaginary
language
    as definition of human being, 7
    dimensions of, "locutionary," "il-
        locutionary," "perlocutionary,"
        80, n. 11
    efficacy of, 91, 123
    essentially "poetic" or "sym-
        bolic," 77–78
    as instrument, 3–6
    "language games," 98–99

as mediation, 6–13
milieu in which the subject be-
    comes subject, 7
performative function of, 79–80
language of rite
    different from ordinary language,
        103–106
    operative, 99–101
    programmed, therefore repeat-
        able, 106–110
    serving to assign positions, 110–111
    symbolic, 101–103
liturgical year, 157–158
liturgy
    conservative nature of, 107
    ethics and, in tension, 65
    evangelization and, 52
Lord's Supper in 1 Cor 11:17–34,
    140–141

manna. *See* grace
market exchange,
    different from symbolic exchange,
        117
    See also symbolic exchange; sign
        and symbol
Mass on television, 38
mediation
    of the body, xii
    of the church, 26–28
    of language, 6–12
    See also immediacy
memorial
    of Jesus' death, 135
    in Jewish worship, 54–56
mirror, stage of the, 10–11

narrative analysis. *See* Eucharistic
    Prayer Number 2
narrative program. *See* Eucharistic
    Prayer Number 2

other. *See* symbolic order

paschal mystery, 156–161
pastoral interview, 184–199
pastoral negotiation between too
    much and too little, 104, 106, 108
priest
    not celebrant but presider, 33
    not an intermediary but a mani-
        festation of the one mediation
        of Christ, 64

"real presence." *See* eucharistic
    presence
rite
    evangelization of, 111–113
    language of (see language of rite)
    rites of passage, 173–174

sacrament
    body and, xii, 113–114
    definition of, xiv, 29–30
    ethics and, 54
    evangelization of, 51–54
    overvaluation of, 40
    point of passage, 146–147
    scriptures and, 47
    word and, 47–49
sacramental theology, three theoreti-
    cal models of
    objectivist model, xiv–xvii
    subjectivist model, xvii–xxi
    Vatican II model, xxi–xxv
Scriptures
    connected to liturgy and ethics,
        41
    definition of, 29
    one of the three elements of Chris-
        tian identity, 29–30
    overvaluation of, 40
    sacrament of God's word, 43–47
sign. *See under* symbol, sign and
    symbol
Spirit
    paradoxes of the, 165–169

in its relation to Christ and the
Church, 166–167
in its relation to sacraments,
167–169
See also epiclesis
structure. *See* Christian identity;
symbolic order
subject
Christian, and language and culture of the Church, 19–20
existing only in relation to other
subjects, 163
human, and language and culture,
7–9, 11
Sunday. *See* assembly; liturgical year
symbol
analysis of, 70–74
in antiquity, 14
different from comparison, 72
examples of, 69–70
liturgical, needing spareness and
reserve, 101–102
representation of the real, 72
semantic drift of term, 72

sign and, 74–83
symbolic exchange
on the anthropological level,
117–123
in the Eucharistic Prayer, 143
on the theological level, 123–127
See also market exchange
symbolic order
definition of, 2
description of, 13–17
symbolization, act of, 83–91

Van Gogh, painting of the peasant
woman's shoes by, 81–82. *See also*
Heidegger
vocabulary of worship. *See* Christian
worship

Word
as bread, 91–92 (see also bread of
life, discourse on)
and sacrament, 47–49
sacraments of the, 92–96
and scriptures, 43–47

Helen 238-3488